PRO/CON VOLUME 15

HUMAN RIGHTS

Published 2004 by Grolier,
an imprint of Scholastic Library Publishing
Old Sherman Turnpike
Danbury, Connecticut 06816

Library of Congress Cataloging-in-Publication Data
Pro/con
  p. cm
Includes bibliographical references and index.
  Contents: v. 13. U.S. History – v. 14. International Development – v. 15. Human
Rights – v.16. Education – v. 17. New Science – v. 18. Commerce and Trade.
  ISBN 0-7172-5927-7 (set : alk. paper) – ISBN 0-7172-5930-7 (vol. 13 : alk. paper) –
ISBN 0-7172-5929-3 (vol. 14 : alk. paper) – ISBN 0-7172-5931-5 (vol. 15 : alk. paper)
– ISBN 0-7172-5928-5 (vol. 16 : alk. paper) – ISBN 0-7172-5932-3 (vol. 17 : alk.
paper) – ISBN 0-7172-5933-1 (vol. 18 : alk. paper)
  1. Social problems. I. Scholastic Publishing Ltd Grolier (Firm)

HN17.5 P756 2002
361.1–dc21

                                                                2001053234

Printed and bound in Singapore

SET ISBN 0-7172-5927-7
VOLUME ISBN 0-7172-5931-5

For The Brown Reference Group plc
Project Editor: Aruna Vasudevan
Editors: Chris Marshall, Phil Robins, Lesley Henderson, Jonathan Dore
Consultant Editor: Nadine Strossen, President, American Civil Liberties
Union, and Professor of Law, New York Law School
Designer: Sarah Williams
Picture Researchers: Clare Newman, Susy Forbes
Set Index: Kay Ollerenshaw

Managing Editor: Tim Cooke
Art Director: Dave Goodman
Production Director: Alastair Gourlay

GENERAL PREFACE

"All that is necessary for evil to triumph is for good men to do nothing."
—Edmund Burke, 18th-century English political philosopher

Decisions

Life is full of choices and decisions. Some are more important than others. Some affect only your daily life—the route you take to school, for example, or what you prefer to eat for supper—while others are more abstract and concern questions of right and wrong rather than practicality. That does not mean that your choice of presidential candidate or your views on abortion are necessarily more important than your answers to purely personal questions. But it is likely that those wider questions are more complex and subtle and that you therefore will need to know more information about the subject before you can try to answer them. They are also likely to be questions where you might have to justify your views to other people. In order to do that you need to be able to make informed decisions, be able to analyze every fact at your disposal, and evaluate them in an unbiased manner.

What is *Pro/Con*?

Pro/Con is a collection of debates that presents conflicting views on some of the more complex and general issues facing Americans today. By bringing together extracts from a wide range of sources—mainstream newspapers and magazines, books, famous speeches, legal judgments, religious tracts, government surveys—the set reflects current informed attitudes toward dilemmas that range from the best way to feed the world's growing population to gay rights, from the connection between political freedom and capitalism to the fate of Napster.

The people whose arguments make up the set are for the most part acknowledged experts in their fields, making the vast difference in their points of view even more remarkable. The arguments are presented in the form of debates for and against various propositions, such as "Should Americans Celebrate Columbus Day?" or "Are human rights women's rights?" This question format reflects the way in which ideas often occur in daily life: in the classroom, on TV shows, in business meetings, or even in state or federal politics.

The contents

The subjects of the six volumes of *Pro/Con 2—U.S. History, International Development, Human Rights, Education, New Science,* and *Commerce and Trade*—are issues on which it is preferable that people's opinions are based on information rather than personal bias.

Special boxes throughout *Pro/Con* comment on the debates as you are reading them, pointing out facts, explaining terms, or analyzing arguments to help you think about what is being said.

Introductions and summaries also provide background information that might help you reach your own conclusions. There are also tips about how to structure an argument that you can apply on an everyday basis to any debate or conversation, learning how to present your point of view as effectively and persuasively as possible.

3

VOLUME PREFACE
Human Rights

Human rights—rights to which everyone is entitled simply by being alive—are a familiar idea in modern society. TV news programs report violations of human rights, courts judge whether new laws are compatible with human rights, and protest groups campaign to improve human rights at home and abroad.

Although they are prominent, however, human rights are difficult to define. Some definitions that appear to be straightforward do not work in practice. The Declaration of Independence, for example, referred to "certain inalienable Rights" granted by God to all men. Among those rights it included "Life, Liberty, and the pursuit of Happiness," which today are still acknowledged as basic human rights. Yet in the Southern states the economy was dependent on slavery, which was incompatible with the idea that every person had a right to liberty. Nor was the right to life "inalienable." The justice system removed that right from criminals such as murderers who were sentenced to death.

Another source of difficulty is separating human rights from other types of rights. Human rights are those that people possess simply by being born. Civil rights, on the other hand, are usually more political and can vary from culture to culture: They include the right to vote and to equal treatment in a justice system. Such rights are fundamental to most western democracies, but are not equally considered in some other countries. Economic rights—such as the right to be paid a fair wage in return for one's labor or the right to own property—again vary in societies, for example, based on collective or communal ownership. Religious freedom is another kind of right that can vary from culture to culture.

A milestone in the history of human rights occurred as a reaction to the upheavals caused by World War II (1939-1945). Under the auspices of the United Nations, the international community drafted a code to define human rights. The Universal Declaration of Human Rights created in 1948, established the first international standards for measuring rights.

Problems remain in applying the Universal Declaration, however. Individual states have their own political, legal, and cultural systems. Many object to interference by the international community in matters of national sovereignty. The United States itself has refused to ratify certain rights agreements, such as the Convention on the Rights of the Child, because it argues that its own domestic laws provide enough protection.

Pro/Con and critical thinking

Most of the information we receive about human rights comes from newspapers, television, or the Internet. Critical thinking skills will help you interpret this information and to understand, say, why a certain ethnic group might be disliked by another.

Human Rights presents pro and con articles showing both sides of 16 key debates in the field. They will help you develop informed opinions on these important contemporary issues.

4

HOW TO USE THIS BOOK

Each volume of *Pro/Con* is divided into sections, each of which has an introduction that examines its theme. Within each section are a series of debates that present arguments for and against a proposition, such as whether or not the death penalty should be abolished. An introduction to each debate puts it into its wider context, and a summary and key map (see below) highlight the main points of the debate clearly and concisely. Each debate has marginal boxes that focus on particular points, give tips on how to present an argument, or help question the writer's case. The summary page to the debates contains supplementary material to help you do further research.

Boxes and other materials provide additional background information. There are also special spreads on how to improve your debating and writing skills. At the end of each book is a glossary and an index. The glossary provides explanations of key words in the volume. The index covers all 18 books, so it will help you trace topics in this set and the previous ones.

marginal boxes
Marginal boxes highlight key points of the argument, give extra information, or help you question the author's meaning.

summary boxes
Summary boxes are useful reminders of both sides of the argument.

further information
Further Reading lists for each debate direct you to related books, articles, and websites so you can do your own research.

other articles in the *Pro/Con* series
This box lists related debates throughout the *Pro/Con* series.

background information
Frequent text boxes provide background information on important concepts and key individuals or events.

key map
Key maps provide a graphic representation of the central points of the debate.

5

CONTENTS

PART 1

THE IDEA OF RIGHTS

INTRODUCTION

Rights vs. no rights

Over the centuries philosophers, intellectuals, and politicians have discussed the issue of rights: the entitlements to which people are due in their everyday life. The idea of rights implies that such entitlements are protected from those who might take them away, including not only other individuals, but also the government or another ethnic or racial group. The most basic category, which is now know as human rights, includes those rights to which people are entitled simply because they exist. They include the right to life, the right to liberty, and the right to live without fear of violence, persecution, or torture. In many people's eyes they also include the right, in the words of the Declaration of Independence, to "the pursuit of happiness"; in other words, the right to be left alone to behave in a way that makes one's life as enjoyable as possible—so long as it does not affect other people's rights.

There are many other categories of rights, which might be described as, for example, civil rights, economic rights, religious rights, and so on. Civil rights are those rights to which a person is entitled as a citizen of a state. They might be political—such as the right to vote in elections to choose a particular government—or the right to fair and equal treatment under the justice system. A free education in the public school system also qualifies as a civil right. Economic rights often involve work and the right to earn a fair wage for one's labor, or the right to own private property. Religious rights might involve the freedom to worship whichever god one chooses, or to follow no religion.

All these categories of rights, however, vary from country to country: some countries reject democratic voting, others promote collective or communal ownership of property, and others forbid the worship of certain religions. Although some commentators argue that these and similar rights should all be considered basic human rights, most also acknowledge that one of the major problems in any debate about rights is how to define them in ways that both apply to everyone equally and are measurable and enforceable. Topic 1 in this section considers the most basic question of all: Do human rights exist?

A universal standard

International codes of conduct, such as the Universal Declaration of Human Rights (UDHR) adopted by the United Nations in 1948, have attempted to codify rights that can and should be applied to every person in every country. Their supporters argue that without such standards it would be impossible not only to measure whether or not societies are mistreating their citizens but also to effectively put pressure on countries to improve their human rights' record.

Western democracies like the United States took the lead in advocating international human rights. Former first lady and UN commissioner Eleanor Roosevelt (1882–1962) was one of the prime influences in the creation of the UDHR. Critics argue that the UDHR and other such codes are limited precisely

the 20th century as some groups attempted to suppress, drive away, or even wipe out others.

In the United States affirmative action policies have been used to try to redress the balance by promoting the group rights of one minority. Critics, however, argue that taking such action often conflicts with the rights of individuals. There have been numerous legal actions brought against

---

"I have a right to nothing which another has a right to take away."

— THOMAS JEFFERSON, PRESIDENT (1743-1826)

---

because they reflect the ideas and values of the western tradition. As such, they do not take into account varied cultural, social, and religious practices around the world. Is it possible, for example, to judge Islamic followers of Sharia law whose behavior is perceived as violating international codes of human rights, even if that behavior is supported by their own tradition and condoned by elements of their religion? Topic 2 examines universal rights and their application.

Group rights

The UDHR concentrates on the rights of the individual, which it promotes as the most important issue in any debate about human rights. Groups also claim rights, however, and protest the abuse of those rights. In parts of Eastern Europe and the former Soviet Union, for example, regions that historically contain many different ethnic and religious groups suffered tension and occasionally violence at the end of

universities, for example, that employed affirmative action policies. One case brought a clash between the rights of a group—African Americans and Mexican Americans—to an equal chance in higher education and the right of individual white applicants to colleges to an application procedure based on ability alone. Topic 3 examines group and individual rights further.

Group rights may also intrude on national sovereignty issues: the right of a state to make its own laws free from outside interference. The international community might perceive another country to be violating the rights of a particular minority group by detaining them without legal representation, for example. But the country in question might justify its actions if it considers the group has threatened national security through terrorism. In such a case, what can the international community do? Topic 4 examines whether human rights should take precedence over national sovereignty.

Topic 1
DO HUMAN RIGHTS EXIST?

YES
FROM "HUMAN RIGHTS AND UNIVERSAL RESPONSIBILITY"
NON-GOVERNMENTAL ORGANIZATIONS, THE UNITED NATIONS WORLD
CONFERENCE ON HUMAN RIGHTS, JUNE 15, 1993, VIENNA, AUSTRIA
HIS HOLINESS THE XIV DALAI LAMA OF TIBET

NO
FROM "THE TYRANNY OF HUMAN RIGHTS"
THE SPECTATOR, AUGUST 28, 1999
KIRSTEN SELLARS

INTRODUCTION

In the United States everyone learns from an early age that they are "endowed … with certain inalienable Rights, that among these are Life, Liberty, and the pursuit of Happiness."

Thomas Jefferson (1743–1826) wrote those words in the Declaration of Independence (1776). They reflect a political philosophy and outlook that developed in Europe and America during the 17th and 18th centuries. Throughout that period there was a growing belief that people were entitled to certain rights that were not granted by a monarch or government but were "natural" rights due to all human beings regardless of nationality or status. Through the 19th and 20th centuries the concept of natural rights has evolved into what we know today as human rights.

Although some commentators go back to ancient Greece for evidence that human rights are as old as civilization, it was during the 18th century—the so-called Age of Enlightenment, when thinkers became interested in applying reason to questions about life and the world—that thinkers and politicians developed the concept of individuals having certain rights just by being born.

One of the most important contributions came from the English philosopher John Locke (1632–1704) in *Second Treatise on Government* (1690). Locke argued that certain rights pertain to individuals as human beings, the most important being the right to life, liberty, and property. In France Enlightenment philosophers such as Voltaire (1694–1778), Charles de Secondet de Montesquieu (1689–1755), and Jean-Jacques Rousseau (1712–1778) attacked the despotism of the French monarchy and proposed new principles of government based on liberty and reason. Both Locke and the French Enlightenment philosophers influenced Jefferson's Declaration of Independence. Jefferson, in turn, influenced the French republicans when they wrote the 1789 *Declaration of the Rights of Man and the Citizen* after the French Revolution. The declaration proclaimed 17 rights as "the natural, inalienable, and sacred rights of man," and gave birth to the famous phrase "Liberty, Equality, Fraternity." The foundations of the human rights tradition can be seen in both these declarations.

Many prominent contemporary thinkers disagreed with the concept of the "rights of man." In *Reflections on the Revolution in France* (1790) the British political philosopher Edmund Burke (1729-1797) argued that rights are particular to each society and created by tradition. Similarly, the British liberal Jeremy Bentham (1748-1832) was scathing: "[F]rom 'laws of nature' come imaginary rights.... Natural rights is simple nonsense."

> *"[L]ife is nuclear survival, liberty is human rights, the pursuit of happiness is a planet whose resources are devoted to the physical and spiritual nourishment of its inhabitants."*
>
> —JIMMY CARTER,
> 39TH PRESIDENT (1977–1981)

Despite such criticism, the notion of human rights persisted throughout the 19th and 20th centuries, culminating in the United Nations Universal Declaration of Human Rights (UDHR) of 1948, which established a basic code of conduct for the treatment of all people around the world.

Supporters of the existence of human rights argue that humankind needs a universal moral code by which to live, and that human or natural rights are an inextricable part of the history of humankind. As UN Secretary-General Kofi Annan (1938–) explained, "Human rights are the foundation of human existence and coexistence."

Skeptics, on the other hand, claim that human rights are an invention of the western liberal tradition and cannot possibly be universal, given the different cultures and political systems throughout the world. They argue that since there is no way to enforce human rights, so to all intents and purposes those rights do not exist. As former Soviet leader Konstantin Ustinovich Chernenko (1911-1985) once said, "Those who try to give us advice on matters of human rights do nothing but provoke an ironic smile among us. We will not permit anyone to interfere in our affairs." Some western governments have adopted a similar attitude, critics allege, leading to claims that they have been inconsistent in implementing legislation and only raise human rights issues if they suit their own ends.

The articles that follow examine the debate further. In the first His Holiness the XIV Dalai Lama criticizes some governments for still considering "the fundamental human rights of its citizens an internal matter for the state." He urges everyone to take responsibility for those who are being mistreated.

Kirsten Sellars, on the other hand, maintains that most human rights policy is that of political expediency. She argues that "The history of human rights as foreign policy is a story of realpolitik and opportunism."

HUMAN RIGHTS AND UNIVERSAL RESPONSIBILITY
His Holiness The XIV Dalai Lama of Tibet

YES

The Dalai Lama made this speech in June 1993 to the UN World Conference on Human Rights held in Vienna, Austria. The 14th Dalai Lama, Tenzin Gyatso (1935–), is the Buddhist spiritual leader of the Tibetan people. In 1959 he was forced into exile after the Chinese military occupation of Tibet. He was awarded the Nobel Peace Prize in 1989.

Our world is becoming smaller and ever more interdependent with the rapid growth in population and increasing contact between people and governments. In this light, it is important to reassess the rights and responsibilities of individuals, peoples and nations in relation to each other and to the planet as a whole.

Common human needs and concerns

This World Conference of organizations and governments concerned about the rights and freedoms of people throughout the world reflects the appreciation of our interdependence. No matter what country or continent we come from we are all basically the same human beings. We have the common human needs and concerns. We all seek happiness and try to avoid suffering regardless of our race, religion, sex or political status. Human beings, indeed all sentient beings, have the right to pursue happiness and live in peace and in freedom. As free human beings we can use our unique intelligence to try to understand ourselves and our world. But if we are prevented from using our creative potential, we are deprived of one of the basic characteristics of a human being. It is very often the most gifted, dedicated and creative members of our society who become victims of human rights abuses. Thus the political, social, cultural and economic developments of a society are obstructed by the violations of human rights. Therefore, the protection of these rights and freedoms are of immense importance both for the individuals affected and for the development of the society as a whole....

The 1993 Vienna conference was attended by representatives of more than 800 nongovernmental organizations (NGOs). These groups included Human Rights Watch as well as Amnesty International. For more information on Amnesty International see pages 86–87 in this volume.

Love and compassion

The key to creating a better and more peaceful world is the development of love and compassion for others. This naturally means we must develop concern for our brothers and sisters who are less fortunate than we are. In this respect, the non-governmental organizations have a key role to play. You not only create awareness for the need to respect the rights of all human beings, but also give the victims of human rights violations hope for a better future.

Respect for fundamental human rights

When I travelled to Europe for the first time in 1973, I talked about the increasing interdependence of the world and the need to develop a sense of universal responsibility. We need to think in global terms because the effects of one nation's actions are felt far beyond its borders. The acceptance of universally binding standards of Human Rights as laid down in the Universal Declaration of Human Rights and in the International Covenants of Human Rights is essential in today's shrinking world. Respect for fundamental human rights should not remain an ideal to be achieved but a requisite foundation for every human society. When we demand the rights and freedoms we so cherish we should also be aware of our responsibilities. If we accept that others have an equal right to peace and happiness as ourselves do we not have a responsibility to help those in need? Respect for fundamental human rights is as important to the people of Africa and Asia as it is to those in Europe or the Americas.

> *The United States was founded on respect for human rights. How does that respect affect society today?*

Global consensus

…The question of human rights is so fundamentally important that there should be no difference of views on this. We must therefore insist on a global consensus not only on the need to respect human rights world wide but more importantly on the definition of these rights. Recently some Asian governments have contended that the standards of human rights laid down in the Universal Declaration of Human Rights are those advocated by the West and cannot be applied to Asia and others parts of the Third World because of differences in culture and differences in social and economic development. I do not share this view and I am convinced that the majority of Asian people do not support this view either, for it is the inherent nature of all human beings to yearn for freedom, equality and dignity, and they have an equal [right] to achieve that. I do not see any contradiction between the need for economic development and the need for respect of human rights. The rich diversity of cultures and religions should help to strengthen the fundamental human rights in all communities. Because underlying this diversity are fundamental principles that bind us all as members of the same human family. Diversity and traditions can never justify the violations of human rights. Thus discrimination of persons from a different

> *The author refutes the idea that the Universal Declaration of Human Rights (UDHR) promotes only western views. For further discussion see Topic 2 Can human rights be applied universally?*

> *Does economic activity affect rights? Does a factory worker have the same rights as the factory owner?*

For further discussion see "Equality for all (Universal Declaration of Human Rights)" on page 27, Volume 2, Government.

What grounds might there be for the downtrodden to be more hopeful? Or is the writer being too optimistic?

See Topic 4 Should human rights come before national sovereignty? for more views on human rights and national sovereignty.

race, of women, and of weaker sections of society may be traditional in some regions, but if they are inconsistent with universally recognized human rights, these forms of behavior must change. The universal principles of equality of all human beings must take precedence....

There is a growing awareness of peoples' responsibilities to each other and to the planet we share. This is encouraging even though so much suffering continues to be inflicted based on chauvinism, race, religion, ideology and history. A new hope is emerging for the downtrodden, and people everywhere are displaying a willingness to champion and defend the rights and freedoms of their fellow human beings. Brute force, no matter how strongly applied, can never subdue the basic human desire for freedom and dignity. It is not enough, as communist systems have assumed, merely to provide people with food, shelter and clothing. The deeper human nature needs to breathe the precious air of liberty. However, some governments still consider the fundamental human rights of its citizens an internal matter of the state. They do not accept that the fate of a people in any country is the legitimate concern of the entire human family and that claims to sovereignty are not a license to mistreat one's citizens. It is not only our right as members of the global human family to protest when our brothers and sisters are being treated brutally, but it is also our duty to do whatever we can to help them....

Advancement of human rights

It is not enough to merely state that all human beings must enjoy equal dignity. This must be translated into action. We have a responsibility to find ways to achieve a more equitable distribution of [the] world's resources. We are witnessing a tremendous popular movement for the advancement of human rights and democratic freedom in the world. This movement must become an even more powerful moral force, so that even the most obstructive governments and armies are incapable of suppressing it.

This conference is an occasion for all of us to reaffirm our commitment to this goal. It is natural and just for nations, peoples and individuals to demand respect for their rights and freedoms and to struggle to end repression, racism, economic exploitation, military occupation, and various forms of colonialism and alien domination. Governments should actively support such demands instead of only paying lip service to them. As we approach the end of the twentieth century, we find that the world is becoming one community.

We are being drawn together by the grave problems
of over population, dwindling natural resources, and an
environmental crisis that threaten the very foundation of
our existence on this planet. Human rights, environmental
protection and great social and economic equality, are all
interrelated. I believe that to meet the challenges of our
times, human beings will have to develop a greater sense of
universal responsibility. Each of us must learn to work not
just for one self, one's own family or one's nation, but for
the benefit of all humankind.

> Does the Dalai Lama make a convincing case that human rights are linked to care for the environment?

Universal responsibility

Universal responsibility is the key to human survival. It is the
best foundation for world peace. This need for co-operation
can only strengthen humankind, because it helps us to
recognize that the most secure foundation for a new world
order is not simply broader political and economic alliances,
but each individual's genuine practice of love and
compassion. These qualities are the ultimate source of human
happiness, and our need for them lies at the very core of our
being. The practice of compassion is not idealistic, but the
most effective way to pursue the best interests of others as
well as our own. The more we become interdependent the
more it is in our own interest to ensure the well-being of
others. I believe that one of the principal factors that hinder
us from fully appreciating our interdependence is our undue
emphasis on material development. We have become so
engrossed in its pursuit that, unknowingly, we have
neglected the most basic qualities of compassion, caring
and cooperation. When we do not know someone or do
not feel connected to an individual or group, we tend to
overlook their needs. Yet, the development of human
society requires that people help each other. I, for one,
strongly believe that individuals can make a difference in
society. Every individual has a responsibility to help more
our global family in the right direction and we must each
assume that responsibility. As a Buddhist monk, I try to
develop compassion within myself, not simply as a religious
practice, but on a human level as well. To encourage
myself in this altruistic attitude, I sometimes find it helpful
to imagine myself standing as a single individual on one
side, facing a huge gathering of all other human beings
on the other side. Then I ask myself, "Whose interests are
more important?" To me it is quite clear that however
important I may feel I am, I am just one individual while
others are infinite in number and importance.

> Can you think of examples of individuals and their actions that make a difference to society?

> Using a visual image is an effective way to convey a point. Is the Dalai Lama successful?

THE TYRANNY OF HUMAN RIGHTS
Kirsten Sellars

NO

When the Swiss attorney-general Carla Del Ponte takes up her post as chief prosecutor of the Yugoslavia and Rwanda war crimes tribunals next month, she will assume the role of high priestess of human rights, the secular religion for the millennium. She will be responsible both for putting Milosevic and the rest behind the bars of Scheveningen prison and for healing the wounds of a troubled world. Her job is to see that good vanquishes evil.

Political expediency

That's the theory, anyway. The reality is more complicated. When viewed with a dispassionate eye, the war-crimes tribunals look less like paragons of justice and more like the political tools of Clinton and Blair. These trials, like the recent bombing campaign, are motivated first and foremost by political expediency. This is not a popular point of view. Indeed, it is heresy. The consensus rules that anything done in the name of human rights is right, and any criticism is not just wrong but tantamount to supporting murder, torture and rape.

Coercive consensus

This coercive consensus gives the most powerful nations carte blanche to interfere in the affairs of any country they choose. In his book *Crimes Against Humanity*, the British-based QC, Geoffrey Robertson, a passionate advocate of human rights, argues for an end to the age of impunity in which repression is allowed to flourish within the protective borders of the nation state. In place of this he envisages a new "age of enforcement" in which interventionist global law ensures that the Pinochets and Pol Pots get their just desserts.

It is a seductive but invidious scenario which ignores the fact that a humanitarian crusade offers a lot more to the crusaders than to those on whose behalf the battle is supposedly fought. History teaches us two important lessons. First, the human-rights ideal was itself born of political convenience, as a smokescreen behind which the great powers could pursue their own interests, oblivious to the needs of those they purported to help. Second, intervention, whatever banner it goes under, is a direct challenge to national self-determination. That is to say, it undermines a people's right to govern themselves. This assault on sovereignty is constantly reinforced by institutions such as the United Nations, Nato and the World Bank.

Attacks on sovereignty, while considered all right for faraway countries, are not acceptable when they affect the United States or Britain. America, the crucible of human rights and chief architect of the UN's 1948 Declaration on Human Rights, refused to accept the Genocide Convention until 1986, on the grounds that it encroached on American sovereignty.

British governments have been equally cautious. Although the Atlee government signed the European Convention on Human Rights, it did so only after securing the condition that UK citizens were banned from taking cases to the human-rights courts in Strasbourg. This ban was lifted in 1964 and there was a succession of high profile cases against the UK on such issues as police powers and press freedom, homosexual rights and the treatment of paramilitary suspects in Northern Ireland. Westminster has reluctantly accepted the court's authority, but there is still, understandably, widespread resentment of meddling Strasbourg Eurocrats.

Do stronger nations apply double standards in their approach to the sovereignty of weaker nations? Or does their strength mean that their sovereignty is more valid than that of other nations?

Human rights as foreign policy

The history of human rights as foreign policy is a story of realpolitik and opportunism. At the 1919 Paris Peace Conference, the US President Woodrow Wilson invoked limited minority rights, while significantly opposing the principle of racial equality. In the second world war, Franklin Roosevelt rallied a hitherto isolationist public's support for the "Good War" in order to extend America's global reach. Later, the Carter and Clinton administrations both launched human-rights missions in order to restore public confidence in the integrity of government after Watergate and Monicagate. Tony Blair and Canada's Lloyd Axworthy have followed their vote-catching example. Official interest in human rights has waxed and waned inversely with the other 20th-century Western idea, anticommunism, and at the end of the Cold War "human-rights abuse" has replaced the "red menace" as the enemy of civilised values.

The Watergate affair was a series of scandals involving the administration of President Richard M. Nixon (1969–1974). For more information see The Watergate Affair (1972–1975) in Volume 2, Government, pages 172–173. "Monicagate" was the name given to the sex scandal involving former president Bill Clinton (1993–2001) and Whitehouse intern Monica Lewinsky. For further details see The case of President Clinton: politics and morality in Volume 2, Government, pages 200–201.

War crimes tribunals

War crimes tribunals have traditionally been the cutting edge of such crusades. The post-Second World War Nuremberg and Tokyo trials established the blueprint for the modern ad hoc tribunals on former Yugoslavia and Rwanda. From the start, politics impinged openly upon the legal process, and there were accusations of double standards from both conservatives ("our generals would have done the same") and from radicals ("Dresden and Hiroshima were war crimes too"). Some lawyers questioned the legal basis of the newly created "crimes against peace" and "crimes against humanity". The Tokyo trial aroused particular controversy, and the Indian judge Radhabinod Pal, rejected all guilty verdicts as victors' justice. William Douglas of the US Supreme Court later wrote of the Tokyo trials: "It took its law from the creator and did not act as a free and independent tribunal. It was solely an instrument of political power."

Allied prosecution

The Allied prosecution of German and Japanese leaders was primarily prompted by political concerns, however high-minded the judges and vile the crimes of many of those involved. Justice had to be seen to be done, but within the framework of broader post-war strategies. At Tokyo, some defendants were scapegoated while a blind eye was turned to others—notably Emperor Hirohito—in order to bolster American occupation policies in Japan.

Justice for conquerors

At Nuremberg, evidence of Allied atrocities (e.g. the Soviet massacre of Poles at Katyn) or aggressive war plans (e.g. Britain's proposed invasion of Norway) was ignored. And once the political and propaganda value of the trials began to wane, the Allied authorities simply wound up the proceedings. Thus, when the lesser tribunals became an obstacle to the creation of the Federal Republic, the Allies shortened the sentences of many Nazi war criminals. Most were freed by the mid-Fifties. History, as we know, is written by the winners. The ensuing justice is conquerors' justice, so only losers ever stand trial for war crimes.

Importance of winning a war

Perhaps, as one Tokyo trial judge noted, a lost war is itself a crime. When Churchill was told that 12 top Nazis had been sentenced to the gallows after the Nuremberg trials in 1946, he mused to General Hastings Ismay, "It shows that if you enter a war, it is supremely important to win it— if we had lost, we would have been in a pretty pickle." After Nato's bombardment of Serbia, these words have a powerful contemporary resonance.

In 1940 in the Katyn woods near Smolensk in Russia Soviet troops, acting on orders from Joseph Stalin (1879–1953), shot and buried more than 4,000 Polish officers. The officers had been captured during the invasion of Poland in 1939. In 1943 the Nazis exhumed the bodies and blamed the Soviets. The next year (Katyn had been retaken from the Nazis) the Soviets exhumed the bodies and blamed the Nazis for the massacre. Forensic evidence showed that the Nazis' version was true. It was only in 1989 with the collapse of Soviet power that it was finally admitted that the Soviet troops had executed the Poles. Stalin's order to execute some 25,700 Poles was also disclosed.

Just and noble wars are back in fashion and so, as night follows day, are war crimes tribunals. A new International Criminal Court looks set to follow on the heels of the courts dealing with former Yugoslavia and Rwanda. Supporters of the enterprise argue that modern humanitarian law can rise above politics and dispense truly impartial justice. The portents are not good, though.

Yugoslavia tribunal

The courts are far from independent. The Yugoslavia tribunal, for example, was set up by the UN Security Council in 1993. Since then it has danced to the tune of the Big Five, especially the more aggressively interventionist members, America and Britain. Occasionally the strings show. In 1997, for example, the United States ruffled the court's feathers when it promised indicted Croats a speedy trial if they surrendered themselves to The Hague.

A tribunal spokesman complained: "By making such statements they are making us look like a politically driven tribunal that you can switch on and switch off every day, according to political circumstance."

Western intelligence

In reality, that is precisely what happens—the current chief prosecutor, Louise Arbour, has admitted as much. She is heavily reliant on Western intelligence to put together prosecution cases and, as she indicates, Security Council members can either "slow down the flow of information or accelerate it" in line with their political aims.

The Kosovo bombardment stripped away lingering illusions of tribunal impartiality. The court acted as the judicial arm of Nato, with Louise Arbour as the Alliance's witchfinder-general. She was glad publicly to accept a bulging dossier of British intelligence on Kosovo from Robin Cook.

Human rights courts

By contrast, when a delegation from a Paris-based organization tried to deliver a petition calling for Bill Clinton's indictment as a war criminal, they were told that the prosecutors were "too busy" to receive it. In the end, they had to hand it in to a UN guard on the gate. Ironically, human rights courts show precious little regard for the legal rights of the accused. The Croat general Tihomir Blaskic has been held in custody for almost three years and still awaits the outcome of his trial....

The International Criminal Court (ICC) in The Hague was established on July 17, 1998. The ICC was established as an independent organization and not as an organ of the United Nations. Its job is to provide justice for genocide, crimes against humanity, and war crimes. The court is supported by 89 governments, but not the United States, Russia, or China. The statute became law on July 1, 2002. On March 11, 2003, 18 judges were sworn in, formally inaugurating the court. See Topic 16 Should the United States recognize the jurisdiction of the International Criminal Court?

Should U.S. presidents have to justify their actions to international organizations?

Summary

In the first article His Holiness the XIV Dalai Lama of Tibet declares that in an increasingly interdependent world it is more important than ever to emphasize the existence of rights and responsibilities. He argues that all human beings are the same and have a right to political, cultural, and social development so that they may freely pursue happiness in peace. All the standards laid down in the Universal Declaration of Human Rights should be accepted and applied universally, not as an ideal, but as the practical basis for all human societies. He believes that it is the inherent nature of all human beings to strive for freedom, equality and dignity. He asserts that human beings have a moral duty to achieve more equitable distribution of the world's resources. Above all, it is compassion, he argues, that is the key to a better world.

In the second article Kirsten Sellars argues that the current political climate makes it difficult to criticize anything done in the name of human rights. She believes that the resulting silence allows powerful nations to interfere in the affairs of other countries. Human rights, she argues, is a smokescreen to aid the great powers in pursuing their own interests. She asserts that certain U.S. administrations have used human-rights campaigns to divert attention from domestic problems. In her discussion of war-crimes tribunals she argues that politics has always impinged on such trials and stresses that the courts are far from being independent. Using the example of the International Criminal Tribunal for the former Yugoslavia, she casts doubt on the idea that humanitarian law can rise above politics and dispense impartial justice.

FURTHER INFORMATION:

Books:

Ahmed, Abdullahi An-Na'Im, *Human Rights in Cross-Cultural Perspective: A Quest for Consensus.* University Park, PA: University of Pennsylvania Press, 1992.

Donnelly, Jack, *International Human Rights*. 2nd edition. Boulder, CO: Westview Press, 1998.

Galtung, Johan, *Human Rights in Another Key.* Cambridge, MA: Polity Press, 1994.

Perry, Michael J., *The Idea of Human Rights: Four Inquiries.* New York: Oxford University Press, 1998.

Useful websites:

www.un.org.icty

United Nations site maintained by the public information service of the International Criminal Tribunal for the former Yugoslavia. Contains comprehensive information on the criminal proceedings. There is a separate site for the International Criminal Tribunal for Rwanda: www.un.org.ictr

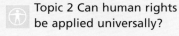

The following debates in the Pro/Con series may also be of interest:

In this volume:

Topic 2 Can human rights be applied universally?

Topic 4 Should human rights come before national sovereignty?

DO HUMAN RIGHTS EXIST?

YES: A society can only function if people act responsibly and do not always exercise individual rights

INDIVIDUAL RIGHTS AND SOCIETY
Do human rights conflict with the general good of society?

NO: The rights of the individual are basic and universal. Society can only benefit if citizens have protection.

YES: Governments should be free to consider the fundamental rights of its citizens as an internal matter of state

NATIONAL SOVEREIGNTY
Are human rights at odds with national sovereignty?

NO: Claims to national sovereignty are not a license to mistreat citizens; human rights are a greater priority

DO HUMAN RIGHTS EXIST? KEY POINTS

YES: The International Criminal Court (ICC) will provide justice in cases of crimes against humanity, genocide, and war crimes

HUMAN RIGHTS AND THE LAW
Can human rights be protected by international law?

YES: War crimes tribunals, such as at Nuremburg and Tokyo after World War II, brought to justice the perpetrators of crimes against humanity

NO: International courts are inevitably biased, and a uniform and global legal system is an impossibility

NO: Individual governments are free to ignore international courts, and sometimes they can take matters into their own hands

Topic 2
CAN HUMAN RIGHTS BE APPLIED UNIVERSALLY?

YES
FROM "ARE HUMAN RIGHTS UNIVERSAL?"
WORLD POLICY JOURNAL, VOLUME XVI, NO. 4, WINTER 1999/2000
SHASHI THAROOR

NO
FROM "HUMAN RIGHTS IN ISLAMIC PERSPECTIVES"
HUMAN RIGHTS: CULTURAL AND IDEOLOGICAL PERSPECTIVES
ABDUL AZIZ SAID

INTRODUCTION

Are human rights universal? In other words, do the same rights apply to all people everywhere? For many commentators the answer is an emphatic yes; all people have the same rights simply by being born. For other commentators, however, the question is far more complex. The basis of their reservations often depends on definitions. What exactly are human rights, and who gets to define them? There is, critics say, no agreement on the question. Without a universally accepted definition, they argue, universal human rights simply cannot be claimed to exist. Even if there is a common definition, they add, the impossibility of guaranteeing human rights in societies with, for example, nondemocratic or military governments effectively means that human rights cannot be called universal.

At first glance the idea of what human rights actually are is easy to answer. In the United States and most

of the western world the idea of rights emerged in the 18th century, when philosophers formulated theories based on the rights of the individual. Such theories underpinned landmark documents such as the English Bill of Rights (1688), the French Declaration of the Rights of Man and of the Citizen (1789), and the American Declaration of Independence (1776). The last asserts that "All men are endowed by their creator with certain unalienable rights," and that "among these are Life, Liberty, and the Pursuit of Happiness." Such a formulation, though radical at the time, is now the accepted norm throughout the western world.

In western societies today human rights include freedom of speech, religion, and assembly; the right to fair and equal treatment under the law; and the right to vote. Economic and social rights, such as the right to work or obtain an education, are also regarded as basic rights. Today most Americans agree that everyone should be entitled to all these rights regardless of age, nationality, race, religion, sex, or economic status.

Supporters of the idea of universal human rights argue that these and similar rights were enshrined in the United Nations Universal Declaration of Human Rights (1948). The declaration acknowledged that everyone shared the same rights and implied a commitment by the international community to guarantee those rights where possible.

"Let the fundamental rules of human rights and human dignity apply to every state and every armed group, every individual and every collective...."

—SERGIO VIEIRA DE MELLO, HIGH COMMISSIONER FOR HUMAN RIGHTS, DECEMBER 6, 2002

Critics counter that the reality in many countries is different. Even within the United States human rights have often appeared to be applied in ways that are far from being universal. Some of the men who signed the Declaration of Independence, opponents claim, believed in equality but themselves owned slaves. Contradictions still exist today. One of the fundamental rights enshrined in the Declaration of Independence, for example, is the right to life. Throughout U.S. history, however, the idea of capital punishment has been based on the idea that

murderers and other serious criminals forgo that right. Today 37 states and the federal government punish first-degree murder with the death penalty. In the other 13 states, however, even a convicted murderer is adjudged to have a right to life. If crossing a state line can make the difference between living or dying, can the right to life be universal?

Critics also point out that there are different ideas of human rights in different societies. Human rights, they argue, are rights associated largely with Christian, democratic, western societies. They are based on ideas of individual freedom of action that are alien to some religions, such as Islam. They are based on rights to property that are alien in many communal or communist societies. And they are based on religious freedoms that have no place in a strict theocracy. Simply because they are economically dominant in the modern world, western societies have no right to impose their own values on other societies.

Among the examples such critics often cite is that of arranged marriages, which are common in countries like India. While westerners are accustomed to ideas of free choice of marriage partner, they argue, the Indian cultural tradition is different. Such ideas do not fit into Indian society, which should be left to follow its own course.

Advocates of universal human rights counter that the tradition is indeed wrong and should be changed. They support their view by pointing to once traditional practices that have now become unacceptable thanks to international pressure, including suttee—the self-sacrifice of Hindu widows—and anti-Semitism.

The following two articles present the different sides of the debate.

ARE HUMAN RIGHTS UNIVERSAL?
Shashi Tharoor

YES

...Those who champion the view that human rights are not universal frequently insist that their adversaries have hidden agendas. In fairness, the same accusation can be leveled against at least some of those who cite culture as a defense against human rights. Authoritarian regimes who appeal to their own cultural traditions are cheerfully willing to crush culture domestically when it suits them to do so. Also, the "traditional culture" that is sometimes advanced to justify the nonobservance of human rights, including in Africa, in practice no longer exists in a pure form at the national level anywhere. The societies of developing countries have not remained in a pristine, pre-Western state; all have been subject to change and distortion by external influence, both as a result of colonialism in many cases and through participation in modern interstate relations.

You cannot impose the model of a "modern" nation-state cutting across tribal boundaries and conventions on your country, appoint a president and an ambassador to the United Nations, and then argue that tribal traditions should be applied to judge the human rights conduct of the resulting modern state.

In any case, there should be nothing sacrosanct about culture. Culture is constantly evolving in any living society, responding to both internal and external stimuli, and there is much in every culture that societies quite naturally outgrow and reject. Am I, as an Indian, obliged to defend, in the name of my culture, the practice of suttee, which was banned 160 years ago, of obliging widows to immolate themselves on their husbands' funeral pyres? The fact that slavery was acceptable across the world for at least 2,000 years does not make it acceptable to us now; the deep historical roots of anti-Semitism in European culture cannot justify discrimination against Jews today.

The problem with the culture argument is that it subsumes all members of a society under a cultural framework that may in fact be inimical to them. It is one thing to advocate the cultural argument with an escape clause—that is, one that does not seek to coerce the dissenters but permits individuals to opt out and to assert their individual rights.

The author is suggesting that double standards are at work if a country wishes to be considered as a modern state but at the same time claims that cultural traditions apply in the case of human rights. Do you agree?

Suttee is the ancient Hindu practice of a widow killing herself on her husband's funeral pyre.

Those who freely choose to live by and to be treated according to their traditional cultures are welcome to do so, provided others who wish to be free are not oppressed in the name of a culture they prefer to disavow.

A controversial but pertinent example of an approach that seeks to strengthen both cultural integrity and individual freedom is India's Muslim Women (Protection of Rights upon Divorce) Act. This piece of legislation was enacted following the famous Shah Banu case, in which the Supreme Court upheld the right of a divorced Muslim woman to alimony, prompting howls of outrage from Muslim traditionalists who claimed this violated their religious beliefs that divorced women were only entitled to the return of the bride price paid upon marriage. The Indian parliament then passed a law to override the court's judgment, under which Muslim women married under Muslim law would be obliged to accept the return of the bride price as the only payment of alimony, but that the official Muslim charity, the Waqf Board, would assist them.

Many Muslim women and feminists were outraged by this. But the interesting point is that if a Muslim woman does not want to be subject to the provisions of the act, she can marry under the civil code; if she marries under Muslim personal law, she will be subject to its provisions. That may be the kind of balance that can be struck between the rights of Muslims as a group to protect their traditional practices and the right of a particular Muslim woman, who may not choose to be subject to that particular law, to exempt herself from it.

It needs to be emphasized that the objections that are voiced to specific (allegedly Western) rights very frequently involve the rights of women, and are usually vociferously argued by men. Even conceding, for argument's sake, that child marriage, widow inheritance, female circumcision, and the like are not found reprehensible by many societies, how do the victims of these practices feel about them? How many teenage girls who have had their genitalia mutilated would have agreed to undergo circumcision if they had the human right to refuse to permit it? For me, the standard is simple: where coercion exists, rights are violated, and these violations must be condemned whatever the traditional justification. So it is not culture that is the test, it is coercion.

Not with faith, but with the faithful

Nor can religion be deployed to sanction the status quo. Every religion seeks to embody certain verities that are applicable to all mankind—justice, truth, mercy,

The Muslim Women (Protection of Rights on Divorce) Act was passed in India in 1986. It was "an act to protect the rights of Muslim women who have been divorced by, or have obtained divorce from, their husbands and to provide for matters connected therewith or incidental thereto." The act provides that the wife is only entitled to claim mehr, or dower (bride price), on divorce, and the husband is not responsible to maintain the wife after a specified period of time. It states that the relatives of the wife are responsible for supporting the wife. How is that different from the way wives are treated under U.S. law?

For more information and discussions of the rights of women see Topic 9 Are human rights women's rights?

Why would the form of government and the media affect the existence of famine?

compassion—though the details of their interpretation vary according to the historical and geographical context in which the religion originated. As U.N. secretary general Kofi Annan has often said, the problem is usually not with the faith, but with the faithful. In any case, freedom is not a value found only in Western faiths: it is highly prized in Buddhism and in different aspects of Hinduism and Islam.

If religion cannot be fairly used to sanction oppression, it should be equally obvious that authoritarianism promotes repression, not development. Development is about change, but repression prevents change. The Nobel Prize–winning economist Amartya Sen has pointed out in a number of interesting pieces that there is now a generally agreed-upon list of policies that are helpful to economic development— "openness to competition, the use of international markets, a high level of literacy and school education, successful land reforms, and public provision of incentives for investment, export and industrialization"—none of which requires authoritarianism; none is incompatible with human rights. Indeed, it is the availability of political and civil rights that gives people the opportunity to draw attention to their needs and to demand action from the government. Sen's work has established, for example, that no substantial famine has ever occurred in any independent and democratic country with a relatively free press. That is striking; though there may be cases where authoritarian societies have had success in achieving economic growth, a country like Botswana, an exemplar of democracy in Africa, has grown faster than most authoritarian states....

For a further discussion on the existence of human rights see Topic 1 Do human rights exist?

When one hears of the unsuitability or inapplicability or ethnocentrism of human rights, it is important to ask what the unstated assumptions of this view really are. What exactly are these human rights that it is so unreasonable to promote? If one picks up the more contentious covenant—the one on civil and political rights—and looks through the list, what can one find that someone in a developing country can easily do without? Not the right to life, one trusts. Freedom from torture? The right not to be enslaved, not to be physically assaulted, not to be arbitrarily arrested, imprisoned, executed? No one actually advocates in so many words the abridgement of any of these rights. As Kofi Annan asked at a speech in Tehran University in 1997:"When have you heard a free voice demand an end to freedom? Where have you heard a slave argue for slavery? When have you heard a victim of torture endorse the ways of the torturer? Where have you heard the tolerant cry out for intolerance?"

Rhetorical questions are a strong way to make a point.

Tolerance and mercy have always, and in all cultures, been ideals of government rule and human behavior. If we do not unequivocally assert the universality of the rights that oppressive governments abuse, and if we admit that these rights can be diluted and changed, ultimately we risk giving oppressive governments an intellectual justification for the morally indefensible. Objections to the applicability of international human rights standards have all too frequently been voiced by authoritarian rulers and power elites to rationalize their violations of human rights—violations that serve primarily, if not solely, to sustain them in power. Just as the Devil can quote scripture for his purpose, Third World communitarianism can be the slogan of a deracinated tyrant trained, as in the case of Pol Pot, at the Sorbonne. The authentic voices of the Third World know how to cry out in pain. It is time to heed them....

Universality, not uniformity

But it is essential to recognize that universality does not presuppose uniformity. To assert the universality of human rights is not to suggest that our views of human rights transcend all possible philosophical, cultural, or religious differences or represent a magical aggregation of the world's ethical and philosophical systems. Rather, it is enough that they do not fundamentally contradict the ideals and aspirations of any society, and that they reflect our common universal humanity, from which no human being must be excluded.

Indigenization of human rights

Most basically, human rights derive from the mere fact of being human; they are not the gift of a particular government or legal code. But the standards being proclaimed internationally can become reality only when applied by countries within their own legal systems. The challenge is to work towards the "indigenization" of human rights, and their assertion within each country's traditions and history. If different approaches are welcomed within the established framework—if, in other words, eclecticism can be encouraged as part of the consensus and not be seen as a threat to it—this flexibility can guarantee universality, enrich the intellectual and philosophical debate, and so complement, rather than undermine, the concept of worldwide human rights. Paradoxical as it may seem, it is a universal idea of human rights that can in fact help make the world safe for diversity.

The Cambodian political leader Pol Pot (1925–1998) was originally named Saloth Sar. He was educated at the Sorbonne in Paris and in 1960 became communist leader of the Khmer. He led Khmer Rouge guerillas against the government, and in 1975 he proclaimed the Democratic Republic of Kampuchea and served as its premier (1976–1979). He was responsible for forced labor in the "killing fields" and the systematic murder of members of various groups. The Khmer Rouge government fell in 1979, when Vietnam invaded. Pol Pot continued as leader until the end of the 1980s. After an internal power struggle he was arrested in 1997 by his former colleagues and charged with treason.

Would flexible definitions and approaches to human rights automatically deny rather than guarantee universality?

HUMAN RIGHTS IN ISLAMIC PERSPECTIVES
Abdul Aziz Said

NO

Human rights are concerned with the dignity of the individual—the level of self-esteem that secures personal identity and promotes human community. While the pursuit of human dignity is universal, its forms are designed by the cultures of people. Politics is a cultural activity reflecting tradition and environment. The debate on human rights assumes that in spite of the differences that characterize the spectrum of world cultures, political conduct can be conceptualized by certain common norms and attitudes. In the modern global system, Westerners have concentrated on discovering common denominators rooted in Judeo-Christian traditions and from which a calculus of human rights would emerge. This emphasis on Western common denominators projects a parochial view of human rights that excludes the cultural realities and present existential conditions of Third World societies.

What has occurred is the reshaping of politics to accommodate various theories of political behavior gleaned from Western traditions. These theories of politics proceed from the assumption that all states share a common agenda of goals—reinforcing the perception of the universality of Western values. Western states assert their interests in an unequivocal litany of demands, including human rights, whose character is determined in the Western experience. The problem with such analogies is that they seek to reduce to a formula their internal milieu—a wholly arbitrary and artificial separation of the political organism. Reality is quite different. The character and nature of human rights are determined in the crucible of a specific sociopolitical culture. Politics is essentially an ascriptive phenomenon: it is culture-specific. The goals that states maximize are a reflection of these factors, and human rights are no exception.

The purpose of the state in Islam is to enforce the principles of the Shariah, the laws derived from the Quran, the Sunnah—the Hadith and decisions of Muhammad, Ijma'— the consensus of opinion of the Ulama (Judges) and, Ijtihad—the counsel of judges on a particular case. The

The author argues that human rights are based on Judeo-Christian values and therefore do not apply to non-western countries. Is that argument convincing?

Hadith is a collection of the traditions of the Prophet Muhammad. It includes his sayings and deeds. A hadith is composed of two parts: the matn (text) and the isnad (chain of reporters). A text needs an authentic isnad with reliable reporters to be acceptable. The authority of Hadith is viewed as second only to the Koran.

implementation of the Shariah means inter alia that the Islamic state must create an environment in the territory under its jurisdiction that satisfies the socioreligious needs of the people. In the Islamic state, sovereignty belongs to God alone. Both the rulers and the ruled are working for the glory of God whose wishes and commands must be fulfilled for achieving happiness here and in the hereafter. Since sovereignty belongs to God alone, the process of legislation becomes less significant in an Islamic state than it is in its counterpart in the West.

In Islam the state surrenders its sovereignty to God and accepts the position of Caliphate (vice-regency) under God's suzerainty. The power of the Caliphate does not reside in any person or a community, but in those who believe and do good. Since the purpose of the individual is service to God, the existence of an organized community of believers requires the establishment of government. Accordingly, the legitimacy of government is its ability to ensure the service of God through counsel (Shurah) among the Muslims.

Do human rights depend on religious foundations? If so, which particular religions, and why?

The Islamic state combines elements of theocracy with democracy. It is theocratic insofar as it is predicated on the doctrine of sovereignty of God. However, it does not delegate the vice-regency of God to a priesthood: the Caliphate is given to believers who are virtuous. The state is democratic since the right to govern derives from counsel among the believers, a form of general will. However the rights of the people to change the law of the state are limited. The Shariah, the Sunnah, Ijma', and Ijtihad provide a check ensuring that the life of the community (Ummah) remains consistent with the law of God and protected from executive, legislative, and judicial revisionism.

Shariah is the religious law of Islam, which covers every aspect of life. The various roots of the Shariah (Sunnah, Ijima', Ijtihad, and Hadith) provide the means to establish prescriptive codes of action and for the evaluation of individual and social behavior.

Viewed against this background, the state in Islam does not exist merely to maintain law and order and provide external protection for its territory. It strives to achieve social justice and promote public good. The viability of the state depends on its ability to balance the relationship between individuals and government, ensure that the government does not become absolute, and prevent individual freedom from threatening the interest of the community....

The concept of freedom

The Western emphasis on freedom from restraint is alien to Islam. While in the liberal tradition freedom signifies the ability to act, in Islam it is the ability to exist. Existence, which is a reflection of the Supreme Being itself, is paramount.

How would redefining freedom in this way affect life in the United States?

The word "Khalifah" (Caliph) refers to the successor or the representative of Prophet Muhammad. Another use for this word is for humanity in general. The human being is considered the Khalifah (representative) of Allah on earth.

If individuals are compelled to seek God, how can the result be defined as freedom?

In Islam human beings are created in the image of God. They are God's representatives (Khalifah) on earth, empowered by the Divine Being to govern themselves, and they seek perfection by following the perfected. Human beings have certain God-granted rights, and right by definition is the exercise of power. As the reflection of God, who is complete freedom and complete necessity, the human being participates in both freedom and necessity. Personal freedom lies in surrender to the Divine Will, and this must be sought within oneself. It cannot be realized through liberation from external sources of restraint. The salvation of the individual lies in the recognition of the link between Divine freedom and political freedom. The freedom of the individual is the supreme end, not only a means to an end; but its limit is the freedom of the community.

Since absolute freedom belongs to God alone, the individual realizes freedom by seeking God, the author of human freedom. There is no freedom possible through rebellion against this principle which is the source of human existence. To rebel against it in the name of freedom is to become separated from the potency and grace of the Divine and to lose inner freedom, the only real freedom. The freedom offered by the material world is the pursuit of happiness—a life of action without purpose. Infinity resides within the human spirit; it cannot be felt by those who live on the periphery of existence. Only when individuals are in touch with this inner reality may they realize absolute freedom. Otherwise, individuals undermine both their power and right in relation to God, nature, and other human beings.

These principles inform Islamic thought on freedom, but their articulation depends on the perspective advanced by the jurists, the theologians, and philosophers within the Islamic tradition. The jurists see human freedom in terms of personal surrender to the Divine Will—it is not an inherent right. Human beings are created by God and have no personal power to create. They are dependent on God and can only receive what is given to them by the source of their own being—the Divine. Human rights exist only in relation to human obligations. Individuals possess certain obligations toward God, fellow humans, and nature, all of which are defined by the Shariah. When individuals meet these obligations they acquire certain rights and freedoms which are again prescribed by the Shariah. Those who do not accept these obligations have no rights, and any claims of freedom that they make upon society lack justification....

The concept of freedom in Islam implies a conscious rejection of a purely liberal and individualistic philosophy of "doing one's own thing" as the meaning of life or the goal of society. The goal of freedom is human creativity, but freedom is defined as belonging to the community and participating in its cultural creation. This egalitarian, community-oriented approach denies some of the essential Western liberal conceptions of freedom. From the Islamic perspective, the anarchy of liberal individualism cannot be a creative seed-bed of culture.

Because societies have been variously and sometimes nearly completely repressive, there emerged in the West a strong tradition seeing the elimination of repression and want as the goal of human-kind. This gave rise to a false dichotomy between the individual and society, portraying the individual as the victim of society and the ideal society as the servant of the individual. Too often the cultural community in which a major portion of human realization must take place has been almost entirely ignored. It is true that cultural systems—like political, economic, and social systems—usually contain much that impedes human development: prejudice, chauvinism, competitiveness, racism, sexism, and so on. But in Islam the cultural community must be served by the political, economic, and social systems— rather than the other way around....

Conclusion

[T]he development of a global conception of human rights is impeded by lack of agreement on the sources of rights including the very foundations of international law. The lack of a philosophical common core poses additional obstacles. The very conception of the organization of society differs from one culture to another. The West emphasizes rights while Japan values obligations; the West emphasizes individual interests while Islam values collective good. The Western tradition poses freedom against despotism, while Islam emphasizes virtue in order to perpetuate traditions that often support a coercive system. ... The concept of human rights must incorporate Islamic and other Third World traditions or it will continue to provoke irreconcilable quarrels. ...

The agenda of human rights is dictated by the historical necessity of the time. ... Social systems impose upon societies a logic of behavior; but social conditions change. As law reflects the achievement of society so too the "rightness" of human rights is determined by time, place, and experience.

Does the idea of individualism contradict the idea of universal human rights?

For discussions of various issues in the complex relationship between individuals and society see Volume 1, Individual and society.

Do you agree that the Universal Declaration of Human Rights does not incorporate Islamic or other Third World traditions? How could it be changed? Go to www.udhr.org to look up the declaration.

Summary

The first article begins with an attack on the idea that culture can ever be used as a defense against violations of human rights. The author, Shashi Tharoor, cites suttee and anti-Semitism as long-established practices that are no longer acceptable to international values. Both these examples involve violence, so it is easy to justify opposition to them. However, she also suggests a way forward in less extreme cases. The example she uses is that of Muslim divorce, in which the woman receives no alimony. She commends the response of the Indian government, which was to introduce a civil marriage in parallel to the Islamic ceremony—a wife with no rights under the laws of her faith would be able to seek redress in the courts of the state. This, in her view, is a happy solution to the problem of human rights legislation being seen as religious intolerance. Her conclusion is that it may be necessary to impose human rights in order to create freedom—she admits that this may seem a paradox, but regards it as a small price to pay for a greater good.

In the second article Abdul Aziz Said argues that the modern notion of human rights is derived exclusively from western traditions, and that it does not pay sufficient attention to people who live by different rules. Politics, he says, is by its nature culture specific—people in the developed world regard themselves as self-determining, whereas citizens of Islamic nations see themselves and their governments as servants of the will of God. In the west, if there is poverty, people want to eliminate it. In the Arab world, by contrast, there is a strong sense of the need to endure adversity. The difference between Muslim and western values is therefore philosophical and relative, not absolute. The fact that Muslims do not have the same definition of human rights does not make them cruel or uncivilized and does not justify attempts by the west to impose values on them.

FURTHER INFORMATION:

 Books:

Donnelly, Jack, *Universal Human Rights in Theory and in Practice.* 2nd edition. Ithaca, NY: Cornell University Press, 2003.

Dunne, Tim, and Nicholas J. Wheeler, *Human Rights in Global Politics.* Cambridge and New York: Cambridge University Press, 1999.

Ignatieff, Michael, *Human Rights as Politics and Idolatry.* Princeton, NJ: Princeton University Press, 2001.

Lauren, Paul Gordon, *The Evolution of International Human Rights.* University Park, PA: University of Pennsylvania Press, 1998.

Patman, Robert G. (ed.), *Universal Human Rights.* New York: St. Martin's Press, 2000.

 Useful website:

www.hri.ca

Site of Human Rights Internet. Comprehensive information on human rights worldwide.

The following debate in the Pro/Con series may also be of interest:

In this volume:
Topic 4 Should human rights come before national sovereignty?

CAN HUMAN RIGHTS BE APPLIED UNIVERSALLY?

YES: Murder, for example, is always perceived as wrong wherever it is committed

YES: Some practices may not be to western taste, but that does not give us the right to impose our own preferences on others

MORALITY
Are values the same everywhere?

CULTURE
Can local traditions ever be above or beyond human rights considerations?

NO: Morals are often based on religious foundations. Islamic countries have differing notions of morals than Christian countries.

NO: Cultural and religious practices must bow to right and wrong, which are not relative but absolute

CAN HUMAN RIGHTS BE APPLIED UNIVERSALLY? KEY POINTS

YES: Liberal democracies must do everything in their power to raise the whole world to their own level of political freedom and social sensitivity

YES: If no one opposes the denial or abuse of human rights in one country, the injustice will spread to other nations. This must be prevented whenever possible.

WHOSE BUSINESS?
Is it right for one nation to interfere in the affairs of another on moral grounds?

NO: The idea that any one nation occupies the moral high ground is arrogant, and any attempt to impose its will by force on another nation is cultural imperialism

NO: Efforts to impose western-style governments and value systems on countries with no such traditions do not necessarily lead to just governments

Topic 3
ARE THE RIGHTS OF THE INDIVIDUAL MORE IMPORTANT THAN GROUP RIGHTS?

YES
FROM "LIBERALISM AND HUMAN RIGHTS: A NECESSARY CONNECTION"
THE HUMAN RIGHTS READER
RHODA E. HOWARD AND JACK DONNELLY

NO
FROM "MINORITY RIGHTS: THE FAILURE OF
INTERNATIONAL LAW TO PROTECT THE ROMA"
HUMAN RIGHTS BRIEF, SPRING 2002
MARY ELLEN TSEKOS

INTRODUCTION

International human rights laws are grounded in the notion of equal rights for all individuals. The 1948 Universal Declaration of Human Rights avoided putting people in cultural contexts and specified that individual rights were paramount. Its model has set the standard for justice internationally ever since, but there is a growing demand for more recognition of group rights. The issue of whether individual rights are more important than group rights is a subject of fierce debate.

Modern human rights laws emerged in a political and cultural climate that favored individuals over the state. In the aftermath of World War II (1939–1945) many governments realized that individuals needed protection against abuse by the state, and that individuals should be seen not merely in terms of their role in society but as human beings "born free and equal in dignity and rights."

Many people, however, argue that laws based on liberal, western ideas of the individual are not appropriate for societies or groups in which the individual is *not* paramount. In tribal societies, such as among Native Alaskans, land is owned communally, whereas in western societies it is owned individually. Similarly, the western idea of women's rights might not fit a society in which wearing a veil and remaining at home are integral to a woman's dignity.

Others claim that existing international human rights laws are the only fair standard to protect individual liberty and justice for everyone. They argue that all groups ultimately benefit from these laws because groups are made up of individuals. That may be so, argue advocates of group rights, but existing laws are still inadequate to protect aspects of group identity, such as language or religious beliefs, that are fundamental to their personal dignity.

Many supporters of group rights want specific laws to protect minorities, such as those that have been introduced in Macedonia, where Roma, Turks, Albanians, and Vlachs are all equal under a constitution drawn up after the breakup of former Yugoslavia in 1991. It is hoped that laws protecting these minorities' traditions and beliefs will prevent a buildup of the ethnic tension that typifies many modern societies.

"The smallest minority on earth is the individual. Those who deny individual rights cannot claim to be defenders of minorities."
—AYN RAND (1905–1982),
NOVELIST

Advocates of group rights, though, question how international law can protect "minorities" when it has yet to adequately define the term. In recent years the term "national minorities" has been used to define minority peoples who are tied to a sovereign state. This term cannot be applied, for example, to the Roma (Gypsies), who are nomadic and choose not to be citizens of any country.

Historically, the United States has favored individual over group rights. The Constitution is founded on the Bill of Rights, which champions the individual. Critics say that this tradition has led to the oppression of minority groups, such as the Native Americans. The solution in the Native American case has been to allow them to follow their own laws and beliefs, while the government retains the right to intervene to protect the individual where necessary.

Affirmative action, the reserving of jobs and places for minorities in employment and education, also comes up in any discussion of individual versus group rights. The policy has come under attack for denying basic rights to individuals who do not belong to the protected group.

The United States has occasionally come into conflict with the rest of the world in its defense of individual rights. In April 2002, for example, the United States left unsigned the treaty ratifying the International Criminal Court (ICC), aimed at prosecuting perpetrators of genocide, war crimes, and crimes against humanity. The United States preferred to retain the right to prosecute, if necessary, its own diplomats or soldiers in its own courts.

Since September 11, 2001, the war on terrorism has become yet another challenge to individual versus group rights. In October 2001 President George W. Bush signed the USA PATRIOT Act granting sweeping new powers to authorities to prevent terrorism. The act allows individual Americans to be spied on more easily by intelligence agencies. Critics argue that such laws infringe on civil liberties.

In the first of the following two articles Rhoda E. Howard and Jack Donnelly argue that individual rights are superior to group rights. In the second article Mary Ellen Tsekos uses the case of the Roma to disagree.

LIBERALISM AND HUMAN RIGHTS: A NECESSARY CONNECTION
Rhoda E. Howard and Jack Donnelly

YES

✓ …The practice of seeking social justice and human dignity through the mechanism of rights held equally by every citizen, and which can be exercised even against society, first originated in the modern west.

This historical fact, however, should not lead us to commit the genetic fallacy of judging an argument or practice by its origins. Quite the contrary, we argue that the historical particularity of human rights is fully compatible with their moral and international normative universality. In fact, we contend that internationally recognized human rights, which are based on a liberal conception of justice and human dignity, represent the only standard of political legitimacy that has both wide popular appeal (in the North, South, East, and West alike) and a concrete record of delivering a life of dignity in modern social and political conditions....

It helps to be clear; explain any unusual terms. "International normative universality" refers to the fact that most world governments now accept as the norm the idea of human rights for everyone.

Liberalism, equality, and personal autonomy

Following Ronald Dworkin, we contend that the heart of liberalism is expressed in the basic political right to equal concern and respect:

"Liberalism" refers generally to a belief in liberal, or free, opinions, practices, or politics.

> *Government must treat those whom it governs with concern, that is, as human beings who are capable of suffering and frustration, and with respect, that is, as human beings who are capable of forming and acting on intelligent conceptions of how their lives should be lived. Government must not only treat people with concern and respect, but with equal concern and respect. It must not distribute goods or opportunities unequally on the ground that some citizens are entitled to more because they are worthy of more concern. It must not constrain liberty on the ground that one citizen's conception of the good life … is nobler or superior to another's.*

The authors are quoting from Taking Rights Seriously (1977) by Ronald Dworkin, professor of law at New York University School of Law.

The state must treat each person as a moral and political equal; it need not assure each person an equal share of social resources, but it must treat all with equal concern and respect. Inequalities in goods or opportunities that arise directly or indirectly from political decisions (and many such inequalities are easily justified within a liberal regime) must be compatible with the right to equal concern and respect.

Personal liberty, especially the liberty to choose and pursue one's own life, clearly is entailed in the principle of equal respect. If the state were to interfere in matters of personal morality, it would be treating the life plans and values of some as superior to others. A certain amount of economic liberty is also required, at least to the extent that decisions concerning consumption, investment, and risk reflect free decisions based on personal values that arise from autonomously chosen conceptions of the good life. But liberty alone cannot serve as the overriding value of social life, nor can it be the sole end of political association. Unless checked by a fairly expansive, positive conception of the persons in relation to whom it is exercised, individual liberty readily degenerates into license and social atomization. If liberty is to foster dignity, it must be exercised within the constraints of the principle of equal concern and respect.

> Why are some inequalities easily justified within a liberal regime? Can you think of any examples?

> What is your definition of "the good life?" Do you think factors like culture, religion, or politics influence people's expectations of what the good life may be?

The inherent dignity of individuals

In fact, autonomy and equality are less a pair of guiding principles than different manifestations of the central liberal commitment to the equal worth and dignity of each and every person. Each human being has an equal, irreducible moral worth, whatever his or her social utility. Regardless of who they are or where they stand, individuals have an inherent dignity and worth for which the state must demonstrate an active concern. Furthermore, everyone is *entitled* to this equal concern and respect. Minimum standards of political treatment are embodied in human rights; they are not merely desirable goals of social policy.

This implies a particular conception of the relation of the individual to the community and the state. Man is a social animal. Human potential, and even personal individuality, can be developed and expressed only in a social context. Society requires the discharge of certain political functions, and large-scale political organization requires the state. The state, however, also can present serious threats to human dignity and equal concern and respect if it seeks to enforce a particular vision of the good life or to entrench privileged inequality. Therefore, human rights have a special reference to the state in order to keep it an instrument to realize rather than undermine equal concern and respect.

The author argues that conflicts between the state and the individual are inevitable. Do you agree?

In the inevitable conflicts between the individual and the state, the liberal gives prima facie priority, in the areas protected by human rights, to the individual. For the liberal, the individual is not merely separable from the community and social roles, but especially valued precisely as a distinctive, discrete individual—which is why each person must be treated with equal concern and respect. The state and society are conceived, in more or less contractarian terms, as associations for the fuller unfolding of human potential, through the exercise and enjoyments of human rights. Human dignity, for the liberal, is largely encompassed in the vision of a life in which each person is an equal and autonomous member of society enjoying the full range of human rights.

The rise of the individual

This view of man is rooted in structural changes that began to emerge in late medieval and early modern Europe, gained force in the eighteenth and nineteenth centuries, and today are increasingly the norm throughout the world. The "creation" of the private individual separate from society is closely linked to the rise of a new and more complex division of labor, the resulting changes in class structure (particularly the rise and then dominance of the bourgeoisie), and a new vision of the individual's relationship to God, society, and the state.

The "bourgeoisie" is a term for the middle classes.

Do not make assumptions about what your audience might know. Always provide explanations and examples.

These developments are well known and need not be recounted here. The social changes of modernization—especially migration, urbanization, and technological development, in the context of capitalist market economies—replaced the all-encompassing moral role of traditional or feudal society with a much more segmented social order. Politics was separated from religion, the economy, and law (which were likewise separated from one another). Individuals too were separated from society as a whole; no longer could they be reduced to their roles, to parts of the community. With the recognition of separate individuals possessing special worth and dignity precisely as individuals, the basis for human rights was established.

The modern state and the individual

Occurring parallel to these changes in society was the equally well known development of the modern state. The newly rising bourgeois class was initially a principal backer of the newly ascendant princes and kings, who also wanted to free themselves from the constraints of the old feudal order.

As the state's power grew, however, it increasingly threatened the individual citizen. Bourgeois "freemen" thus began to demand that they indeed be free.

Such demands eventually took the form of arguments for the universal natural rights and equality of all people. In this socially mobile society in which entrance to and exit from the bourgeois class was relatively unpredictable, a new set of privileges could not readily be reserved for a new elite defined by birth or some similar characteristic.... In order for some (the bourgeoisie) to be able to enjoy these rights, they had to be demanded and at least formally guaranteed for all. Thus human rights came to be articulated primarily as claims of any individual against the state. Human rights lay down the basic form of the relationship between the (new, modern) individual and the (new, modern) state, a relationship based on the prima facie priority of the individual over the state in those areas protected by human rights.

Human rights are morally prior to and superior to society and the state, and under the control of individuals, who hold them and may exercise them against the state in extreme cases. This reflects not only the equality of all individuals but also their autonomy, their right to have and pursue interests and goals different from those of the state or its rulers. In the areas and endeavors protected by human rights, the individual is "king"—or rather an equal and autonomous person entitled to equal concern and respect.

> *"Natural rights" was a term that has now been replaced by "human rights." Natural rights, according to the 17th-century philosopher John Locke, were those rights enjoyed by humans in their original "state of nature," before they began forming complex societies. For more on this see Topic 1 Do human rights exist?*

The ideal of human rights

In practice, these values and structural changes remain incompletely realized even today, and for most of the modern era they have been restricted to a small segment of the population. Nevertheless, the ideal was established and its implementation begun. And even if the demand for human rights began as a tactic of the bourgeoisie to protect its own class interests, the logic of universal and inalienable personal rights has long since broken free of these origins.

Although these processes of sociopolitical individuation and state-building were first played out in Europe, they are increasingly the rule throughout the world. The structural basis for a society of equal and autonomous individuals is thus being universalized despite its historically particular ... origin. Social structure today increasingly parallels the near universal diffusion of the idea of human rights and the ... claim that human rights are universal. Individual human rights increasingly appear not merely as moral ideals but as ... necessary to protect and realize human dignity.

> *Do you agree with the authors that individual human rights are a necessity rather than an ideal?*

MINORITY RIGHTS...
Mary Ellen Tsekos

NO

The Roma people are also known as Gypsies.

...Historians disagree about the origins of the Roma. Most believe, however, that the ancestors of the Roma migrated from northwest India at around 1000 A.D. Contrary to the common misconception, the name Roma did not originate in the country of Romania. Rather, the name comes from the Sanskrit-related language spoken by the Roma in which the word "Rom" is the masculine singular noun meaning "man." "Roma" is the plural for "Rom."

The Roma first appeared in Western Europe in the 1400s. Early tolerance soon turned to suspicion, partly due to the Roma's unique cultural practices. Romani culture, for example, is infused with both mistrust and fear of outsiders. This distrust stems in part from their semi-religious beliefs, which divide the world into the clean and the unclean. To the Roma, the perception of the rest of the world as unclean justifies treating outsiders differently. ...Thus, while stealing would never be accepted within the Roma group, stealing from outsiders is considered acceptable so long as what is stolen is needed for subsistence. These cultural differences have placed the Roma at great odds with citizens of the countries to which they emigrate....

Do you think that cultural practices that bring a specific group into conflict with the wider society are acceptable?

The Roma's beliefs and practices have fostered great discrimination and prejudice against them. For centuries, the Roma have endured banishment, deportation, cultural destruction, enslavement, mutilation, and murder....

In the 20th century, acceptance of the Roma has not changed significantly. During World War II, the Roma were among the first targets of Nazi policies; at least half a million to a million Roma were killed under the Nazi regime. From 1920 to 1972, the Swiss government enacted a policy of taking Romani children from their parents to be raised by non-Roma families. Until 1954, Sweden prohibited the Roma from entering the country, and banished the Roma population already there....

For more information on the human rights situation of the Roma go to www.errc.org/index.shtml—the European Roma Rights Center website.

The definition of minorities in international law
Existing international mechanisms are inadequate to protect the rights of the Roma as a minority group. The issue is partly one of definition. Currently there are no universally accepted

definitions within international law for the terms "people,"
"nation," or "minority"…

[R]ecent international human rights declarations have used
the term "national minorities," but have failed to define it. The
term "national minority," however, generally has been used to
identify minority groups who fall into one of two groups: (1)
minority groups who are nationals of one state but have
ethnic ties to another; or (2) minority groups who reside on
the territory of a state, are citizens of that state, and maintain
long standing and lasting ties to the state.

The Framework Convention for the Protection of National
Minorities (Framework Convention), which was adopted by
thirty-nine European states in 1994, is the first legally binding
multilateral instrument devoted exclusively to the protection
of minorities. Despite the fact that [it] is legally binding, it
fails to provide a conclusive definition of minority.…

Current definitions remain limited in scope and apply only
to minorities who are either nationals of a particular state, or
those who are colonized peoples. Neither of these definitions
extends minority status to the Roma. The Roma were not a
colonized people, they do not have a homeland, and they do
not bear ties to any currently existing state. The Roma also
are not citizens of any given state, in part because of their
nomadic way of life, which developed in response to
centuries of fleeing persecution.…

Minorities as actors in the international system

International law…is structured around the concept of the
sovereign state as the most effective organizing framework
for law and order.… Modern history has, however, been
marked by abhorrent abuses committed by states against
their own citizens, and thus it has become necessary to allow
individuals to have some personal redress at an international
level. The modern international human rights framework has
begun to afford individuals a small degree of recognition as
independent actors within the international system. For
example, states are bound by numerous international
conventions guaranteeing individuals certain rights, and
pursuant to these conventions, individuals may now bring
claims independently to the European Court of Human
Rights, the Inter-American Commission on Human Rights,
and the Inter-American Court of Human Rights when states
violate the rights guaranteed within these conventions.

This minimal recognition of the individual as an
international actor has not expanded sufficiently to
effectively include minority groups as actors. The human

Go to www.word
reference.com to
research possible
definitions of
these terms.

Why do you
think there are
so many problems
surrounding the
definition of the
word "minority"?

Look back to the
first article in this
debate. How
does the author's
perception of
individual rights
differ from
that of the
previous authors?

rights system in Europe serves as a key example of the problem. Europe's primary human rights instrument is the European Convention for the Protection of Human Rights and Fundamental Freedoms (European Convention). This document obliges states to guarantee the protection of human rights to all persons within their jurisdiction.... Significantly, however, the document guarantees all those rights to individuals. No rights are granted to groups....

What about the argument that if individuals have rights, groups do not need rights?

The European Convention also established the European Court of Human Rights (ECHR) and granted it the authority to hear cases from individuals. Notably, the Convention continues to require that all domestic remedies be exhausted before redress is sought at the ECHR. This is particularly problematic for minority groups such as the Roma, who often are not recognized as a minority group by the states in which they reside. If such unrecognized minority groups are not granted minority status, they will lack the requisite standing to bring a claim against the state based on discrimination, and thus will be unable to satisfy the exhaustion of domestic remedies requirement set by the European Convention....

If states do not recognize minorities, who should dictate whether a group is a minority or not?

Collective rights of minorities in international law

Some might argue that the international human rights regime, which is increasingly granting individuals standing as actors within the international system, is sufficient to protect members of a minority group against discrimination and abuse. This approach, however, ignores the necessity of protecting group identity, and disregards the fact that the rights to develop a group's culture, religion, language, traditions, and cultural heritage are fundamental in protecting their human rights.

It is an effective debating technique to state the opposing argument and then argue against it.

The 1935 advisory opinion of the Permanent Court of International Justice (Court) concerning minority schools in Albania highlights the importance of fundamental group rights, and conveys the Court's opinion that protection of individual rights alone is not sufficient to protect minorities. In this case, the Albanian Constitution was amended to abolish all private schools in 1933. The Albanian government asserted that this amendment was non-discriminatory since it applied equally to all private schools. In effect, however, the amendment disproportionately discriminated against the minority Greeks since the group relied heavily on its private school system to protect its identity, faith, and culture. The Court found that the abolition of the private school system denied the Greeks equal treatment as a culture, and that

Greece and Albania share a common border. Greeks have lived in the region that is now Albania since the seventh century B.C. It has been estimated that in the early 20th century about 35,000 Greeks lived in Albania.

without the ability to teach their children, the Greek minority's culture would slowly be eradicated.

The *Minority Schools in Albania* case is analogous to the problems faced by the Roma population today in protecting their group culture. The current system continues to emphasize protection of individual rights, which includes the right to practice one's own cultural beliefs, but fails to include state protection of group practices. Thus ... the Roma are not allowed to have a separate legal system, nor are they guaranteed that their children would learn Romanes in school. The Roma culture, language, and traditions exist within groups, and a failure to protect their group rights essentially undermines the rights of the Romani individual to practice his or her beliefs. Despite the *Minority Schools in Albania* decision, [some] international conventions, including the ICCPR and, more recently, the European Framework Convention, fail to afford protection to minority groups. ...

Tsekos makes her argument stronger by making a comparison between the Roma and the Greeks in Albania, a case clearly defined in international law.

This is the crux of the author's argument—that the rights of the individual cannot be separated from those of the group. They are synonymous.

Disentangling sovereignty

In order for the Roma to be able to flourish as a group, they must be granted certain group rights. Granting them these rights, however, will mean that states will have to give up some measure of sovereignty over the Roma. Thus, solving the problems faced by the Roma requires rethinking the notion of sovereignty. One proposed alternative is to disentangle the notion of sovereignty, or group autonomy, from the concept of land....

In this way, minority groups could be granted status as a "nation" without destroying the physical jurisdiction of the state. Although the concept may sound radical, it is not novel. In the United States, for example, Native American tribes retain their own legal traditions and their own schools, while the U.S. government retains ultimate jurisdiction. Diplomatic and consular immunities show the same type of division, and allow the state to retain territorial control....

Make your argument more convincing by offering possible solutions to problems. Tsekos suggests that minority groups can be granted nationhood, as have the Native Americans, in a way that is also compatible with the state's authority.

It is clear that the international system, with the sovereign state as its main actor, is not going to change quickly. The international system, however, increasingly has begun to operate outside the realm of state control, and the panoply of players in the international system has expanded significantly. The development of international legal frameworks that allow individuals to have a personal voice in the international system, as well as the creation of supra-national associations that are composed of entities that are not sovereign states, suggest an increasing role for non-state actors in the international system....

Summary

The articles in this debate explore whether individual rights are more important than group rights. In the first article Rhoda E. Howard and Jack Donnelly examine the origins of modern human rights. They take issue with the suggestion that human rights based on the rights of the individual serve mainly the liberal west because that is where they originated. They argue that human rights represent the only standard of political legitimacy that is acceptable worldwide. Howard and Donnelly claim that human rights are morally superior to the rights of society or the state and reflect the autonomy and equality of individuals. They say that the notion of human rights has now broken free of its origins and provides the basis for a society of equal and autonomous individuals throughout the world.

In the second article Mary Ellen Tsekos looks at the failure of international law to protect the Roma, an ethnic group that has endured discrimination for centuries. She argues that international human rights law has focused too much attention on individuals at the expense of minorities. Tsekos says the recognition of individuals having rights against the state has not expanded to include groups. She points out that existing laws on the rights of minorities are unclear and rely too much on the groups' ties to and residence in a sovereign state. This is particularly problematic for the nomadic Roma, who have no links to one particular state and are not recognized as a minority in any of the states in which they reside. Tsekos proposes that minority groups such as the Roma could be granted status as a nation, enabling them to retain their own traditions, while the state they live in maintains territorial control.

FURTHER INFORMATION:

 Books:

Bloom, Irene, *Religious Diversity and Human Rights*. New York: Columbia University Press, 1996.

Useful websites:

www.hrw.org/summaries/s.albania952.html
Article from 1995 on the Human Rights Watch site, Human Rights Watch report from 1996, "A Threat to 'Stability': Human Rights Violations in Macedonia."
www.minorityrights.org
Site of the campaigning organization Minority Rights Group International.
www.ecmi.de/doc/index.html
Site of nonpartisan institute engaged in projects concerned with minority-majority relations in Europe.
www.udhr.ch
Site dedicated to Universal Declaration of Human Rights.

The following debates in the Pro/Con series may also be of interest:

In this volume:

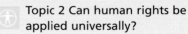 Topic 2 Can human rights be applied universally?

Topic 4 Should human rights come before national sovereignty?

Topic 7 Do stateless people have rights?

Amnesty International, pages 86–87.

ARE THE RIGHTS OF THE INDIVIDUAL MORE IMPORTANT THAN GROUP RIGHTS?

YES: Individuals need protection against abuse by the state

YES: Since groups are made up of individuals, they benefit from these rights

EQUALITY
Should individuals be given more rights than groups?

HUMAN RIGHTS
Is it right that human rights focus on equal rights for all individuals?

NO: The rights of certain minority groups, such as the Native Americans, have largely been ignored, and that has led to oppression

NO: Existing laws do not protect aspects of group identity, such as language or religious beliefs

ARE THE RIGHTS OF THE INDIVIDUAL MORE IMPORTANT THAN GROUP RIGHTS?
KEY POINTS

YES: At times, for example, since September 11, 2001, the rights of the individual become less important than preserving group rights

YES: Sometimes individual rights are in conflict with group rights, and the government may have to make difficult but necessary decisions

BEST INTERESTS
Are the rights of the individual ever justifiably overlooked for the greater good of the country?

NO: Since September 11 both individual and group rights have been eroded. Individuals have less right to privacy, and some groups are suspected of terrorism simply because of their religion.

NO: The notion of individual human rights is crucial to a commitment to international standards of human rights even in times of national crisis

HOW TO WRITE A BOOK REPORT

"Books are the bees which carry the quickening pollen from one to another mind."

— J. RUSSELL LOWELL (1819–1891), U.S. POET AND EDITOR

A book report should not be confused with a book review. Book reviews, often found in magazines and newspapers, are usually personal and persuasive and can focus on a particular issue or theme. Book reports, on the other hand, are a descriptive summary of the plot or main themes. Students are often asked to write book reports at school and college. The actual writing of the report helps the reader analyze the main points of the book, clarify opinions, and demonstrate knowledge and understanding.

Preparation

You must be certain that you understand the main ideas and focus of your chosen book before you begin your report. It is good practice to read the book more than once. Use a notebook to write down impressions (always note the page number for later reference). The use of quotations will demonstrate your ability to highlight key events or ideas within the text.

Introduction

Write down the title of the book, the author's name, and publishing details (publisher, publication date, number of pages). The first section of your report should inform the reader of the main idea, thesis, or argument of the book. Provide some background information on the author.

Summary of content

The summary should clarify the main themes or events in the book. If the book is divided into sections, summarize the main points of each section and how it relates to the overall content of the book. For fiction the summary should include an overview of the plot, as well as descriptions of character, mood, and setting. This section of your report should be concise.

Analysis of text

In this section you can write about your opinions, but make sure you explain and back them up with examples, such as quotations from the text. Examine the author's use of literary techniques or writing styles to communicate ideas. Discuss the author's point of view and how the argument is structured.

Evaluation of text

Conclude your report with an evaluation that emphasizes your key points. Indicate whether you think the author has been successful in representing his or her ideas. Remember that the book report should be informative rather than persuasive.

GENRE DIFFERENCES

Your report will vary in content and style depending on whether your chosen book is fiction or nonfiction. Check the required criteria with your teacher. Use the points below to help.

Fiction

If your book is a fictional or creative piece of writing, you will need to describe elements such as the setting, the time period, the main characters, and the plot. Try to avoid recording every small detail, but do the following:

- Define the opening situation involving the main character(s)
- Identify the needs/desires/ambitions of the main character(s)
- Describe events and their effect on the main characters
- Conclude briefly by giving an overall opinion of the book

Nonfiction

Biographical, historical, or factual texts will differ slightly. In an academic or factual book report your introduction should include a clear statement about the topic. The summary should expand on the themes and describe the author's intentions. For a biographical book describe key events and their relevance to the individual's life. Consider the main theme to help you analyze the text, for example, does Henry David Thoreau's *Walden* effectively communicate his ideas about the importance of living in harmony with nature?

CREATIVE MODELS

Your book report does not necessarily have to be in essay format. Discuss with your teacher the model you use to present a creative book report. Some of the following ideas may appeal to you:

- Work in groups, and adapt your book reports into a short film
- Present your report to your class, and use visual aids as support
- Debate your report in teams, taking opposing view points
- Use the school/college website to present reports with photographs/images
- Animate your report

USEFUL WEBSITES

Visit these websites for further information on writing your book report:
http://www.sdc.uwo.ca/writing/owlhandout/book_report.html
http://www.infoplease.com/homework/wsbookreporths/html

Topic 4
SHOULD HUMAN RIGHTS COME BEFORE NATIONAL SOVEREIGNTY?

YES
FROM "SOVEREIGNTY, HUMAN RIGHTS AND LEGITIMACY IN THE POST-COLD WAR WORLD"
TOWARD A NEW PARTNERSHIP: INTERNATIONAL NORMS IN THE U.S.-EUROPEAN RELATIONSHIP SINCE 1980
MICHAEL JOSEPH SMITH

NO
"HANDS OFF DOMESTIC POLITICS, SAY ASIAN NATIONS"
INTERPRESS THIRD WORLD AGENCY, SEPTEMBER 27, 1999
THALIF DEEN

INTRODUCTION

National sovereignty is broadly defined as the freedom of every country to carry on its internal affairs without external interference. The concept is usually held to have originated with the Peace of Westphalia, a series of treaties between major European powers that ended the Thirty Years' War in 1648.

Human rights are fundamental entitlements that all persons are meant to enjoy as protection against unjust conduct by the state in which they live. Among the forms of mistreatment most widely condemned as violations of human rights are extrajudicial or summary execution; disappearance (in which people are taken into custody and never seen again); kidnapping; torture; arbitrary detention; slavery or involuntary servitude; discrimination on racial, ethnic, religious, or sexual grounds; and violation of the rights to due process of law, free expression, and peaceful assembly.

National sovereignty and human rights have often come into conflict. Ideally, the internationally recognized boundaries of any state should never be violated, and the government of each state should be left to determine what is best for its citizens. Yet in fact, if the government of one country legalizes or permits any of the aforementioned abuses, other countries or the international community as a whole may express disapproval. In extreme cases they may intervene to stop violations either by imposing economic sanctions or by military action.

The overriding problem is that neither national sovereignty nor human rights can be satisfactorily defined. Some countries are so powerful that they can behave much as they like. China, for example, carries out summary executions for crimes that other nations, such as those of western Europe, regard as petty. Yet it would be futile for a liberal democracy like Denmark to issue the Chinese government an ultimatum to end capital punishment—it lacks the might to dictate terms.

Meanwhile, countries that are more concerned than China about foreign approval have been compelled to recognize external authority structures, such as the European Union and the United Nations (UN). Those bodies have successfully demanded changes in nations' domestic laws. Britain, for example, was ordered in 1999 by the European Union to lift its ban on gays in the armed forces. In the same year the UN sanctioned military intervention to end the persecution and murder of minority ethnic Albanians in Kosovo, a province of the rapidly disintegrating state of Yugoslavia

---

> *"The respect for human rights is one of the most significant advantages of a free and democratic nation in the peaceful struggle for influence, and we should use this good weapon as effectively as possible."*
>
> —JIMMY CARTER, 39TH PRESIDENT (1977–1981)

Other less powerful nations exist only by the agreement of the international community. Taiwan, for example, has Westphalian sovereignty, but not international legal sovereignty. If the United States withdrew support for the island-state, its present government could not be maintained. Monaco remains independent only with the agreement of neighboring France. Both nations must therefore be more responsive than a great power to external criticism.

Many political commentators have observed that the issue of human rights has less to do with the preservation of basic freedom than with the pursuit of foreign policy—rich countries use it as a stick with which to beat poor countries. During the presidency of Jimmy Carter (1977–1981) the United States placed a greater emphasis than ever before on the worldwide pursuit of human rights. While many applauded that initiative, it created serious diplomatic problems in countries where it was regarded as a form of neocolonialism. African and Asian leaders objected that although the United States called for democracy, one-person, one-vote was not synonymous with human rights—despite the success of this form of government in North America, in parts of the developing world the system was unworkable.

In the first article Michael Joseph Smith argues that human rights should and must take precedence over the rights of states. In his view the international community has a moral duty to eradicate injustice whenever and wherever it can.

The second article, by Thalif Deen, looks at the recent case of three Asian nations—Sri Lanka, India, and China. Each of the nations argues against external intervention in its domestic policies, and each claims that human rights issues should be dealt with internally.

SOVEREIGNTY, HUMAN RIGHTS AND LEGITIMACY IN THE POST-COLD WAR WORLD
Michael Joseph Smith

YES

"Gunboat diplomacy" is the threat of, or resort to, force in diplomatic initiatives. The term originated in the first Opium War (1839–1842), when the Chinese rebelled against the British importation of opium into China, and the British response was to send a gunboat up the Yangtze River. Can you think of other, more recent examples?

…My argument in this chapter is straightforward: norms of human rights have fundamentally and irrevocably challenged traditional norms of national sovereignty…. Consider the following statements:

[1] Such arguments as "human rights taking precedence over sovereignty" and "humanitarian intervention" seem to be in vogue these days. But respect for sovereignty and non-interference are the basic principles governing international relations and any deviation from them would lead to a gunboat diplomacy that would wreak havoc in the world.

[2] Not all the ideas that have arisen in the course of the discussion about the future of Europe seem to us to be justified. I'm thinking in particular of the appeals for humanitarian interference—this is a new idea—in the internal affairs of another state, even when this is done on the pretext of protecting human rights and freedoms.

The OSCE (Organization for Security and Cooperation in Europe) is an international association of more than 50 eastern and western countries that work to increase their security.

Both these speakers—China's Foreign Minister Tang Jiaxuan at the United Nations [1] and Russian President Boris Yeltsin [2] at the November 1999 meeting of the OSCE in Istanbul— regard themselves as reaffirming the fundamental international norm of the sovereign independence of states, and a corresponding duty to respect the domestic jurisdiction of states. (At the same [UN] debate in September 1999, the Indian Foreign Minister warned that international action should not in anyway diminish state sovereignty.)

Both China and Russia condemned the NATO action in Kosovo: "…A regional military organization, in the name of humanitarianism and human rights, bypassed United Nations and took military action against a sovereign state. It created an ominous precedent in international relations."…

Responding to Mr. Tang, the Chinese Foreign Minister, at the September UN debate, German Foreign Minister Joschka Fischer said, "The Kosovo conflict marks a change in the direction of the development of international relations—one in which human rights are valued as much as sovereignty." Václav Havel, President of the Czech Republic, has expressed this interpretation with his usual eloquence…:

If it is possible to say about war that it is ethical, or that it is fought for ethical reasons, it is true of this war [in Kosovo].... This war gives human rights precedence over the rights of states.... I see this as an important precedent for the future....

… And in his answer to Boris Yeltsin at the OSCE meeting in November 1999, President Bill Clinton said "… I do not believe there will ever be a time in human affairs when we will ever be able to say we cannot criticize [an] action simply because it happened within the territorial borders of a single nation." …

Why multiply these quotations? In themselves they prove nothing, but they do, I think, illustrate an important change in the international normative environment: the traditional norm of sovereignty, as both the supreme source and location of values worth protecting, is increasingly being questioned. To put it differently, the legitimacy of state sovereignty—both as a commanding value and as the organizing principle of international relations—is being challenged by the cluster of values we associate with human rights. …

But what precisely is meant here by the norm of sovereignty? The term is notoriously prone to conflicting definitions. "Sovereignty" can be defined as "supreme authority" in a domestic political context, as juridical, international legal sovereignty, or as so-called "Westphalian" sovereignty, the characteristic institutional arrangement of the world into separate, independent territorial units…. This version of sovereignty, i.e., a particular institutional arrangement of nation-states, is obviously the most relevant to the present discussion. Of course, as many have recognized, sovereignty has always been more an ideal-type than a faithful description of reality … and departures from the ideal type version are by no means new. This has led to another kind of distinction—formal or legal sovereignty versus operational sovereignty. States with formal, or legal, sovereignty may in fact have limited capacity to guarantee, or enforce, their autonomy from outside actors and influences. In a world of

> *In 1998 Albanians in Kosovo, a region within Serbia, openly rebelled against the Serbian government. In an attempt to stop the two sides fighting, the UN drew up a peace plan. When the Serbian government refused to sign the plan, NATO, backed by the UN, launched air attacks on Serbia—the first attack on a sovereign European country in NATO's history. The Serbians agreed to full military withdrawal from Kosovo 11 weeks after the air strikes began.*

> *In what ways do the values associated with human rights challenge state sovereignty?*

Can you think
of many states
that claim to be
independent but
have to rely on
other nations to
maintain them?

interdependence, in which currency values, capital flows, communications and energy are subject to no centralized control, states may claim to be independent and autonomous, but the operational reality obviously belies this claim....

In a process well described by Immanuel Kant in 1784, the system of sovereignty finds itself struggling against the universalism of human rights and a new set of institutions designed explicitly to guarantee these rights. The process is slow and evolutionary. A human rights regime is not straightforwardly replacing Westphalian sovereignty. Rather, it exists in a kind of creative tension with it.... [I]n this view, the Westphalian system will gradually give way to a different "state of affairs," as a result of a process of internal and external change.... Gradually, the European states have moved to constrain their own sovereign independence in service of a broader goal of achieving a peaceful, more extensive, social order. This has not occurred all at once, nor has it meant the end of European sovereign states. But the EU does represent a significant normative and institutional change in the way heretofore quite independent states relate to each other. And it has, to a considerable extent, made war among its members quite unthinkable....

Normative beliefs are based on norms, principles that serve to guide, control, or regulate proper or acceptable behavior.

Norms of human rights: Future directions

For too long, states have coasted on a kind of presumptive legitimacy derived simply from their status as nation-states. The internal legitimacy of their rule has gone unexamined, unquestioned, as if a government's treatment of its own citizens were opaque to outside scrutiny. States have (largely correctly) assumed that they could maltreat their own citizens or subjects with impunity: the outside world could not, or would not, critically examine such behavior, much less interfere with it. But the advance of human rights ideas has ended this opacity: we can now see in. Sovereignty no longer means that internal actions are beyond scrutiny. A state that oppresses and violates the autonomy and integrity of its citizens and subjects can no longer claim that sovereignty shields it from such scrutiny and "outside interference." Indeed, the European Court of Human Rights has frequently sided with individuals who press a human rights claim against their home state, as in the recent ruling against Britain's exclusion of gays and lesbians from its military. And although Western protestations against Russian military action against Chechnya proved to be ineffectual, these protests and inspections at least affirmed the principle that no state actions that so clearly violate human rights are

In September 1999 the European Court of Human Rights ruled that Britain's dismissal of gay service personnel breached Article 8 (right to respect for private and family life) of the European Convention on Human Rights. See Volume 7, The Constitution, Gays and lesbians in the military, pages 112–113.

beyond international attention, even when these actions are represented as internal matters.

Of course, the gap between international "attention" and effective action of prevention or enforcement is huge, and the image of a devastated Grozny haunts our collective conscience. Too many such images—from Srebenica, to Sarajevo, to Rwanda or East Timor—have crowded the landscape of sovereignty and international inaction. Not even Dr. Pangloss could look at such pictures with satisfaction. As Judith Shklar has written in her remarkable essay, "The Liberalism of Fear," "We say 'never again,' but somewhere someone is being tortured right now, and acute fear has again become the most common form of social control. To this the horror of modern warfare must be added as a reminder."

Thus, the next challenge for those who value human rights is to find ways to translate principle into action.... A condition for securing this kind of most basic freedom, I suggest, is to remove, or at least qualify, the protection or shield which sovereignty has afforded to all sorts of oppressive states. We must continue to press the notion that recognition of and respect for human rights must come before the principles of state sovereignty and non-interference. An egregious violation of human rights is no less so because it occurs within the borders of a particular state. "Today, what is internal doesn't remain internal for very long," UN Secretary-General Kofi Annan has said, "... We need a new consensus....The founders of the United Nations in 1945 came out of a world war determined to stop conflicts between states. The time has come for our generation to look at its responsibilities toward civilians who in today's wars are deliberately targeted."

The deepening legitimacy of the ideas of human rights provides the context for Annan's assertion. It is perhaps remarkable that the leader of an interstate organization is able to promote an agenda that many states, qua states, would find troubling, if not offensive. The Secretary-General surely understands this, but perhaps takes more seriously the article that opens the Universal Declaration on Human Rights: "All human beings are born free and equal in dignity and rights. They are endowed with reason and conscience and should act towards one another in a spirit of brotherhood." The Declaration may now be more a statement of lofty aspiration than a list of enforceable rights in a world of conflict within and between sovereign states. But this defines our task ahead: to translate the norms of human dignity and rights into practices and institutions that can make these norms realities.

Dr. Pangloss is a character in Candide *by the French writer Voltaire (1694–1778). Pangloss epitomizes optimism and believes that "everything is for the best."*

If a sovereign country is not free to govern itself, would the result be constant interference by powerful nations in the affairs of weaker states?

See Topic 5 Has the Universal Declaration of Human Rights achieved anything significant?

HANDS OFF DOMESTIC POLITICS, SAY ASIAN NATIONS
Thalif Deen

NO

Sri Lanka, India and China—three Asian countries long involved in civil unrest—have warned the United Nations to keep its hands off domestic political issues.

Chinese Foreign Minister Tang Jiaxuan set the tone of the argument against interference in any country's internal affairs by brushing aside repeated arguments that human rights should take precedence over national sovereignty.

"When the sovereignty of a country is put in jeopardy, its human rights can hardly be protected effectively," he said.

Sovereign equality, mutual respect for state sovereignty and non-interference in each other's internal affairs are the basic principles governing international relations today, Tang said.

China's strong stand against "humanitarian intervention" was prompted primarily by fears of a Kosovo-type intervention in Tibet—whose separatist movement has strong support in the United States. The issue of human rights, in essence, was the internal affair of a country and should be addressed mainly by the government of that country through its own efforts, Tang stressed.

Sri Lanka and the LTTE

Sri Lanka, where an insurgency by Tamil separatists has dragged on for 18 years, also rejected proposals for a UN role in mediating the dispute.

Responding to statements last week on civilian casualties in the ongoing battle, Sri Lankan Foreign Minister Lakshman Kadirgamar said that UN officials and non-governmental organisations (NGOs) had no right to inject themselves into the domestic politics of a country because they did not possess any mandate to do so.

"With the exception of the Office of the UN High Commissioner for Refugees—involved in issues relating to humanitarian aid and refugees—other UN agencies have mandates only to be involved in social and economic development of a country," Kadirgamar said.

"They should be more concerned with malaria and mosquitoes—not domestic political issues," he told IPS.

Chinese Foreign Minister Tang Jiaxuan argues that the sovereignty of a country is vital to the protection of its citizens. Do you agree that a state should have the right to govern without external interference? Does that apply equally to all forms of government?

During the second half of the 20th century the Tamils, an ethnic minority in Sri Lanka, began to accuse the Sinhalese majority of discrimination. In the 1970s there were increasing calls for the creation of a separate Tamil state. After years of ethnic conflict civil war broke out in 1983 between the separatist Liberation Tigers of Tamil Eelam (LTTE) and the Sinhalese-dominated government.

Women soldiers from the Liberation Tigers of Tamil Eelam (LTTE) in Sri Lanka. The Tamil Tigers, as they are popularly known, were formed on May 5, 1976.

Lakshman Kadirgamar (1932–) is Sri Lanka's presidential adviser. He trained as a lawyer in the UK and practiced law at the Ceylon Bar from 1955 to 1960 and 1971 to 1974 respectively. He was minister of foreign affairs from 1994 to 2000. He was the only Tamil in the government and took a firm stand on international terrorism.

Kadirgamar was furious about the move taken by unnamed UN officials in Colombo in expressing "deep concern" over the "extensive civilian killings in two separate incidents" in Sri Lanka recently.

The mandate of most UN agencies operating in the field is confined primarily to development, he said, "But yet some of them are trying to expand their mandates," he complained.

Criticism

Kadirgamar also criticised a statement attributed to the Geneva-based International Committee of the Red Cross (ICRC) which said it was "deeply concerned at the recent outburst of violence in the conflict in Sri Lanka, which is resulting in an alarming increase in the number of civilian casualties." The minister said the ICRC was wrong in equating the killing of 50 civilians by the Liberation Tigers of Tamil Eelam (LTTE) with an air attack by the Sri Lanka air force in which 22 civilians died.

"They should have drawn a distinction between the two – and not refer the two incidents in the same breath," he said. "It looks as if one justifies the other."

The civilian deaths in the air force attack were an accident, but the LTTE killings were not, he added. "It looked as if they were trying to make a virtue out of the retaliation."

The ICRC was not tolerated in India and had been barred from that country, he noted.

Why might a country ban organizations such as the Red Cross?

India and Kashmir

Addressing the 188-member General Assembly, Indian Foreign Minister Jaswant Singh said it would be an error to assume that the days of state sovereignty were over.

"The United Nations was not conceived as a super state, it will not ever become so, principally, because there is no viable substitute to the sovereign state," he added.

To diminish, marginalise or to ignore the state would also be bad practice because, the weaker any state became, the less it would be able to promote the interests of its citizens, Singh said.

India has barred any form of UN intervention in the disputed territory of Kashmir, even refusing to permit senior UN officials including Secretary-General Kofi Annan, to raise the issue at a diplomatic level. Singapore's Foreign Minister S. Jayakumar argued that, notwithstanding Kosovo where a US-led military force intervened without Security Council authorisation, "it does not appear that the majority of states have much to fear if they treat their citizens well."

Many countries ignore world organizations such as the United Nations. Do such bodies ever do any good?

If there was to be any form of "humanitarian intervention," said Jayakumar, there should be rules and objective criteria for such intervention.

"Failure to do so will breed uncertainty and instability," he warned. "If a new balance has been struck between sovereignty and other values, it should be struck knowingly, and with our eyes open."

Jayakumar said this would pose a major challenge in the coming century if the United Nations was to remain relevant in the coming century.

"This is because we can expect to face many more situations which will pose the dilemma of reconciling state sovereignty with international intervention to redress violations of human rights," he said.

Jayakumar implies that there are different understandings of sovereignty and human rights. Is it possible to establish accurate definitions of those terms?

Summary

According to Michael Joseph Smith in the first article, human rights are now so widely accepted as a desirable norm that the need to protect them has superseded national sovereignty. The precedent for this new world order was created by the UN-backed NATO intervention in Kosovo in 1999. Today independent nations may not have the economic or political power to guarantee human rights, and their maintenance must therefore be the responsibility of the international community. Smith says that this is an evolutionary process, exemplified in the progress of the states of the European Union away from what he calls Westphalian sovereignty—in other words, self-sufficiency at home with no accountability to outsiders—into an interdependent community of nations. Even where the will of the international community cannot be imposed, as, for example, during Russia's bloody intervention in Chechnya, the fact that injustice was condemned by the outside world underlines the fact that human rights are now more important than the sanctity of a state's political borders.

In the second article Thalif Deen outlines some of the objections of various Asian foreign ministers to external intervention in their countries' domestic affairs. The Chinese foreign minister is quoted as saying that a country cannot protect its inhabitants' human rights if its sovereignty is threatened. The Sri Lankan states that the UN and the Red Cross should concern themselves only with the social and economic development of a country, and should not become involved in domestic political struggles, even if they are violent. In the view of the Indian foreign minister the UN has its uses, but it is not an alternative to the sovereign state.

FURTHER INFORMATION:

Books:

Felice, William F., *Taking Human Rights Seriously: The Importance of Collective Human Rights*. New York: SUNY Press, 1996.

Lauren, Paul Gordon, *The Evolution of International Human Rights*. Philadelphia, PA: University of Pennsylvania Press, 1998.

Newman, Frank, and David Weissbrodt, *International Human Rights: Law, Policy and Process*. Cincinnati, OH: Anderson, 1996.

Useful websites:

www.hrw.org

Human Rights Watch site. Contains extensive information on human rights conditions worldwide arranged by country and by region.

The following debates in the Pro/Con series may also be of interest:

In this volume:

Topic 2 Can human rights be applied universally?

Topic 3 Are the rights of the individual more important than group rights?

Topic 5 Has the Universal Declaration of Human Rights achieved anything significant?

SHOULD HUMAN RIGHTS COME BEFORE NATIONAL SOVEREIGNTY?

YES: A country that suffers outside interference cannot protect human rights

YES: Nations are both less independent and more interdependent than ever

NATIONS ARE SACROSANCT
Should countries be left to run their own affairs?

GLOBALIZATION
In the modern world is one nation's problem every nation's problem?

NO: The international community must do everything in its power to stamp out injustice wherever it occurs

NO: The most powerful countries use human rights as a pretext for intervening in the affairs of weaker countries to further their own economic and political interests

SHOULD HUMAN RIGHTS COME BEFORE NATIONAL SOVEREIGNTY?
KEY POINTS

YES: It is both possible and necessary to oust evil rulers and replace them with good ones

YES: If the free world turns a blind eye to violations of human rights, the practice will continue

HUMAN RIGHTS ARE SACROSANCT
Are liberal values worth fighting for?

NO: Freedom is place-specific: A system that works in the United States may be impracticable in the developing world

NO: If we use force to combat injustice, we will commit worse crimes than those we were trying to eradicate

PART 2
POLITICS AND HUMAN RIGHTS

Politics is a crucial factor in both establishing and protecting human rights and in causing human rights abuses. The conditions that support or undermine rights are usually created at a political level. Some of the most brutal abuses of human rights—such as the murder of the Jews in Germany during the Holocaust of the 1930s and 1940s or the murder of millions of Cambodians in the 1970s by the Khmer Rouge led by Pol Pot—have been orchestrated by governments. On the other hand, it is often only the apparatus of the state, such as the legal system and the police force, that supports the rights of minorities in the face of the majority.

1948: a good and bad year

The adoption of the Universal Declaration of Human Rights by the United Nations on December 10 made 1948 a key year in human rights history. The declaration stated, among other things, that all human beings, no matter where they were born, had a right to liberty and freedom, equality before the law, and freedom of opinion and expression. It also declared that torture and slavery were unacceptable practices. For many observers the UDHR was a great step forward. The international community—and the national governments that it comprised—had come together to make an agreement aimed at preventing a recurrence of the atrocities that had occurred during World War II (1939–1945), including the Holocaust.

The same year, however, also provided a stark reminder of the limits of any such declaration. In 1948 the Afrikaner National Party that governed South Africa introduced a policy called apartheid. The system legally classified the country's large majority nonwhite population as second-class citizens. It forbade black and colored South Africans the vote, limited them to living in separate areas from those of the white minority, and effectively ruled them out of economic advancement.

Despite the optimism fueled by the creation of the UDHR, the international community failed to react. It was only in the 1970s that an antiapartheid movement emerged, led initially by the United Nations and human rights groups. The United Nations placed an embargo on selling arms to South Africa in 1977, which was followed by emargoes on computer equipment and other goods. Sanctions and international pressure eventually led to the dismantlement of the apartheid system. It was only in 1994, however, that apartheid was destroyed and South Africa held its first all-race elections.

In the case of apartheid, politics played a vital role not only in the initial abuse of human rights but also in their eventual restoration. For critics, however, the South African example displayed the weakness of the UDHR. Topic 5 examines if the declaration has achieved anything significant in over 50 years of its existence.

Reality vs. ideals

In 2002 the human rights organization Amnesty International (see pages 86–87) received reports of people

issues and the individual right to dissent or criticize.

Topic 7 considers the position of stateless people, or those who have been displaced from their country of citizenship, perhaps by war or by pressure from other ethnic or religious groups within the country. Without a government to uphold them, do such

---

"Governments exist to protect the rights of the minorities. The loved and the rich need no protection— they have many friends and few enemies."

— WENDELL PHILLIPS (1811–1884), U.S. REFORMER

---

being tortured or ill-treated by security forces, police, or other state representatives in 106 countries, including several African nations, Switzerland, and the United States.

Some observers believe that such figures reflect many governments' concern with national security following the terrorist actions of September 11, 2001, in the United States. Governments have, they say, ignored the rights of the minority— dissenters against the ruling political party, for example—in an attempt to safeguard the majority.

The passing of the USA PATRIOT Act in the United States, for example, prompted much debate. It both addressed the loose national security that some people blamed for the attacks of 9/11 and stifled the traditional right of citizens to criticize the government on the grounds of protecting national security. Topic 6 considers the balance between security

people have any rights at all? Or is the protection of a state really the only guarantee of rights?

Violent struggle

Throughout history, people have asserted their own rights only by violating the rights of others. Individuals, groups, and nations have all used violence to try to further their claim, for example, to independence from foreign rule. Sometimes the violence takes the shape of warfare; at others it comprises terrorist outrages such as the attacks of 9/11 or the Palestinian intifada, or uprising, against Israel. In other cases, too, it comprises individual acts of violence, such as when campaigners for the rights of the unborn child murdered staff from birth control clinics in the United States. The last topic in this section examines whether violence is an acceptable way to attain human rights, or whether it negates what it sets out to receive.

Topic 5

HAS THE UNIVERSAL DECLARATION OF HUMAN RIGHTS ACHIEVED ANYTHING SIGNIFICANT?

YES

"THE UNIVERSAL DECLARATION OF HUMAN RIGHTS: A GUARANTEE OF UNIVERSAL GOOD"
AMNESTY INTERNATIONAL, NOVEMBER 1, 1997
ASMA JAHANGIR

NO

FROM "50 YEARS OF THE UNIVERSAL DECLARATION OF HUMAN RIGHTS AND 50 YEARS OF HUMAN RIGHTS ABUSES"
AMNESTY INTERNATIONAL, JUNE 17, 1998
AMNESTY INTERNATIONAL

INTRODUCTION

The Universal Declaration of Human Rights (UDHR) was adopted by the United Nations on December 10, 1948. World War II (1939-1945) had prompted the international community to make an agreement to foster respect for the fundamental rights of all people throughout the world.

Among the many rights outlined in the 30 articles of the UDHR were: the right to life; the right to liberty and freedom of movement; the right to equality before the law; freedom of thought, conscience, and religion; freedom of opinion and expression; and freedom of assembly and association. The UDHR forbade torture, slavery, arbitrary arrest, and the exploitation of children. Economic, social, and cultural rights, which it also acknowledged, included the right to wages sufficient to support a minimum standard of living, the right to equal pay, the right to form trade unions, and the right to free primary education.

However, while the UDHR has been praised for its noble intentions, its opponents claim that in the decades since it was passed, human rights have not improved that much. Large parts of the world have been affected by hunger and extreme poverty. Not a year has passed without the world witnessing war, government repression of opposition groups, interethnic strife, and huge numbers of refugees. Such events have provoked questions about whether the UDHR has really achieved anything significant.

The 1998 world report by the human rights organization Amnesty International (see pages 68-71) estimated that in 1997 alone at least 1.3 billion people lived on less than

$1 a day, 117 governments practiced torture, 55 governments executed people without trial, and at least 87 governments jailed people for their religious or political beliefs. Such figures prove, critics claim, that in practice the UDHR has achieved little.

> *"[T]he advent of a world in which human beings shall enjoy freedom of speech and belief and freedom from fear and want has been proclaimed as the highest aspiration of the common people...."*
>
> —UNIVERSAL DECLARATION OF HUMAN RIGHTS (1948)

On the other hand, supporters of the UDHR assert that without it the incidence of human rights abuses would only be worse. They argue that the declaration is invaluable for the United Nations and for rights groups such as Amnesty International and Human Rights Watch, enabling them to monitor human rights abuses and to raise awareness of rights issues internationally. Even advocates admit, however, that change has been slow.

As a result of the UDHR and subsequent international agreements, as well as awareness campaigns and monitoring by various human rights organizations, there has been increased international recognition of children's rights, for example, and the widespread abuse of those rights through child labor. However, that practice has been difficult to combat effectively, since in many countries business relies on that cheap, available, and abundant source of labor, and governments often believe it is not in their interest to legislate against it. According to the International Labour Organization (an agency of the United Nations), 246 million children—one out of every six children in the world—were involved in child labor in 2002.

Critics argue that many countries only pay lip service to the UDHR because it is not legally binding, and governments cannot be penalized or fined for abuses. Some argue that despite professed support for the UDHR, the United States has itself been guilty of human rights abuses, including the internment without trial of Al Qaeda suspects at the Guantanamo Bay naval base in Cuba (See *Topic 13 Does the United States have a good human rights record?*).

Advocates counter that despite the difficulties of putting the UDHR into practice, it has established a code of conduct that has attained universal recognition. They also point out that the UDHR is backed by several legally binding international treaties (see the commentary box on page 66) and has, in fact, led to significant improvements in human rights.

In the first of the articles that follow, human rights lawyer Asma Jahangir argues that the UDHR is an invaluable instrument for bringing about a better world. The second article, a summary of Amnesty International's 1998 world human rights report, indicates that enormous gaps exist between reality and the UDHR's ideals.

THE UNIVERSAL DECLARATION OF HUMAN RIGHTS: A GUARANTEE OF UNIVERSAL GOOD
Asma Jahangir

YES

Asma Jahangir, a founding member of Pakistan's Human Rights Commission, became the Special Rapporteur of the UN Commission on Human Rights on Extrajudicial, Summary, or Arbitrary Executions in 1998. She wrote this article in 1997, a year before the 50th anniversary of the UDHR.

In the decades ahead the Universal Declaration of Human Rights will increasingly become the criterion by which societies will be judged and the achievements of governments measured. The contest between ideologies of old is more likely to yield the arena to the supremacy of the Declaration's concerns than to any new clash of civilizations.

It would be naive, however, not to temper that optimism with certain doubts. While the achievements of the past cannot be minimized, it has to be recognized that the hurdles ahead will sorely test all our will and resources. Progress will depend both on finding practical ways to surmount these hurdles, and on generating a genuine political will on the part of those leading global politics to accept, wholeheartedly, a non-discriminatory application of human rights values and norms.

"Proselytization" means the attempt to convert people to a particular religion or cause. Is it an appropriate word to use here?

Double standards undermine western credibility

Western countries' ardent proselytization of human rights will continue to be needed. However, the occasional evidence that their faith is subject to the limits of their political and economic interests, undermines the power of their message. Their increasing reluctance towards economic equitability in relation to developing countries; their failure sufficiently to apply concern about nuclearization and arms expenditure to their own arsenals; lingering traces of historical bias reflected in their tolerance of massacre and other atrocities in parts of the world and the alacrity of their response in others, including the relentless regimen of sanctions; the dragging of their feet over such issues as nuclear waste dumping. All this hints at a double standard that does not go down well in the Third World and blemishes the West's human rights credentials.

The apparent conflict between political and economic rights has not disappeared with the Vienna Conference's solemn declaration that all rights are indivisible. It is not even

For information about the 1993 Vienna Conference see the commentary box on page 66.

COMMENTARY: Eleanor Roosevelt

Eleanor Roosevelt (1884–1962), cousin and later wife of President Franklin D. Roosevelt (1882–1945), was instrumental in the creation of the Universal Declaration of Human Rights. An unhappy childhood—her mother and her alcoholic father both died before she was 10, and she was subsequently brought up strictly by her grandmother—made her especially sensitive to the plight of others. In her adult life she dedicated herself to improving the rights of the underprivileged and campaigned tirelessly against all forms of racial and sexual discrimination. She assisted her husband—who suffered from polio—both in his fight to become presidential candidate for the Democratic Party and also as 32nd President of the United States, when she became an influential voice in his administration (1933–1945). After his death in 1945 she was appointed a member of the U.S. delegation to the first United Nations General Assembly, which met in London in January 1946. She chaired the first United Nations Commission on Human Rights, as well as the subcommittee that actually drafted the Universal Declaration. Eleanor Roosevelt played a crucial role in guiding the subcommittee through that process, and also in ensuring that—in spite of opposition from China and the Soviet Union—the declaration was adopted by the UN General Assembly on December 10, 1948.

Eleanor Roosevelt remained active, both in politics and as a writer, until her death in 1962.

Eleanor Roosevelt holds a copy of the Universal Declaration of Human Rights, which was drafted and adopted while she chaired the UN Commission on Human Rights.

COMMENTARY: Agreements after the UDHR

The International Bill of Rights

Although it set an internationally recognized standard, the 1948 Universal Declaration of Human Rights (UDHR) was not a legally binding treaty. The United Nations (UN) therefore tried to develop a treaty, using the UDHR as a basis, that would transform the principles of human rights into an effective instrument of international law. However, disagreements about the relative value of the different kinds of rights listed in the UDHR soon emerged, partly as a result of the ideological conflicts of the Cold War (the rivalry between the west and the Soviet Union and its allies that lasted from 1945 until 1989). While western democracies emphasized the importance of political freedom above all other rights, communist governments preferred to emphasize the value of economic and social rights. As a result, the UN finally divided the rights outlined in the UDHR into two treaty agreements, both adopted by the UN General Assembly in 1966. The International Covenant on Civil and Political Rights (ICCPR) included the right to life, the right to liberty and security of person, and the right to freedom of thought, conscience, and religion. The International Covenant on Economic, Social, and Cultural Rights (ICESCR) included the right to work, the right to be free from hunger, and the right to education. In 1976 both covenants became legally binding treaties for the 35 countries that had by then ratified them, that is, formally adopted them into their domestic legal systems. Although the covenants were on the whole complementary, many governments have had problems with parts of the agreements, and the process of ratification has taken many years. By the end of 2001, 148 countries had ratified the ICCPR, and 145 countries had ratified the ICESCR. The United States ratified the ICCPR in 1992; but although it has been a signatory to the ICESCR since 1979, reservations about the legitimacy of some of the rights listed meant that by 2004 it had still not ratified it. The two covenants, together with the UDHR and a number of additional optional agreements, make up what is known as the International Bill of Human Rights.

The Vienna Declaration

At a World Conference on Human Rights held in June 1993 in Vienna, Austria, 171 countries signed the Vienna Declaration and the Program of Action. The treaty reaffirmed a commitment to existing human rights agreements and stressed the universality of fundamental human rights—their applicability to all people everywhere—and their indivisibility—that rights should not be divided into fundamental kinds and other relatively dispensable ones. It also declared all rights to be interlinked, interdependent, and of equal value. The declaration also stressed the UN's commitment to human rights.

answered by citing examples of established democracies which are also prosperous. It took them some centuries to attain that stage, and in attaining it they themselves were no models of respect for the rights of peoples, their own or the others they happened to trade with or rule over.

Certain countries have been able to show enduring stability and sustained progress at the cost of varying curtailment of civil or political rights. Many, even among their own people, wonder if the price was worth paying. Often, too, the choice is not one of freedom or hunger; it is, less of one for the sake of less of the other.

The dilemma is not helped by the nostrum on offer—that of privatization and the market economy. At least initially, this effectively delivers the economy into the hands of the few who, at various levels, control the market. Whatever economic good it will do in the long run, in the shorter term it looks almost certain to exact a heavy price from the underprivileged sections of the population.

Merriam-Webster's dictionary defines "nostrum" as "a usually questionable remedy or scheme." Is the author justified in using the word here?

A universal declaration

Progress may continue to be hampered in certain societies by problems peculiar to them. In Muslim countries, these universal rights confront orthodox interpretations of Islam which seem to contradict them. This impacts particularly on the rights of women and on freedom of worship and conscience. Women are regarded as a subject section of the population, entitled to less than equal shares and vulnerable to a variety of hazards. Religious minorities continue to be discriminated against. They are persecuted and exploited in the name of religion. The state feels obliged to appease religious orthodoxy, which only breeds fanaticism and an air of intolerance. This atmosphere of militancy silences many followers of the human rights movement and keeps the movement from growing as fast as it should.

See Topic 9 Are human rights women's rights?

Great as the challenges still are, there is no question that next to the holy texts, few documents have had more lasting and universal an impact than the Universal Declaration of Human Rights (UDHR).

Even more than the past, the future belongs to it.

The author compares the UDHR to a "holy text." What does she mean? Is it a justifiable comparison?

50 YEARS OF THE UNIVERSAL DECLARATION OF HUMAN RIGHTS AND 50 YEARS OF HUMAN RIGHTS ABUSES
Amnesty International

NO

For more information about Amnesty International see pages 86–87.

"Prisoners of conscience" are those who are jailed for their beliefs and convictions.

Pierre Sané was born in 1949 in Senegal, West Africa. He was secretary-general of Amnesty International from 1992 until 2001.

See Topic 2 Can human rights be applied universally?

X Fifty years on from the adoption of the Universal Declaration of Human Rights (UDHR), the victims of human rights violations have yet to see the world without cruelty and injustice promised by governments in 1948, Amnesty International said today as it released its 1998 Annual Report.

The report—covering human rights abuses in 141 countries during 1997—details atrocities committed by governments and armed opposition groups including unlawful killings, torture, "disappearances" and the jailing of prisoners of conscience.

"For most people around the world, the rights in the UDHR are little more than a paper promise," said Pierre Sané, Secretary General of Amnesty International.

A promise which has not been fulfilled for the 1.3 billion people who struggle to survive on less than US$1 a day; for the 35,000 people who die of malnutrition and preventable diseases every day; for the billion adults, most of them women, who cannot read or write; for the prisoners of conscience jailed in half the world's countries, and for the victims of torture in a third of the world's countries.

Driven by political expediency and self interest, governments continue to trample on their citizens' rights in order to maintain power and privilege for the few. What is relatively new, and deeply worrying, is that some governments are trying to excuse this behaviour by challenging the whole ethos of the universality and indivisibility of human rights set out in the UDHR.

Countering the arguments put by their governments are thousands of human rights defenders around the world—men, women and children who risk their lives protecting and promoting the human rights of others. Many of them have been killed, "disappeared", jailed and harassed for their work, and Amnesty International dedicates this year's annual report to these courageous individuals.

"The UDHR has been called 'the world's best kept secret', despite governments agreeing in 1948 to actively promote it wherever possible," Mr Sané said. "Our current campaign to promote the UDHR in the run up to the 10 December anniversary hopes to change that. We all owe it to the victims, their families and future generations to ensure that the next 50 years really do see that promise of a better world realized."

During 1997, Amnesty International documented extrajudicial executions in 55 countries and judicial executions in 40 countries. Prisoners of conscience were in jail in at least 87 countries. The organization recorded cases of torture in 117 countries and "disappearances" in 31 countries, although Amnesty International believes the true figures for all these statistics to be much higher.

"Extrajudicial executions" occur without trial. Are judicial executions more acceptable, or is any form of execution contrary to human rights?

Regional highlights:

Africa

In 1997, ongoing armed conflicts and further social and political unrest led to appalling human rights violations in Africa. There was little accountability for these abuses and the perpetrators continued to act with impunity. In the Great Lakes Region, mass killings were widespread and the human rights situation continued to worsen, while in the Democratic Republic of Congo, the new government obstructed the United Nations investigation on massacres. In Liberia, Amnesty International stressed the necessity of accountability and of rebuilding institutions to uphold the rule of law and international human rights standards.

The "Great Lakes Region" refers to the African countries of Rwanda, Uganda, Burundi, and the Democratic Republic of the Congo.

Torture, lack of medical care or cruel, inhuman or degrading prison conditions were believed to have led to the death of hundreds of people in 14 countries. Freedom of expression and freedom of association were seriously curtailed, and in 27 countries confirmed or possible prisoners of conscience were held. Across Africa, the debate on the tragic impact of female genital mutilation became one of urgency and reflected widespread concern.

"Freedom of association" means the right to organize with others for political or other purposes.

Americas

Cases of torture, ill-treatment, "disappearances" and extrajudicial executions were regularly reported throughout the Americas, where human rights defenders and journalists

The removal of female genitalia is a traditional practice in some cultures. Human rights groups have sought to ban it globally. See Topic 9 Are human rights women's rights?

denouncing these and other abuses often themselves became victims. In Argentina and Mexico, for instance, information received in some cases of intimidation, repeated death threats and attacks against journalists indicated the possible involvement or acquiescence of the security forces.

In Mexico, where President Zedillo increased the participation of the army in law enforcement, cases of torture, "disappearances" and extrajudicial executions by members of the security forces and paramilitary groups showed a marked increase. In Cuba, several hundred prisoners of conscience were believed to be imprisoned, while the government of Fidel Castro continued to justify repression of political dissent on the grounds of persistent hostility from the USA. The main victims of the spiralling conflict in Colombia continued to be civilians, mostly peasant farmers in disputed areas. Hundreds of people were killed by the security forces or paramilitary groups, and at least 140 "disappeared" after detention.

Asia

In the 50th anniversary year of the Universal Declaration of Human Rights, challenges to the universality and indivisibility of human rights were prevalent throughout the Asia Pacific region. Amnesty International was particularly concerned about the effects on human rights of the economic crisis in many countries. Economically disadvantaged groups, migrant labourers, and ethnic minority groups all faced the consequences of political and economic instability.

Workers in China protesting against corruption were injured by police and many were arrested. In Indonesia, independent trade union activist Muchtar Pakpahan began serving a four-year prison sentence for his peaceful activities, while also facing a separate trial for subversion, and 26 people were detained for three days for organizing a labour rights workshop. The Myanmar [Burmese] military were responsible for extrajudicial killings, forcible relocations and torture of ethnic minorities.

Thousands of people were reportedly detained because of their ethnicity or "un-Islamic" behaviour in Afghanistan, where torture and ill-treatment were widespread. Tens of thousands of women remained physically restricted to their homes by Taliban edicts. In Cambodia, at least 16 people were killed in a grenade attack on a peaceful opposition demonstration in March, and government forces deliberately killed more than 43 suspected opposition supporters following the July coup.

Have human rights improved in Mexico since the presidency of Ernesto Zedillo came to an end in 2000? Go to www.hrw.org/americas/mexico.php for reports on Mexico.

The communist leader Fidel Castro (1927–) has governed Cuba since 1959. The United States has accused Castro of abuses of power. It imposed economic sanctions against Cuba in 1962.

Among other issues, Muchtar Pakpahan (1953–) argued for the independence of East Timor from Indonesia. He was released by President B.J. Habibie (1936–) when he came to power in Indonesia in May 1998. East Timor became independent in 2002.

The Taliban fell from power in Afghanistan in November 2001 after a military response by the United States and its allies to the September 11, 2001, terrorist attacks in New York and Washington, D.C.

Australia moved to introduce legislation effectively allowing the authorities to disregard any human rights treaty previously ratified by the government.

Europe

Torture and ill-treatment by security forces, police or state authorities continued to be the most widely reported human rights violations in the Europe region, with cases recorded in 28 countries. Victims died as a result of torture in at least five European countries during 1997; nevertheless, there were some positive moves in the region. In October [1997], President Yeltsin signed a decree which envisaged step-by-steps reform of the penitentiary system in the Russian Federation, where cases of torture and ill-treatment by law enforcement officers and in the military are regularly reported. In Turkey, where torture continued to be widespread, a new law shortening the maximum terms of police detention in provinces under state of emergency legislation had some positive impact. However, incommunicado detention, widely recognized as being conducive to torture, continued. Approximately 1.4 million people from Bosnia-Herzegovina remained refugees or internally displaced due to bureaucratic obstacles or because it was still unsafe for them to return home.

Middle East

In 1997, thousands of people were victims of systematic torture or unlawful killings, and were denied the minimum of justice. Hundreds of cases of unfair trials were recorded in most countries in the Middle East and North Africa, leading to widespread human rights violations and a significant rise in the number of death sentences and executions

In October [1997], Amnesty International, together with other human rights organizations, issued a joint appeal calling for an international investigation into the human rights situation in Algeria. The UN Committee against Torture stated that methods of interrogation used by Israel constituted torture. Cruel and inhuman judicial punishments, such as amputations, flogging and stoning were widely imposed in various countries in the Gulf Region, including Iran, Saudi Arabia and Yemen. In Ras al-Khaimah (United Arab Emirates), a Sri Lankan woman and an Indian man were reportedly sentenced to 130 and 90 lashes respectively.... In Egypt, the Supreme Administrative Court upheld the decree banning female genital mutilation from being carried out in state hospitals.

Between 1987 and 2002 the Turkish government placed several of its mainly Kurdish southeastern provinces under emergency rule. It aimed to suppress a separatist group—the Kurdish Workers Party (PKK)—that was fighting for Kurdish self-rule.

In 1991 Bosnia won independence from Serbian-dominated Yugoslavia. Some Bosnian Serbs objected, however, because of their ethnic and religious ties to Serbia. Ethnic violence erupted between them and the Muslim Slavs and Catholic Croats who made up the rest of Bosnia's population. Civil war ensued (1992–1995), during which many human rights abuses were reported.

The Addis Ababa Declaration was issued in Addis Ababa, Ethiopia, in September 1997. It called on African governments to adopt clear policies and measures aimed at eradicating female genital mutilation by 2005.

Summary

The 1948 Universal Declaration of Human Rights (UDHR) has received praise from some people for its role in improving the global human rights situation, while others have criticized it for its lack of effectiveness.

In the first article Asma Jahangir argues that "few documents have had more lasting and universal an impact" than the UDHR. She believes that societies will be judged against the benchmark that it provides, although she recognizes many obstacles preventing achievement of all its objectives. She argues that the political and economic interests of the west—especially its commitment to free markets—can undermine its advocacy of human rights.

The second article, summarizing Amnesty International's 1998 world report, lists many examples of human rights abuses in every region of the world. The piece carries a statement from Amnesty's secretary general, Pierre Sané, who believes that "for most people around the world, the rights of the UDHR are little more than a paper promise." Sané argues that the simple fact that 35,000 people die every day from malnutrition and preventable diseases makes the success of the UDHR highly questionable. Despite international agreements, he says, political expediency ensures that rights are often sacrificed in order to maintain the power and privilege of ruling elites.

FURTHER INFORMATION:

Books:

Allison, Graham T., and Samantha Power (eds.), *Realizing Human Rights: Moving from Inspiration to Impact*. New York: St. Martin's Press, 2000.

Chomsky, Noam, *The Umbrella of U.S. Power: The Universal Declaration of Human Rights and the Contradictions of U.S. Policy*. New York, Seven Stories Press, 2002.

Glendon, Mary Ann, *A World Made New: Eleanor Roosevelt and the Universal Declaration of Human Rights*. New York: Random House, 2002.

Ignatieff, Michael, et al., *Human Rights as Politics and Idolatry*, edited by Amy Gutmann. Princeton, NJ: Princeton University Press, 2001.

Johnson, M. Glen, and Janusz Symonides, *The Universal Declaration of Human Rights: A History of Its Creation and Implementation, 1948-1998*. Paris: UNESCO, 1998.

Morsink, Johannes, *The Universal Declaration of Human Rights: Origins, Drafting, and Intent*. Philadelphia, PA: University of Pennsylvania Press, 2000.

Sellars, Kirsten, *The Rise and Rise of Human Rights*, Stroud, Gloucestershire: Sutton Publishing, 2002.

Useful websites:

www.amnesty.org
Amnesty International site.
www.gwu.edu/~erpapers
The Eleanor Roosevelt Papers site, with essays and links.
www.udhr.org/index.htm
Site celebrating 50 years of the Universal Declaration.
www.unhchr.ch
United Nations Office of the High Commissioner for Human Rights site, with texts of many human rights agreements, including the Universal Declaration of 1948.

The following debates in the Pro/Con series may also be of interest:

In this volume:
Topic 2 Can human rights be applied universally?

Part 2: Politics and human rights

HAS THE UNIVERSAL DECLARATION OF HUMAN RIGHTS ACHIEVED ANYTHING SIGNIFICANT?

YES: The Universal Declaration of Human Rights (UDHR) has set a standard for the treatment of minorities by all nations

YES: It is true that human rights abuses still occur, but the UDHR has improved conditions for many people of different creeds, colors, and races

ETHNIC MINORITIES
Has the declaration helped stop the persecution of minority groups?

A "PAPER PROMISE"
Is it realistic to think that a paper agreement can stop human rights abuses?

NO: Despite the UDHR, every country has some record of human rights violations of minority groups

NO: It is far too idealistic to believe that a piece of paper can stop people's discriminatory practices. Only education or policing can do that.

HAS THE UNIVERSAL DECLARATION OF HUMAN RIGHTS ACHIEVED ANYTHING SIGNIFICANT?

KEY POINTS

YES: Cultural diversity makes the existence of the UDHR and other such agreements more important, since they can provide a workable set of common values for all countries

YES: The UDHR sets a standard for the protection of human rights that no state can legitimately ignore

ONE AGREEMENT FOR THE WORLD
Is it possible to have one human rights agreement that can be applied universally?

NO: The individual must sometimes sacrifice his or her rights to the greater good of the state

NO: The UDHR does not take into account cultural diversity and cannot be applied to countries that value duties over rights

Topic 6

DO THREATS TO NATIONAL SECURITY EVER JUSTIFY RESTRICTIONS ON HUMAN RIGHTS?

YES

"IS THERE A TORTUROUS ROAD TO JUSTICE?"
LOS ANGELES TIMES, NOVEMBER 8, 2001
ALAN M. DERSHOWITZ

NO

FROM "ITEM 4: REPORT OF THE
UNITED NATIONS HIGH COMMISSIONER FOR HUMAN RIGHTS AND FOLLOW-UP TO THE
WORLD CONFERENCE ON HUMAN RIGHTS"
COMMISSION ON HUMAN RIGHTS, 58TH SESSION, MARCH 20, 2002
MARY ROBINSON

INTRODUCTION

The terrorist attacks of September 11, 2001, have intensified a long-standing debate: Do threats to national security ever justify restricting human rights? Some people argue that the nature of the new security threat facing the United States today requires the use of whatever means necessary to protect the public's safety. Therefore, they argue, the demands of national security must take precedence over all other considerations. But others are concerned that in waging the so-called "War against Terrorism," the Bush administration sacrificed the values of democracy. They point to the fact that after September 11, Bush's administration detained more than 1,000 aliens living in the United States. The government also ordered many deportation hearings, held in secret, and

the arrest and indefinite detention of any American whom the president designates an "enemy combatant" without trial, access to a lawyer, or effective review in any court.

The administration said that such actions were necessary for dealing with real threats to national security. Critics, however, argued that in dealing with such threats, the government must not violate its moral obligation to respect constitutionally protected and internationally recognized standards of human rights, such as legal rights for the accused.

Throughout U.S. history the federal government has struggled to balance individual civil liberties or human rights against the interests of national security. In time of war support for civil liberties has often bowed to claims of national security—claims that often turned out later to be exaggerated.

The 1918 Sedition Act virtually eliminated free speech in the United States during World War I. It forbade Americans to "utter, print, or publish disloyal, profane, scurrilous, or abusive language about the form of government, the Constitution, soldiers and sailors, the flag, or uniform of the armed forces … or by word or act oppose the cause of the United States."

> *"[M]y country … has a long history of failing to preserve civil liberties when it perceived its national security threatened."*
>
> —JUSTICE WILLIAM J. BRENNAN, JR. (1906–1997)

During World War II the fear of enemy sabotage or espionage in the United States prompted President Franklin D. Roosevelt to order the internment of thousands of Japanese living in the United States. Over 110,000 people spent the next three years of their lives in camps in remote areas throughout the western United States, making the episode, critics claim, one of the most blatant examples of political repression in U.S. history. In 1983 a government study found that there was no national security threat to justify the internments, and Congress paid survivors modest compensation.

Similarly, the Cold War years were often characterized by a fear of communism so intense that the demands of national security sometimes overwhelmed the demands of democracy both at home and abroad. "McCarthyism," named for Senator Joseph R. McCarthy of Wisconsin, was the label for a domestic campaign to silence critics of the Cold War through intimidation and other tactics (see Volume 13, *U.S. History*, *Topic 11 Did the United States overestimate the threat of communism?*)

Not every wartime suspension of civil liberties during the course of American history was later discredited. During the Civil War, for example, President Abraham Lincoln suspended in certain parts of the country the writ of habeas corpus, the constitutional guarantee against the detention of a person by authorities without legal cause. Lincoln justified the suspension by arguing that it made no sense to observe constitutional niceties while the ultimate purpose of the Constitution— to preserve the Union—was under attack. Lincoln's argument was that some threats to national security are so serious that they justify placing certain (at least temporary) restrictions on civil liberties or human rights.

Are threats to national security in the age of terrorism so serious as to justify government restrictions on human rights to get vital information about terrorist activity? The following articles provide two compelling answers to the question. In the first Professor Alan M. Dershowitz argues that under some extraordinary circumstances, threats to national security do justify extreme measures such as torture to elicit vital information. Mary Robinson, on the other hand, strongly disagrees. She argues that some human rights are so fundamental that their violation can never be justified.

IS THERE A TORTUROUS ROAD TO JUSTICE?
Alan M. Dershowitz

YES

The FBI's frustration over its inability to get material witnesses to talk has raised a disturbing question rarely debated in this country: When, if ever, is it justified to resort to unconventional techniques such as truth serum, moderate physical pressure and outright torture?

The constitutional answer to this question may surprise people who are not familiar with the current U.S. Supreme Court interpretation of the Fifth Amendment privilege against self-incrimination: Any interrogation technique, including the use of truth serum or even torture, is not prohibited. All that is prohibited is the introduction into evidence of the fruits of such techniques in a criminal trial against the person on whom the techniques were used. But the evidence could be used against that suspect in a non-criminal case—such as a deportation hearing—or against someone else.

If a suspect is given "use immunity"—a judicial decree announcing in advance that nothing the defendant says (or its fruits) can be used against him in a criminal case—he can be compelled to answer all proper questions. The issue then becomes what sorts of pressures can constitutionally be used to implement that compulsion. We know that he can be imprisoned until he talks. But what if imprisonment is insufficient to compel him to do what he has a legal obligation to do? Can other techniques of compulsion be attempted?

> The Fifth Amendment of the Constitution concerns the rights of persons. The part referred to here states that "no person shall be compelled in any criminal case to be a witness against himself."

Is using truth serum ever justified?

Let's start with truth serum. What right would be violated if an immunized suspect who refused to comply with his legal obligation to answer questions truthfully were compelled to submit to an injection that made him do so?

Not his privilege against self-incrimination, since he has no such privilege now that he has been given immunity.

What about his right of bodily integrity? The involuntariness of the injection itself does not pose a constitutional barrier. No less a civil libertarian than Justice

> For more information about "truth serum" see page 78.

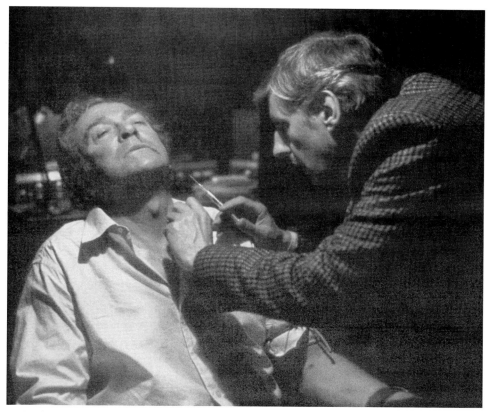

In the film Blue Ice *(1992) Michael Caine (left) plays an ex-MI6 (secret service) agent. This still from the film shows him being injected with truth serum by Jack Shepard.*

William J. Brennan rendered a decision that permitted an allegedly drunken driver to be involuntarily injected to remove blood for alcohol testing. Certainly there can be no constitutional distinction between an injection that removes a liquid and one that injects a liquid.

What about the nature of the substance injected? If it is relatively benign and creates no significant health risk, the only issue would be that it compels the recipient to do something he doesn't want to do. But he has a legal obligation to do precisely what the serum compels him to do: answer all questions truthfully.

Is torture ever justified?

What if the truth serum doesn't work? Could the judge issue a "torture warrant," authorizing the FBI to employ specified forms of non-lethal physical pressure to compel the immunized suspect to talk?

In 1987 Justice William J. Brennan, Jr., gave a speech entitled "The Quest to Develop a Jurisprudence of Civil Liberties in Times of Security Crises." You can download a copy of the speech from the Brennan Center for Justice website (www.brennan center.org).

COMMENTARY: Truth serum

The drug that is commonly called "truth serum" is a barbiturate (a drug that induces sleep or sedation) called thiopental sodium, better known by its trademark name of sodium pentothal. It is a yellow crystal that can be dissolved in water or alcohol, and it is given to people by mouth or by being injected directly into a vein.

What does it do?

Sodium pentothal is used as a sedative and as an anesthetic during surgery. In common with all sedatives, it depresses the central nervous system, slows the heart rate, and lowers the blood pressure. Patients who are anesthetized with the drug usually lose consciousness very quickly (less than a minute) after it enters their veins. The drug causes only a few minutes of sedation. Because it is such an effective sedative, sodium pentothal is used in U.S. prison systems to sedate prisoners on death row who are about to be executed.

The drug is used in milder doses as a so-called "truth serum." People who are under its influence lose their inhibitions and become very communicative and more likely to share their thoughts. Although sodium pentothal is nicknamed the "truth serum," it will not make a person tell the truth against his or her will. Its effects are simply to make a person less inhibited and therefore more likely to tell the truth. Some people have argued that the drug's use as a "truth serum" is flawed for this very reason—those with strong self-control will be able to resist revealing what they do not want others to know.

Other uses and properties of sodium pentothal

Psychiatrists use sodium pentothal with some patients as a part of narcotherapy—a form of therapy in which patients are sedated. The drug makes patients fully relaxed and more susceptible to suggestion, allowing psychiatrists to uncover any repressed feelings or memories.

Veterinarians use sodium pentothal to sedate injured animals that need to be examined and also to minimize stress in large animals that need to be handled or moved.

Another important property of sodium pentothal is that it is a radioprotective agent—that is, it minimizes the effects of radiation (short wavelengths with high energy) on the body. If abnormally high levels of radiation are present in the atmosphere—such as might occur after an accident at a nuclear power plant, for example—radiation will attack the molecules in body cells, changing the molecules' original functions and causing irreparable and often lethal damage. If sodium pentothal is taken three to four hours before the exposure to radiation, it protects body cells and prolongs their life even if the dose of radiation is ultimately lethal.

Here we run into another provision of the Constitution—the due process clause, which may include a general "shock the conscience" test. And torture in general certainly shocks the conscience of most civilized nations.

If a nation employs torture, does that automatically make it uncivilized?

The ticking bomb situation

But what if it were limited to the rare "ticking bomb" case—the situation in which a captured terrorist who knows of an imminent large-scale threat refuses to disclose it?

Would torturing one guilty terrorist to prevent the deaths of a thousand innocent civilians shock the conscience of all decent people?

To prove that it would not, consider a situation in which a kidnapped child had been buried in a box with two hours of oxygen. The kidnapper refuses to disclose its location. Should we not consider torture in that situation?

All of that said, the argument for allowing torture as an approved technique, even in a narrowly specified range of cases, is very troubling.

The author deliberately uses an extreme case to make his point. How would you argue against him? Is the argument here about specific cases or about principles?

We know from experience that law enforcement personnel who are given limited authority to torture will expand its use. The cases that have generated the current debate over torture illustrate this problem. And, concerning the arrests made following the Sept. 11 attacks, there is no reason to believe that the detainees know about specific future terrorist targets. Yet there have been calls to torture these detainees.

I have no doubt that if an actual ticking bomb situation were to arise, our law enforcement authorities would torture. The real debate is whether such torture should take place outside of our legal system or within it. The answer to this seems clear: If we are to have torture, it should be authorized by the law.

See the USA Today article "Ex-CIA Chief Revitalizes 'Truth Serum' Debate" at www.usatoday.com/ news/nation/2002/ 04/26/torture.htm for more on the debate on tactics to be used on uncooperative Al Qaeda and Taliban captives at Guantanamo Bay in Cuba.

Judges should have to issue a "torture warrant" in each case. Thus we would not be winking an eye of quiet approval at torture while publicly condemning it.

Democracy requires accountability and transparency, especially when extraordinary steps are taken. Most important, it requires compliance with the rule of law. And such compliance is impossible when an extraordinary technique, such as torture, operates outside of the law.

ITEM 4: REPORT OF THE UNITED NATIONS COMMISSIONER FOR HUMAN RIGHTS...
Mary Robinson

Mary Robinson (1944–) was the United Nations High Commissioner for Human Rights from 1997 to 2002. Born in County Mayo, Ireland, Robinson served as president of Ireland from 1990 to 1997. She was the first head of state to visit Somalia in 1992 after the humanitarian crisis and received the CARE Humanitarian award for her work there.

Is it possible to say that something is "never" justified? Can you think of any examples?

The ICCPR came into force in 1976. Article 7 states: "No one shall be subjected to torture or to cruel, inhuman or degrading treatment or punishment. In particular, no one shall be subjected without his free consent to medical or scientific experimentation."

NO

My report to the Commission on Human Rights under agenda item 4 is devoted to the questions of human rights, human security and terrorism. I know that these issues are central to your concerns in this Commission, and I welcome the opportunity to share some further thoughts with you. In the report I argue that human rights should act as a unifying framework within which we can address the human insecurity that results from terrorism and from other causes....

National security vs. human rights

The issue of terrorism is not new on the human rights agenda. Terrorism is a threat to the most fundamental human rights. Finding common approaches to countering terrorism serves the cause of human rights. Some have suggested that it is not possible to effectively eliminate terrorism while respecting human rights. This suggestion is fundamentally flawed. The only long-term guarantor of security is through ensuring respect for human rights and humanitarian law. The essence of human rights is that human life and dignity must not be compromised and that certain acts, whether carried out by State or non-State actors, are never justified no matter what the ends. At the same time human rights and humanitarian law are tailored to address situations faced by States, such as a public emergency, challenges to national security, and periods of violent conflict. This body of law defines the boundaries of permissible measures, even military conduct. It strikes a fair balance between legitimate national security concerns and fundamental freedoms.

These balances are most notably reflected in the International Covenant on Civil and Political Rights (ICCPR). As you know the ICCPR recognizes that States could take measures to derogate from certain rights at a time when the life of the nation is threatened, or to restrict rights in other defined exceptional circumstances. There are conditions however to ensure the transparency, proportionality and necessity of the measures taken. Some rights such as the right to life, freedom of thought, conscience and religion, freedom from torture or cruel, inhuman or degrading treatment, and the principles of precision and non-retroactivity of criminal law, must be safe guarded at all times. The right to fair trial is also explicitly guaranteed under international humanitarian law. The principles of legality and rule of law require that the fundamental requirements of fair trial must be respected even under an emergency. In particular, any trial leading to the imposition of the death penalty during a state of emergency must conform to the provisions of the ICCPR.

These standards have survived the Cold War, times of armed conflict, and economic instability. The Commission has a responsibility to ensure that they are not disregarded today.

Before I go any further, let me stress that as High Commissioner for Human Rights, I share the legitimate concern of States that there should be no avenue for those who plan, support or commit terrorist acts to find safe haven, avoid prosecution, secure access to funds, or carry out further attacks. Security Council Resolution 1373 creates an important framework for action in this regard. This Resolution is binding on all member States and States must cooperate in its implementation. My Office has suggested to the Counter-Terrorism Committee established under this resolution that it issues guidance to States to assist them in complying with Resolution 1373 and their international human rights obligations.

Safeguarding human rights in times of crisis

It is important to recall that the issue of reconciling States' obligations under human rights law with measures taken to eliminate terrorism did not commence on 11 September. The human rights system has extensive experience in addressing the use and abuse of emergency and security laws. This is why the international community has paid particular attention to safeguarding human rights standards in the context of emergency and political instability.

I am particularly concerned that counter-terrorism strategies pursued after 11 September have sometimes undermined efforts to enhance respect for human rights. Excessive measures have been taken in several parts of the world that suppress or restrict individual rights including privacy, freedom of thought, presumption of innocence, fair trial, the right to seek asylum, political participation, freedom of expression and peaceful assembly. On 10 December 2001, on the occasion of Human Rights Day, 17 special rapporteurs and independent experts of the Commission on Human

In January 2002, 20 alleged terrorists of the Taliban and Al Qaeda were transferred from Afghanistan to the U.S. military base in Guantanamo Bay in Cuba. Their detention led to accusations that America was violating basic human rights. Go to www.google.com and search for articles on this subject. What do you think?

Security Council Resolution 1373, adopted by the United Nations just days after the September 11 attacks, states that member nations should suppress or prevent the financing of terrorism and also exchange information and cooperate with one another to prevent acts of terrorism.

Some of the suspected Al Qaeda and Taliban fighters being held at Guantanamo Bay are being detained without charge. In March 2003 the U.S. Court of Appeals in Washington ruled that these captives were aliens outside U.S. sovereign territory and therefore not protected by the Constitution.

Rights expressed their concern over reported human rights violations and measures that have targeted particular groups such as human rights defenders, migrants, asylum-seekers and refugees, religious and ethnic minorities, political activists and the media. Ensuring that innocent people do not become the victims of counter-terrorism measures should always be an important component of any anti-terrorism strategy.

In my Opening Statement to the Commission, I invited you to reflect on whether the Commission might establish a mechanism to examine from a human rights perspective the counter-terrorism measures taken by States. Should you take up this idea, this mechanism could be focused for example on advising States on the best practices in balancing effective anti-terrorism provisions with effective human rights guarantees....

Enhancing human security

This brings me to the concept of human security. The notion of human security, which was first developed by UNDP in its 1994 Human Development Report, places the human person at the centre of the security debate. There is no doubt that people feel insecure today because of threats of terrorism. But human insecurity also results from other sources. Millions experience insecurity as a result of armed conflict, racial discrimination, arbitrary detention, torture, rape, extreme poverty, HIV/AIDS, job insecurity and environmental degradation. The commitment to human security underlines much of United Nations action in the areas of peace and security, humanitarian assistance, crime prevention and development, among others.

The key to enhancing human security is the pursuit by all governments of a comprehensive human rights programme. Next year we will be marking the 10th anniversary of the 1993 Vienna Declaration and Programme of Action. This important platform continues to provide the world with all the elements of a comprehensive, universal human rights approach.

Impunity for those who have committed gross violations of human rights and grave breaches of humanitarian law remains widespread. Impunity for violations induces an atmosphere of fear and terror. It produces unstable societies and delegitimizes governments. It encourages terrorist acts and undermines the international community's efforts to pursue justice under the law. The coming into force of the Rome Statute of the International Criminal Court will strengthen the capacity of international law to respond to impunity. But it is only one of the necessary building blocks. The most effective measures to combat impunity are national

The United Nations Development Program (UNDP) 1994 report is entitled New Dimensions of Human Security. *The UNDP website at www.hdr.undp. org/reports has details.*

The Vienna Declaration and Program of Action summed up proceedings of the World Conference on Human Rights, held in Vienna, Austria, in 1993. One of its recommendations was the establishment of a UN high commissioner for Human Rights. The first high commissioner took office in 1994. See the box on page 66 for further information on this declaration.

legal and judicial systems that do not tolerate exceptions to accountability for gross violations of human rights. In addition, the increasing acceptance of universal jurisdiction by countries is of practical relevance in ending impunity....

Addressing the underlying conditions of violence

Last year, the Secretary-General pledged to move the United Nations from a culture of reaction to a culture of prevention. In summary, my report argues that it is not sufficient to respond only to the immediate manifestations of violence; it is imperative to address the underlining conditions that lead individuals and groups to violence. There is no doubt that the absence of the rule of law and democracy, suppression of expression, disrespect of the rights of ethnic and minority groups in addition to claims of domination, discrimination and denigration are among those underlying conditions....

Terrorism often stems from hatred, and generates more hatred. Behind the resort to terrorism is the assumption of the diminished humanity of the victims. A human rights approach affirms the richness of human diversity and respect for every human life. It offers an antidote to terrorism.

It is widely acknowledged that racism and intolerance can be both a cause and a consequence of violence, and therefore of insecurity....

The Durban Declaration and Programme of Action ... recognizes that promotion of tolerance, pluralism and respect for diversity would produce more inclusive societies. The indispensable role of civil society, including that of non-governmental organizations and the media, in promoting and enhancing the anti-discrimination efforts is particularly highlighted.

This Commission is looked to to assert the fundamental importance of respecting human rights as a core component of enhancing security.... Addressing the challenges to human insecurity requires enhancing international cooperation, taking prevention seriously, reinforcing equality and respect, and fulfilling human rights commitments. It is time for leadership on the basis of values.

Got to Volume 13, U.S. History, Topic 16 Was September 11, 2001, the result of U.S. imperialism?

The Durban Declaration summed up the proceedings of the World Conference on Racism, Racial Discrimination, Xenophobia, and Related Intolerance in Durban, South Africa, in 2001.

Summary

Dershowitz and Robinson take very different stands on the issue of whether threats to national security ever justify restrictions on human rights.

Dershowitz poses the issue in a stark but revealing way when he asks: "… what if [the use of torture] were limited to the rare 'ticking bomb' case—the situation in which a captured terrorist who knows of an imminent large-scale threat refuses to disclose it? Would torturing one guilty terrorist to prevent the deaths of a thousand innocent civilians shock the conscience of all decent people?" Dershowitz concedes that the approved use of torture "… even in a narrowly specified range of cases, is very troubling." But he also acknowledges that it would be unrealistic to suppose that in the case of an actual ticking bomb situation, law enforcement officials would not use torture to elicit information. The important issue for him, then, is whether or not there are specific laws in place to ensure that when such extraordinary actions are required, they are carried out within proper legal limits.

In sharp contrast to Dershowitz, Robinson argues that certain acts, such as the use of torture, "are never justified no matter what the ends." Moreover, Robinson does not see the safeguarding of national security and ensuring respect for human rights as two mutually exclusive goals. For her "the key to enhancing human security is the pursuit by all governments of a comprehensive human rights programme." According to Robinson, protecting human rights should be considered not as a limitation or restriction on protecting national security but as an essential requirement for doing so. "Addressing the challenges to human insecurity," she concludes, "requires enhancing international cooperation, taking prevention seriously, reinforcing equality and respect, and fulfilling human rights commitments."

FURTHER INFORMATION:

 Books:

Cameron, Iain, *National Security and the European Convention on Human Rights*. New York: Kluwer Law International, 2000.

Farrington, Karen, *History of Punishment and Torture: A Journey through the Dark Side of Justice*. London: Hamlyn Publishing Group, 2000.

O'Brien, Edward L., et al., *Human Rights for All*. 11th ed. Lincolnwood, IL: NTC Publishing Group, 1999.

 Useful websites:

www.amnesty.org
The Amnesty International site, an organization working to protect human rights worldwide.

www.hrw.org
Site dedicated to protecting people's human rights.

The following debates in the Pro/Con series may also be of interest:

In *Criminal Law and the Penal System*:

 Topic 5 Do wartime laws violate civil liberties?

 Topic 14 Do prisoners have rights?

DO THREATS TO NATIONAL SECURITY EVER JUSTIFY RESTRICTIONS ON HUMAN RIGHTS?

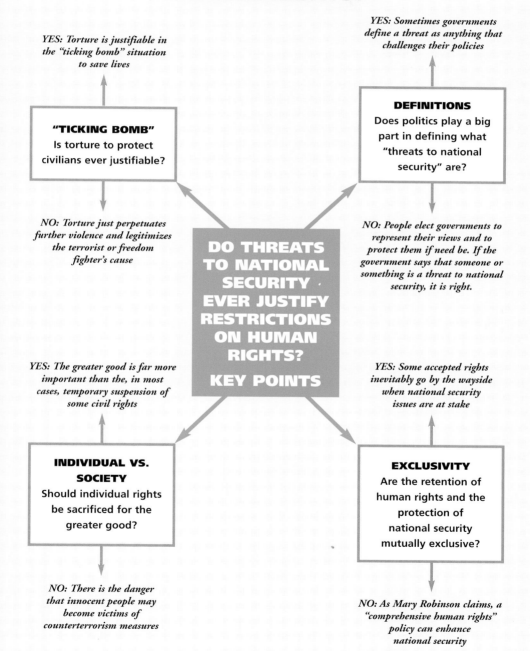

YES: Torture is justifiable in the "ticking bomb" situation to save lives

YES: Sometimes governments define a threat as anything that challenges their policies

"TICKING BOMB"
Is torture to protect civilians ever justifiable?

DEFINITIONS
Does politics play a big part in defining what "threats to national security" are?

NO: Torture just perpetuates further violence and legitimizes the terrorist or freedom fighter's cause

NO: People elect governments to represent their views and to protect them if need be. If the government says that someone or something is a threat to national security, it is right.

DO THREATS TO NATIONAL SECURITY EVER JUSTIFY RESTRICTIONS ON HUMAN RIGHTS?

KEY POINTS

YES: The greater good is far more important than the, in most cases, temporary suspension of some civil rights

YES: Some accepted rights inevitably go by the wayside when national security issues are at stake

INDIVIDUAL VS. SOCIETY
Should individual rights be sacrificed for the greater good?

EXCLUSIVITY
Are the retention of human rights and the protection of national security mutually exclusive?

NO: There is the danger that innocent people may become victims of counterterrorism measures

NO: As Mary Robinson claims, a "comprehensive human rights" policy can enhance national security

AMNESTY INTERNATIONAL

"You can fall asleep in the comfort of your freedom. We can't right all the wrongs, but we can find people who can help to do it. If Amnesty are doing it, why not lend support to them?"

—BONO, LEAD SINGER OF U2

Amnesty International is one of the most influential and widely recognized human rights organizations in the world. Originally established in 1961 as a British organization, by 2003 it had over a million supporters in some 140 countries and territories around the world. Amnesty International's aim is for everyone, regardless of race, gender, religion, sexual orientation, or politics, to enjoy the human rights enshrined in the Universal Declaration of Human Rights (UDHR) and other international human rights legislation. It works to prevent and end abuse, highlighting cases of injustice around the world.

1961 May 28: British lawyer Peter Benenson, prompted by an article about the jailing of two Portuguese students who toasted "freedom," publishes an article called "The Forgotten Prisoners" in the British newspaper *The Observer*. He launches the Appeal for Amnesty '61, with the backing of British lawyers, writers, and publishers. It calls for the release of men and women imprisoned for their beliefs, race, politics, color, or national origin. Benenson calls these people "prisoners of conscience." Constantin Noica, a philosopher from Romania, the Rev. Ashton Jones, a leading member of CORE Freedom Rides against the color bar in the Southern U.S. states, Cardinal Minszenty, under house arrest in the U.S. embassy in Hungary for opposing the communist government, Archbishop Josef Beran of Prague, jailed by the communist government, Toni Ambatielos, a Greek communist jailed for his trade union activities, and Dr. Agostino Neto, an Angolan poet and doctor (who later became the first president of Angola), jailed by the Portuguese authorities for his political activities, are named as the first prisoners of conscience. **July:** Delegates from Belgium, France, Germany, America, Switzerland, Ireland, and Britain decide to establish an international movement in defense of "freedom and religion." The group opens an office in London. Other Amnesty groups are formed in Holland, West Germany, France, Italy, and Belgium.

1962 Louis Blom-Cooper, a London lawyer, goes to Ghana on Amnesty's behalf. He interviews the minister of interior and gets information on members of the opposition being held under the Preventive Detention Act. Other missions follow to Czechoslovakia, Portugal, and East Germany. A prisoner of conscience fund is started; 1,200 prisoners of conscience are documented. In Belgium all the Amnesty groups set up a permanent body called Amnesty International (AI). Seven more countries, including the United States and Denmark, establish groups. Amnesty sends an observer to the trial of Nelson Mandela in South Africa.

1963 Amnesty has 330 groups. Of the 770 prisoners of conscience adopted since its establishment, 140 have been released. International lawyer Sean MacBride becomes chairman of Amnesty's newly established International Executive Committee (IEC).

1964 Peter Benenson is named president of AI. There are 360 groups that have adopted 1,367 prisoners, of which 329 have been released. **August:** The United Nations (UN) gives Amnesty consultative status.

1965 September: Amnesty publishes simultaneous reports on prison conditions in Portugal, South Africa, and Romania.

1966 Eric Baker takes over as president of AI. Amnesty celebrates the release of the 1,000th prisoner since it was founded.

1967 Cardinal Beran lights a candle in Rome for Amnesty, following his release.

1968 Martin Ennals becomes the first Secretary General in July.

1969 Out of 4,000 prisoners, 2,000 are free.

1974 AI announces that its campaigns against torture, ill-treatment, and capital punishment are its most important.

1975 The UN adopts a declaration against torture and other cruel treatment.

1976 The first Secret Policeman's Ball benefit show for AI is held, featuring Monty Python and many other comedians and musicians.

1977 Amnesty receives the Nobel Peace Prize for having contributed to "securing the groundwork for freedom, for justice, and thereby also for peace in the world."

1978 Amnesty is awarded the UN Human Rights prize.

1981 Amnesty celebrates its 20th anniversary with a candle-holding ceremony in London.

1984 On Human Rights Day the UN adopts the Convention against Torture.

1986 AIUSA launches the Conspiracy of Hope rock tour, featuring U2, Sting, Lou Reed, and others. The following year it reports that the United States is guilty of human rights abuse in retaining the death penalty.

1991 AI's 30th anniversary. It pledges to promote all the rights endorsed by the Universal Declaration of Human Rights.

1992 Amnesty's membership exceeds one million; it has 6,000 groups in 70 countries.

1996 Amnesty begins its campaign for an International Criminal Court (ICC), adopted by the UN General Assembly in 1998.

1998 The 50th anniversary of the UDHR. AI celebrates with a concert in Paris.

2001 For AI's 40th anniversary British comedian Eddie Izzard takes journalists in London on a double-decker bus tour of the embassies of countries with bad human rights records.

For further information on Amnesty International:
- Go to www.amnestyusa.org/about/observer.html
  Peter Benenson, "The Forgotten Prisoners," article that originally appeared in *The Observer* in 1961
- www.amnesty.org
  The site of Amnesty International. Individual country sites are listed

Topic 7

DO STATELESS PEOPLE HAVE RIGHTS?

YES

"ALL REFUGEES AND MIGRANTS HAVE RIGHTS"
NGO BACKGROUND PAPER ON THE REFUGEE AND MIGRATION INTERFACE
PRESENTED TO THE UNHCR GLOBAL CONSULTATIONS ON INTERNATIONAL PROTECTION,
GENEVA, JUNE 28–29, 2001, REVISED FINAL VERSION (JUNE 29, 2001)
HUMAN RIGHTS WATCH, INTERNATIONAL CATHOLIC MIGRATION COMMITTEE, AND THE
WORLD COUNCIL OF CHURCHES (WITH OTHER NGOS)

NO

FROM "SADIQ'S STORY"
THE GUARDIAN, SPECIAL REPORT, REFUGEES, MAY 21, 2001
MAGGIE O'KANE

INTRODUCTION

Stateless people are those with no nationality—people who do not enjoy the rights of citizenship in any country. Some such people belong to minority groups, such as the nomadic Roma (Gypsies) of southeastern Europe who do not recognize any state. More often they are refugees—people who flee their country of nationality either because they have been persecuted or because they have good grounds to believe they will be persecuted in the future. Since refugees do not enjoy the rights of citizenship of the country from which they have fled, they are effectively stateless unless or until they are given citizenship elsewhere.

Although the problem of refugees has existed throughout history, it became catastrophic during the 20th century. Since the end of World War II (1939–1945) more than 100 million persons have been uprooted. According to the Office of the United Nations

High Commissioner for Refugees, by the end of 2000 the world refugee total was 11.7 million. As a result of civil wars in Ethiopia, Liberia, Nigeria, Rwanda, Sierra Leone, and Sudan, there are more than 3 million refugees in Africa alone. Some states have to cope with high levels of refugees. For example, Iran and Pakistan host around 3 million Afghan refugees, while there are an estimated 3.7 million stateless Palestinian Arab refugees in Jordan, Lebanon, and the Israeli-occupied territories of the Gaza Strip and the West Bank.

In international law there are several statutory provisions that are designed to protect the rights of refugees and stateless people. In 1948 the Charter of Universal Declaration of Human Rights affirmed the principle that all human beings shall enjoy fundamental rights. The United Nations Geneva Convention Relating to the Status of Refugees (1951) then consolidated the rights of refugees. It defines a refugee as a person who has left his or her country of nationality because of a well-founded fear of being persecuted for reasons of race, religion, nationality, or for membership in a particular social or political group. It also sets out the fundamental principles of protection that signatory states commit themselves to provide. One of the key rights outlined in the 1951 convention is the right of political asylum—the right of an individual who has been forced to flee his or her native country to receive sanctuary or "asylum" in a foreign state.

"Everyone has the right to seek and to enjoy in other countries asylum from persecution."
—ARTICLE 14,
UNIVERSAL DECLARATION OF
HUMAN RIGHTS (1948)

Asylum in theory enables the person seeking it to enjoy both physical safety and the same basic rights as any other foreigner who is a legal resident. People who have committed war crimes or other violations of human rights, however, are excluded from the right to asylum. The convention also stipulates that refugees may not be forcibly returned to countries where they may face danger—a process sometimes known as "refoulement."

However, critics argue that while in theory the rights of stateless people are numerous and set out in detail in international law, in practice such

people are not always dealt with justly. They point out that the monitoring of the treatment of refugees by governments and the protection of refugees' "fundamental rights" is often difficult to enforce. They also assert that economic concerns and prejudice often direct how stateless people are treated in richer nations, leading some refugees to be dealt with as harshly in their host country as in the country from which they fled.

Many critics point to the case of the United States to support their argument. After World War II many thousands of European refugees were allowed to settle in the United States. Suspicions quickly grew, however, that many were seeking U.S. citizenship not in order to escape persecution but merely in order to get a better life. The main problem thus became one of differentiating those refugees seeking asylum for genuine political reasons from those "economic" migrants, who were simply after a better life.

Asylum policies were later liberalized (by, for example, the 1980 Refugee Act), but even then many refugees from war-torn countries—such as El Salvador in the 1980s and Haiti in the early 1990s —were still classed as "economic" migrants by the U.S. Immigration and Naturalization Service. In October 1997 the Illegal Immigration Reform and Immigrant Responsibility Act took effect, which aimed to eliminate cases of fraudulent asylum applications.

The first of the following articles, cowritten by a number of human rights organizations, outlines some of the rights to which refugees are entitled. The second article, by the British journalist Maggie O'Kane, recounts the story of a man hoping for political asylum in Britain.

ALL REFUGEES AND MIGRANTS HAVE RIGHTS
Human Rights Watch, International Catholic Migration Committee, and the World Council of Churches, et al

YES

The migration and asylum nexus interface needs to be addressed from a rights-based perspective. The basic human rights of people who leave their countries cannot be abrogated [nullified or annulled].

Inalienable rights
All human beings have inalienable rights, provided for in internationally recognized human rights standards, irrespective of their status, nationality, or [the] country they find themselves in. These include:

- [the] right to life
- [the right] not to be subject to torture
- [the] right not to be held in slavery or servitude
- [the] right to liberty and not to be arbitrarily detained
- [the right to] security of persons

Shared rights and human rights protection
In addition, foreigners enjoy a number of rights enjoyed by nationals, including the right to move, to leave one's country, [and] to return to one's country. Basic rights guarantees apply to all persons no matter where they are.

Once inside a country, undocumented migrants enjoy a certain level of human rights protection, including:

- [the] right to compensation for human rights and labour violations
- [the] right to emergency health care
- [the] right to education for children

Migrants legally residing in a country often enjoy the same rights as nationals in every respect ...[except] political participation (ICCPR Art. 15.[sic.]) These rights include:

Refugees from Afghanistan line up at the border with Pakistan, November 23, 2001.

- [the right to] equality before the courts
- [the right to] protection against discrimination
- [the right to] protection against arbitrary expulsion
- the right to a fair trial
- the right to family reunion
- the right to work
- the rights to freedom of expression, association and peaceful assembly
- the right to marry
- the right to housing
- the right to a nationality
- the right to education.

Other instruments of protection

The one over-arching human rights instrument specifically focusing on migrants—the International Convention on the Protection of the Rights of All Migrant Workers and Members of their Families—has yet to come into force.

In June 2001, when this article was written, the convention had been ratified—or formally adopted—by 16 countries. By the end of 2002 it had been ratified by 19 countries. It needs to be ratified by 20 countries in order to come into force.

COMMENTARY: Refugees and the UN

The UNHCR

During and immediately after World War II (1939–1945) the United Nations (UN) set up several temporary agencies to give aid to countries liberated from Germany and its allies. In December 1950 it established the United Nations High Commission for Refugees (UNHCR), giving it a three-year mandate to accomplish the task of repatriating and resettling over one million refugees still uprooted as a result of the war. However, the UNHCR has repeatedly had its mandate renewed due to the many subsequent conflicts and emergencies that have led to large numbers of refugees being without homes. In 2002 the UNHCR had a staff of some 5,000 people, and it gave assistance to roughly 20 million people in 120 countries.

The UNHCR's work is based on the Geneva Convention Relating to the Status of Refugees, which was adopted by the UN on July 28, 1951. The convention was the first formal agreement to recognize that international cooperation was essential to protect the rights of refugees. It was designed mainly to protect people who were already refugees in 1951, but was later supplemented by another agreement—the 1967 Protocol Relating to the Status of Refugees—that also included people who had been made refugees after 1951. By 2002, 141 countries had formally adopted the 1951 convention, and 139 had adopted the 1967 protocol. The convention defines a refugee as someone who "owing to well-founded fear of being persecuted for reasons of race, religion, nationality, membership of a particular social group, or political opinion, is outside the country of his nationality and is unable, or owing to such fear, is unwilling to avail himself of the protection of that country; or who, not having a nationality and being outside the country of his former habitual residence as a result of such events, is unable or, owing to such fear, is unwilling to return to it." The convention stipulates that no refugee shall be returned to a country where he or she fears persecution. That obliges governments of countries that are party to the agreement to admit and protect the rights of all those who arrive legitimately seeking asylum (refuge from ill-treatment).

The problems of implementing policies

There are many problems with the actual implementation of those agreements to protect refugees' rights. The main one is the difficulty in determining whether someone really is a legitimate refugee according to the convention's definition. Economic migrants—people who move to another country in order to enjoy a better standard of living—may claim refugee status in order to gain admission into the country of their choice. That presents great problems for governments, which must decide—often with very little evidence—whether each individual claim for asylum is genuine or bogus and act accordingly.

In addition to the rights afforded to all migrants, those in need of protection from persecution or [with] well-founded [fears of future] persecution because of race, religion, nationality, membership in a social group or political opinion are given additional rights by the international community. The 1948 Universal Declaration of Human Rights says, "everyone has the right to seek and to enjoy in other countries asylum from persecution" (art. 14).

Signatories to the 1951 Geneva Convention on the Status of Refugees have agreed to the principle of non-refoulement —that is to uphold the right of people not to be returned to countries where their lives may be in danger. Governments that are party to other instruments, such as the 1966 International Covenant on Civil and Political Rights and the 1950 European Convention for the Protection of Human Rights and Fundamental Freedoms, also agree to this principle under Article [s] 7 and 3 respectively. The prohibition against torture is a peremptory norm of international law and applies to all states. The right to seek and obtain asylum is a fundamental right. It must take precedence over State concern about migration control.

There is no consolidated international regime or designated agency to protect the rights of migrants, neither is there an international consensus on the responsibility of states to respond to migration in an agreed-upon and rights-respecting manner. The International Organization for Migration has a mandate to facilitate orderly migration, but it does not have a mandate to protect the rights of migrants. Given the complex interface between asylum and migration both in terms of the mixed movements of people, and the impact of governmental migration and asylum policies, this is a gap that should be addressed in the context of the Global Consultations.

See www.unhcr. ch/1951convention/ for the full history of the refugee convention. The complete text of the agreement can be found at www.unhchr.ch/ html/menu3/ b/o_c_ref.htm.

The article states that there is no "designated agency to protect the rights of migrants." Do you agree? Does the UNHCR serve a different purpose? Go to www.unhcr. ch/cgi-bin/texis/ vtx/home for information. See www.iom.int for more about the International Organization for Migration.

From June 28–29, 2001, in Geneva, Switzerland, the UNHCR held the Global Consultations on International Protection, a series of international conferences. This paper was presented there.

SADIQ'S STORY
Maggie O'Kane

A *"semi"* is a semidetached house—one half of a pair of houses joined by a shared side wall. They are common in British towns and cities.

The wallpaper in Sadiq Hanafi's bedsit in north London's Kensal Green has the grubby gleam of paint that is layered on, year after year, burying the embossed leaves of the wallpaper. Outside, Hanover Road's once-respectable semis have the scent of slippage: crooked To Let signs and greying net curtains. This is human cargo land—people nobody wants, trying to get somewhere. They have come a long way. Afghans, Kurds, Iranians, Rwandans and Sri Lankans all squashed in behind the window frames blackened by winter damp.

The article was published in the British newspaper The Guardian *in* May 2001. The Taliban regime fell from power in Afghanistan in November 2001 after a military attack by the United States and its allies, which was provoked by the September 11, 2001, terrorist attacks.

Sadiq Hanafi, 26, is from Afghanistan. His journey to Kensal Green began five years ago when the Muslim fundamentalists, the Taliban, took away his army officer father who died in prison two years later. The family fled to neighbouring Pakistan to massive refugee camps where, like two million other Afghans, they waited for things to get better before returning home….

Sadiq Hanafi's journey to London took seven months and almost killed him twice. In Kabul, he had plans to work as a paediatrician. Now he's lined up for a job in an all-night Pakistani grocers in the Elephant and Castle [area of London].

From Afghanistan to Pakistan

In Afghanistan it is spring; a time when even Kabul, trashed by war, parched by drought and suffocated by fundamentalists, can be beautiful….

The Soviet Union invaded Afghanistan in 1979, installing Babrak Kamal as a puppet leader. The mujahideen (fundamentalist resistance fighters) proclaimed war on them, with the backing of some of the Islamic world and with arms and money supplied by the United States. Kabul, the capital, suffered much destruction during the conflict, which lasted until 1989, when the Soviet troops withdrew.

In the marketplace, women who have never dared to speak to foreigners tug on my shirt. "Shut up, let me speak," one shouts at my government-authorised minder. "I am hungry, there are no jobs, no factories, no education for women, just for the men. Where are you from? England? How do you get a visa to London?"

The only road out of Afghanistan to Pakistan is so bad that the bus rocks like a boat on a rough sea. A lizard as long as a wheelbarrow scuttles across. His prehistoric face fits in this country, trapped in a bizarre and brutal time warp.

Next stop for Sadiq was Pakistan—Peshawar, a border town where drugs, antiquities and people are filtered through a giant switchboard of middlemen and smugglers.

The main cargo in Peshawar now is the Afghan sons of
the refugee camps....

The Afghans who have no money have started dying this
summer in exile in Pakistan. In Jalozai camp, the ... dead are
buried on a windy wasteland above the camp that lies about
40km [25 miles] from Sadiq's road to the west—and London.
On Wednesday May 9 there were 11 fresh graves there,
mostly children, parched by the lack of water and dehydrated
with diarrhoea. The international aid agencies are not
allowed to bring enough water or food to keep all of them
alive: Pakistan's way of getting tough with their "spongers"....

After the United
States' attack on
Afghanistan in 2001
more than 200,000
Afghan refugees
fled to Pakistan to
join the roughly
two million already
there. The Pakistan
government began
to introduce tough
measures to limit
the numbers of
those entering the
country. Do you
think governments
should be allowed
to do that? See
www.hrw.org/
campaigns/
afghanistan/
refugees.htm
for information
about refugees
in Pakistan.

Iran and Turkey

Sadiq Hanifi's mother sold the family's land in Afghanistan
to buy her son's passage to London for $9,000 (£6,500). He
left Pakistan by land, going south through Quetta and then
turning west into Iran.

"We got through Iran without too much trouble," he tells
me, back in Kensal Rise.

*The smuggler told us to get off the bus at certain points.
We had no papers to go into Iran. We had to sneak over
the mountain. It took a couple of weeks to get through
Iran to Tabriz near the Turkish border and then we had
to wait around for the next smuggler to take us on.*

By using Saddiq's
own words, O'Kane
makes her story
seem much
more personal
and immediate.

The wolves of the Ararat mountain range that divides
western Iran and eastern Turkey have a special hunting
technique for farm dogs in the winter when the snow
makes them hungry. One wolf lures the farm dog away from
the farm and then the pack pounces ripping at the throat.

*We began climbing at mid-afternoon. We had been in
Tabriz for 15 days waiting for the smugglers to pass
us on to the next person who would take us over the
mountains into Turkey.... It was snowing and very,
very cold. After about five hours, the wolves attacked.
We saw them ... coming across a plateau. There were
five of them. The shepherds with us had sticks and
they started to beat them and they ran off....*

At nights the only sound in the mountains is the barking
of dogs, the only sight a string of white lights that marks
the border stones....

"We had been walking all night and were crossing
when the soldiers started firing at us," Sadiq remembers.

The two smugglers who were with us ran away. We were freezing and had no food so we tried to make our way down. Two shepherds found us and sold us on to another smuggler who put us in a truck that was going to Istanbul.

Turkey is one of the busiest centers in Europe for human traffickers. Do you think that is mainly a result of its geographical position? Go to www.worldatlas.com/webimage/countryslasialtr.htm for a map.

Istanbul is 1,400km (840miles) west of the Iranian border. Sadiq went in a truck. More recently, the smugglers have used oil tankers secretly refitted with seats. He passed through Istanbul quicker than most of the city's human cargo. Afghans, Kurds, Saudis and Iraqis can spend years in the garment districts of Zeytinburnu....

In a basement sweatshop, two men in their early 20s are sewing sheepskin waistcoats for the bazaar. They work from 8am to 3am. Their boss bought two of them from the police for $500 (£347). It will take the fur slaves six months to pay him back the money, another two years to pay for a boat to take them out of this basement to London, Munich or Rome where they can begin to help their families....

Across Europe

Sadiq left Istanbul's slave colony after waiting almost two months for his boat. He took a large fishing boat down the Aegean Sea towards Italy. The boat never made it.

The Koran is the Muslim holy book.

*...The sea was rough and there were 300 people on board. We were below and I remember the water rising up and up, past the porthole. The people started praying and crying, opening their Korans. It was dark. Then the captain came down to us and he got up on a chair in the middle of all the people and he was shouting....
"You want me to try and save you. I am trying to save us but stop screaming." I really thought that night I was dead but then a Greek military boat rescued us.*

Many Afghans, like Sadiq, go directly from Istanbul to Italy on illegal fishing boats or sand dredgers. They have no passports so avoid boats, planes or trains that require customs. Those with the least money take the most dangerous route of all and hand themselves over to the Albanian scafisti [smugglers] who have drowned countless refugees, dumping them in the sea when they are chased by the Italian police to lighten the boats for their getaway. "In Bari, Foggia and Brindisi the morgues are full of their unclaimed bodies," says Marianna Gocola, 28, who has worked with the Italian police on the coastline for eight years.

"You don't have to go to a special school to learn how to dump them out of the boat," says Chichio, a 19-year-old scafisto with cold dead eyes.

It's like taking a sharp bend in the car—you flick the wheel and over they go. There are three of us in the boat, me driving, someone for the diesel and someone watching the cargo. Doesn't matter whether they are women and children on board—they are cargo like guns or women. The most important thing is the boat. If I lose my boat I lose my job....

Sadiq avoided the dreaded scafisti. He was dropped by his military boat on a Greek island whose name he doesn't remember, or maybe never knew. From Bari he took a train to Rome where the Afghan community steered him towards another smuggler who showed him how to sneak into a wholesale depot where trucks were leaving for the UK.

I was under the washing-powder boxes—no one searched us or anything. But the agents had told us, "Don't move, don't shake, don't talk—otherwise you will be found". At Dover, when we jumped out, I asked the driver in English where we were and he replied— "We're in fucking England". He looked really cross and was walking up and down ... talking on the phone.

Britain: journey's end?

Sadiq is a very private and proud man. He wants to work. After seven months on the road, he arrived exhilarated in London. Now he is frustrated and depressed. His mission to earn money to send back has so far failed. He's still waiting for his first interview with the Home Office. The process of accepting or rejecting his asylum hasn't even begun.

In the meantime, he is bewildered by the hatred he sees around him. At a Sainsbury's [supermarket] check-out a few months after he arrived, he was buying food with his £26 [about $40] worth of grocery vouchers when a voice behind him rasped into his ear. "Look at you, eating our taxes."

"I felt so embarrassed at the way she spoke to me but how could I explain?"

For a brief second, this man who has been attacked by wolves in the mountains of Iran and made his peace with Allah on a sinking ship on the Adriatic Sea, came close to tears for the first and only time.

And it happened in Sainsbury's.

By using the term "cargo," Chichio dehumanizes the migrants, making it clear that he thinks they are dispensable. Do you think that governments are doing enough to prevent men like Chicio from exploiting refugees?

The Home Office is the British government department that deals with asylum and immigration. Applications for asylum in Britain increased vastly during the 1990s. In 2001 the British Labour Government suggested that the 1951 Geneva Refugee Convention should be amended so that governments could more easily reject applications, but the UNHCR opposed the suggestion.

Summary

To what extent is it possible for stateless people to enjoy the same human rights as others? Do they really have rights?

The first article is a report coauthored by a number of nongovernmental organizations, including Human Rights Watch, on the rights of refugees and other migrants. It is mainly a summary of current international law, though it also refers to a set of provisions that have yet to come into legal force— the International Convention on the Protection of the Rights of All Migrant Workers and Members of Their Families. The authors state that a refugee's right to seek and obtain asylum is "a fundamental right" and one that "must take precedence over State concern about migration control." They also call for the establishment of a dedicated intergovernmental agency to make sure that the rights of all migrants are properly protected.

The second article, by journalist Maggie O'Kane, originally published in the British newspaper *The Guardian*, suggests that in reality refugees enjoy few of the rights to which they are entitled. The piece recounts the experiences of Sadiq Hanafi, a refugee who fled his native Afghanistan to escape the Taliban, the fundamentalist Muslim regime that ruled the country from 1996 to late 2001. The author describes his journey overland through Pakistan, Iran, and Turkey, then by sea to Italy, and finally England. While waiting for his asylum case to be examined by the British government, Sadiq experienced hostility from local British people who regard him as little more than a parasite, O'Kane recounts. The author examines only a single case, but refers to others and clearly implies that the abuses described are commonplace.

FURTHER INFORMATION:

Books:

Harding, Jeremy, *The Uninvited: Refugees at the Rich Man's Gate*. London: Profile Books, 2000.

Helton, Arthur C., *The Price of Indifference: Refugees and Humanitarian Action in the New Century*. New York: Oxford University Press, 2002.

U.S. Committee for Refugees, *World Refugee Survey 2002: An Annual Assessment of Conditions Affecting Refugees, Asylum Seekers, and Internally Displaced Persons*. Washington, D.C.: U.S. Committee For Refugees, 2002.

Useful websites:

www.amnesty.org/ailib/intcam/refugee/report/ Amnesty International 1997 report on refugees.

www.hrw.org/refugees Refugees section of Human Rights Watch site.

www.iom.int International Organization for Migration site.

www.unhcr.ch/cgi-bin/texis/vtx/home Site of the Office of the United Nations High Commissioner for Refugees, featuring a variety of reports and statistics.

www.refugees.org/index.cfm U.S. Committee for Refugees site, with many articles.

The following debates in the Pro/Con series may also be of interest:

In this volume:
Topic 4 Should human rights come before national sovereignty?

DO STATELESS PEOPLE HAVE RIGHTS?

YES: International human rights agreements act as codes of conduct by which governments have to act, and they grant stateless people certain rights

YES: Every application is considered according to a particular country's criteria for asylum

INTERNATIONAL AGREEMENTS
Do human rights agreements ensure the rights of stateless people?

FAIRNESS
Are applications for asylum always treated fairly?

NO: The poor conditions that many refugees endure in the countries to which they have fled show that international agreements do not automatically ensure even basic rights

NO: Some countries have color bars or quotas, and refugees may be penalized for coming from a particular country or ethnic group

DO STATELESS PEOPLE HAVE RIGHTS?

KEY POINTS

YES: The situation since September 11, 2001, has meant that some liberal democracies have become involved in conflicts as part of the War against Terrorism, and they may lead to greater numbers of people fleeing from particular regimes. Governments have a duty to grant those people asylum.

YES: People in danger in their own countries should be given the opportunity to live without fear

MORALITY
Do governments have a moral duty to give sanctuary to people in need?

NO: It is not just a matter of morality; other factors also come into the equation, and governments must serve the best interests of their own citizens first

NO: Most asylum applicants are bogus ones. Governments have to be careful about who they let into their country.

Topic 8
IS VIOLENCE ACCEPTABLE AS A MEANS TO ATTAIN HUMAN RIGHTS?

YES

FROM "MARTYRDOM (ISTISH-HAD)—THE ONLY OPTION TO ACHIEVE FREEDOM"
HTTP://WWW.MEDIAREVIEWNET.COM/MARTYRDOM.HTM
FIROZ OSMAN

NO

"NONVIOLENT RESISTANCE"
HTTP://WWW.STANFORD.EDU/GROUP/KING/ABOUT_KING/ENCYCLOPEDIA/
NONVIOLENT.RESIST.HTML
THE MARTIN LUTHER KING, JR., PAPERS PROJECT

INTRODUCTION

The idea that the use of violence is justified in the attainment of human rights has always been a subject of debate, but never more so than since the acts of terrorism that occurred in the United States on September 11, 2001. Throughout history there have been many incidents of violent action to bring about change, from the slave rebellions under the Roman Empire to the bombings in Bali in 2002. The incidence of terrorism in the late 20th and early 21st centuries, particularly the actions of so-called "suicide bombers," has drawn mixed reactions: What would drive anyone to sacrifice their own lives and those of others to further their cause? Is violence the only way to attain human rights?

The concept of human rights was formally recognized by the United Nations in 1948. The Universal Declaration of Human Rights (UDHR) sought to create a "world in which

human beings shall enjoy freedom of speech and belief and freedom from fear and want." Despite that ambition, in many societies the struggle to realize these rights is marked by conflict.

Conflict can be resolved through violent or nonviolent means. Violent responses may include overt war or covert guerrilla warfare, which are confrontations between parties directly involved in a conflict, usually the state and a political group. Violent responses may also be acts of terrorism that are aimed at civilians who may not be directly involved in a dispute. Nonviolent strategies may range from official attempts at diplomacy to tactics such as boycotts, strikes, protest marches, petitions, acts of civil disobedience, and resignations.

The use of violence in the name of freedom has a long history; examples include the American Civil War (1861–1865), which was fought, among other things, to abolish slavery, and the French Revolution (1787–1799), which was fought in the name of liberty, equality, and fraternity. Similarly the 20th century saw many violent protests by terrorist groups such as the Tamil LTTE (Liberation Tigers of Tamil Eelam) and Al Qaeda.

While some terrorist groups have support from the local and international community, critics argue that the violent action undertaken by them has lost them the very support that they need to achieve their aims. They say that it is immoral to kill or injure anyone in order to achieve what are essentially political ends, and that violence actually negates someone else's right to live in peace. A more reasonable, peaceful approach would be more effective, they claim.

> *"Nonviolence is a powerful and just weapon.... It is a sword that heals."*
>
> —MARTIN LUTHER KING, JR. (1964)

It is not just politics that drives violent action though. In 1999 anti-abortionists in the "Nuremberg Files" case were charged with threatening to harm doctors who conducted abortions. They argued that they were protecting the right of the unborn child to live. Animal rights groups, such as the ALF (Animal Liberation Front), have also been known to use violent methods, including setting fire to meat companies and blowing up cars.

Supporters of peaceful action point to numerous examples of people using nonviolent means to attain change. Those people argue that the human and material cost of violence is too great. The nonviolence movement draws inspiration from the teachings of a variety of philosophical, religious, and political tracts; for example, Jesus Christ's preaching of forgiveness in the Bible and the Buddha's philosophy of Ahimsa, or "noninjury" to all beings.

It was Mohandas K. Gandhi (1869–1948), however, who used the principles of nonviolence to effect political change. Gandhi used the principle of satyagraha, or "passive resistance," in his fight to remove British rule from India. He persuaded millions of Indians to participate in a nonviolent action: by not paying taxes, refraining from buying British goods, and refusing to obey certain laws. He weakened British authority until India was finally granted independence in 1947. Drawing on Gandhi's principles, Dr. Martin Luther King, Jr. (1929–1968) used nonviolent methods to challenge segregation in the United States. One of the most celebrated examples of his campaign was the Montgomery Bus Boycott (1955). The boycott began when Rosa Parks, a black woman, was arrested for refusing to give up her seat to a white person. For weeks blacks in Montgomery, Alabama, refused to use the buses unless they were allowed to sit anywhere in the bus. After initial resistance the bus companies were forced to change their policy on segregation.

In the first article Dr. Firoz Osman examines Palestine and violent action. The Martin Luther King, Jr., Papers Project asserts, however, that nonviolent means are best in achieving change.

MARTYRDOM (ISTISH-HAD)—THE ONLY OPTION TO ACHIEVE FREEDOM
Firoz Osman

> *May God be the witness that you are martyrs....*
> *You died to honor God's word. (You) committed*
> *suicide? We committed suicide by living like the dead...*

This poem, glorifying the martyrs who blew themselves up in defence of their land of Palestine, has struck a chord with Arabs and Muslims in particular. The heroic resistance of the Palestinian youth … has captured the hearts and minds of the ordinary oppressed throughout the world.

Remarkably it was written by the Saudi Arabian ambassador to Great Britain Ghazi Alghosaibi. This has caused considerable consternation in the West by generating controversy over the issue of martyrdom (ishtish-had) or as the West calls it "suicide bombing", and that's when he penned this poem.

Martyrdom or suicide bombing

The controversial issue of martyrdom (ishtish-had), or as the media calls it "suicide bombing", reflects the polarized views that the Muslim and Western world has on the current crisis in Palestine.

The Western world … endorsed the sentiments expressed by the American president George Bush calling the "suicide bombers … murderers, not martyrs", as representing some horrible new form of terrorist warfare.

America and the Western world's muted response to Israel's invasion of Jenin, Ramallah, Nablus, Bethlehem and Tul Qarem in effect sanctions the massacres and war crimes perpetrated against the Palestinian people.

The myth of Israel's victimhood is consistently propagated by the regime to justify its illegal and increasingly brutal occupation of Palestine. The repetitive and distorted picture of Israel as a victim, rather than the perpetrator of terrorism, can only emerge from a pre-supposed pro-Israeli agenda, which focuses principally on the killing of Israelis by Palestinian human bombs, while completely blocking out … killing of Palestinians by the Israeli Defense Force (IDF).

A "martyr" is a person who defends a principle even though it may mean a great sacrifice—perhaps even the cost of his or her life. Although the Koran forbids the taking of one's own life, suicide bombers often view themselves and are seen by others as martyrs. There were approximately 80 suicide bombings between September 2000, when the Palestinians announced an intifada, and April 2003.

Do Israel's attacks on Palestinian communities justify Palestine's use of violence?

Israel's justification of its invasion rests in the wake of the martyrdom operation that killed 28 people in the resort city of Netanya during the Passover. One needs to view, however, the entire spectrum of violence by all the protagonists and then apportion appropriately with whom the major responsibility for violence lays.

A study conducted by Nafeez Ahmad, a British political analyst and researcher, cites statistics endorsed by the Israeli Human Rights group, B'Tselem. The numbers of fatalities from the first intifada in December 1987 until January 2002, a total of 2,166 Palestinian civilians were killed by Israeli security forces and settlers. In the same period, a total of 454 Israeli civilians were killed by Palestinians. Thus, the approximate ratio of fatalities between the Palestinians and Israeli's is 5:1. In other words, Israeli violence resulting in death against Palestinians is approximately five times that of Palestinian violence resulting in death against Israelis.

"Intifada," which means literally a shaking off, is the term used to describe the popular uprising of Palestinian Arabs against the Israeli occupation of the West Bank and the Gaza strip.

Statistics

Statistical data on the number of injuries on both sides is an even more damning indictment of the Israeli role. The total number of Palestinians seriously injured by the use of live ammunition, rubber/plastic bullets, teargas, shrapnel and bomb fragments amount to 18,761. The total on the Israeli side is 427. Thus the ratio of casualties between the Palestinians and the Israelis is a shocking 44:1…. Israeli violence against Palestinians resulting in civilian casualties is 44 times that of Palestinian violence against Israelis.

Statistics can be highly effective in supporting an argument, but be careful to use credible sources.

Then one needs to bring into the equation the daily humiliation and degradation of Palestinians, demolition of their homes, eviction, uprooting of trees, lack of access to water, electricity, employment, schools, clinics and hospitals.

The only logical conclusion one can draw from this analysis is that the statistical data proves very clearly that Israel bears overwhelming responsibility for violence and terrorism in this conflict, as a matter of record.

There is of course a critical factor obfuscated by the West—that the Palestinians are a resistance force fighting an oppressive and occupying Israeli force. The right of resistance is sanctioned by international law, the UN charter and the Geneva Conventions. The human bombs by courageous martyrs are a response to decades of repression and de-humanization.

The state of Israel was established by international agreement in 1948 as a homeland for the Jews. Its creation in Arab Palestine has been a source of constant controversy ever since.

It seems almost incomprehensible for ordinary Westernized people to grasp the awesome psychological and human dimensions surrounding the concept of ishtish-had—

A Palestinian mother holds up a photograph of her daughter, a suicide bomber.

martyrdom. This form of struggle by tormented Palestinians is vilified because it has challenged the myth of invincibility of the world's fourth most powerful army—the Israeli Defence Force (IDA).

Martyrdom operations and Hamas

Hamas's military wing Ezzeddin Al-Qassam Brigades, have been ... associated with the planning and execution of martyrdom operations. These operations which recently target civilians are considered an aberration from Hamas and for that matter, Islamic Jihad's fundamental position of hitting only military targets. Hamas officials emphasis that these operations represent an exception is necessitated by the Israeli insistence on targeting Palestinian civilians and by Israel's refusal to agree to an understanding prohibiting the killing of civilians on both sides, an understanding comparable to the one reached between Israel and Hizbullah in southern Lebanon.

The first martyrdom operation came in response to the massacre of Muslim worshippers as they kneeled in prayer in the Ebrahimi mosque in Hebron at dawn by a Jewish settler, Dr. Baruch Goldstein. Sheikh Ahmed Yasin, Hamas spiritual leader who offered Israel a truce, explained that his movement does not endorse the killing of civilians, but that it is sometimes the only option it has to respond to the murder of Palestinian civilians. Israel has spurned Hamas's offer....

[S]elf-defense and self-preservation are a religious and moral duty of the first order, however unorthodox and unesthetic the means employed to achieve them may appear to the Western world. If the world is so concerned about Jewish civilians getting killed ... then it should pressurize the racist Israeli Zionist regime to stop massacring and brutalizing innocent Palestinians, including children, which would lead to the saving of Jewish lives as well.

The rage exhibited by thousands of mourners whenever Israel terrorizes, annihilates and butchers Palestinians is a testimony that armed resistance is a true expression of the wishes of the Palestinians whose daily encounters with occupation, humiliation and oppression, reinforces their conviction that only the language of force pays off.

The struggle of the Palestinians is a life and death struggle for survival. Without any Apache helicopters, no tanks, no air force, no navy and no army, they have courageously resorted to resist oppression and occupation with the only weapon available to them—martyrdom.

"Hamas" is an Arabic acronym for the Islamic Resistance Movement, a Palestinian Islamic fundamentalist group established in 1987 during the intifada. Hamas operates in mosques, schools, and social programs but is best known in the west for its military wing, which has carried out terrorist attacks on Israelis.

Hizbullah (or Hezbollah) is a Lebanese group of Shiite militants that is a major force in Lebanese politics and society. The name means "party of God,"and it seeks to create a Muslim fundamentalist state modeled on Iran.

The United States is a major financial supporter of Israel. Should the United States put more pressure on Israel to change its tactics against Palestine?

NONVIOLENT RESISTANCE
The Martin Luther King, Jr., Papers Project

NO

Dismissing the use of violence as "both impractical and immoral," Martin Luther King, Jr., endorsed the method of nonviolent protest stating that this "mentally and spiritually aggressive" technique not only avoids "external physical violence," but "seeks to avoid internal violence [to the] spirit."

Inspired by Gandhi

In his first book, *Stride Toward Freedom: The Montgomery Story*, King writes that, "Gandhi was probably the first person in history to lift the love ethic of Jesus above mere interaction between individuals to a powerful and effective social force on a large scale." King affirmed his conviction that nonviolent resistance is "one of the most potent weapons available to oppressed people in their quest for social justice."

Nonviolent direct action

History had demonstrated to King the power and potential of nonviolence. Upon returning from India, King remarked that India and Gandhi had provided a template of social change, through nonviolent direct action, for blacks in America.

"I left India more convinced than ever before that nonviolent resistance was the most potent weapon available to oppressed people in their struggle for freedom It was a marvelous thing to see the amazing results of a nonviolent campaign. India won her independence, but without violence on the part of Indians.

Nonviolence and redemption

"The aftermath of hatred and bitterness that usually follows a violent campaign was found nowhere in India," King went on to say that, "The way of acquiescence leads to moral and spiritual suicide. The way of violence leads to bitterness in the survivors and brutality in the destroyers.

"But the way of nonviolence leads to redemption and the creation of the beloved community. I returned to America with a greater determination to achieve

Mohandas K. Gandhi (1869–1948) was a spiritual and political leader. He helped free India from British control (1947) by the principle of satyagraha, or nonviolent resistance. For more information on satyagraha see the commentary box on page 108.

In August 1947 the formerly British-ruled India was partitioned into two independent countries, a predominantly Hindu India and a predominantly Muslim Pakistan.

Does violence inevitably create more hatred and violence?

freedom for my people through nonviolent means. As a result of my visit to India, my understanding of nonviolence became greater and my commitment deeper."

The basic steps

In King's Letter From a Birmingham Jail, he laid out the four basic steps within a campaign using nonviolent direct action: (1) collection of facts to determine whether injustices are alive; (2) negotiation; (3) self-purification; (4) direct action. Through these steps, King concluded, the necessary level of constructive nonviolent tension would be created. "Nonviolent direct action seeks to create such crises and establish such creative tension that a community that has constantly refused to negotiate is forced to confront the issue. It seeks to dramatize the ease that can no longer be ignored." In Birmingham and Albany, protesters trained in the discipline of nonviolent resistance responded to the violence of police dogs, Billy-clubs and fire hoses with nonviolence. Their refusal to react violently aided the cause, creating a crisis in Birmingham and creating moral indignation throughout the world.

King further summarized the basis of nonviolent direct action and why it best suited the civil rights movement:

1) This is not a method for cowards; it does resist. The nonviolent resister is just as strongly opposed to the evil against which he protests as is the person who uses violence. His method is passive or nonaggressive in the sense that he is not physically aggressive toward his opponent. But his mind and emotions are always active, constantly seeking to persuade the opponent that he is mistaken. This method is passive physically but strongly active spiritually; it is nonaggressive physically but dynamically aggressive spiritually.

2) Nonviolent resistance does not seek to defeat or humiliate the opponent, but to win his friendship and understanding. The nonviolent resister must often express his protest through noncooperation or boycotts, but he realizes that noncooperation and boycotts are not ends themselves; they are merely means to awaken a sense of moral shame in the opponent. The end is redemption and reconciliation. The aftermath of nonviolence is the creation of the beloved community, while the aftermath of violence is tragic bitterness.

In November 1962 Martin Luther King, Jr., was imprisoned for demonstrating against segregation in Birmingham, Alabama. While in prison, he wrote the Letter from a Birmingham Jail explaining his actions. For further information see Volume 1 Individual and Society, Topic 8 Should people have to obey unjust laws?

Is "moral indignation" useful in the struggle for human rights?

"Nonviolent resistance" is a method of social change that employs strategies such as strikes, sit-ins, and boycotts. The nonviolent theory was developed by the U.S. writer Henry David Thoreau (1817–1862), who argued in his essay On the Duty of Civil Disobedience (1849) that it was morally justified to peacefully resist unjust laws. His views inspired those involved in the struggle against slavery and the fight for trade union rights and women's suffrage.

COMMENTARY: Gandhi and satyagraha

Mohandas K. Gandhi (1869–1948) was educated in India and in London. He was admitted to the English bar in 1889 and practiced law in India for two years. In 1893 he went to South Africa, where he became a successful lawyer and leader of the Indian community, and became involved in the fight to end discrimination against the country's Indian minority. It was in South Africa that Gandhi developed the doctrine of satyagraha (devotion to truth) as a nonviolent way to redress wrongs.

Non-violent resistance

According to Gandhi, "the essence of non-violent technique is that it seeks to liquidate antagonisms but not the antagonists." Gandhi adopted the religious principle of *ahimsa* (doing no harm), which is shared by Buddhism, Hinduism, and Jainism, and developed it as a tool of mass action. He used it to fight discrimination of all kinds and colonial rule.

The principles

Gandhi believed satyagraha to be a weapon of the strong, one that admits no violence under any circumstances and always insists on the truth. He drew up the following rules, which were published in *Young India*, on February 27, 1930:

1. A satyagraha, i.e., a civil resister, will harbor no anger.

2. He will suffer the anger of the opponent.

3. In so doing, he will put up with assaults from the opponent, never retaliate; but he will not submit, out of fear of punishment or the like, to an order given in anger.

4. When any person in authority seeks to arrest a civil resister, he will voluntarily submit to the arrest, and he will not resist the attachment or removal or his own property, if any, when it is sought to be confiscated by authorities.

5. If a civil resister has any property in his possession as a trustee, he will refuse to surrender it, even though in defending it he might lose his life. He will, however, never retaliate.

6. Nonretaliation excludes swearing and cursing.

7. Therefore a civil resister will never insult his opponent and therefore will not take part in many of the newly coined cries which are contrary to the spirit of *ahimsa*.

8. A civil resister will not salute the Union Jack, nor will he insult it or officials, English or Indian.

9. In the course of the struggle if anyone insults an official or commits an assault upon him, a civil resister will protect such an official or officials from the insult or attack even at the risk of his life.

3) This method is that the attack is directed against forces of evil rather than against persons who are caught in those forces. It is evil we are seeking to defeat, not the persons victimized by evil. Those of us who struggle against racial injustice must come to see that the basic tension is not between races. As I like to say to the people in Montgomery, Alabama: "The tension in this city is not between white people and Negro people. The tension is at bottom between justice and injustice, between the forces of light and the forces of darkness. And if there is a victory it will be a victory not merely for 50,000 Negroes, but a victory for justice and the forces of light. We are out to defeat injustice and not white persons who may happen to be unjust."

Is it really possible to separate a person from the evil he or she commits?

4) Nonviolent resistance avoids not only external physical violence but also internal violence of spirit. At the center of nonviolence stands the principle of love. In struggling for human dignity the oppressed people of the world must not allow themselves to become bitter or indulge in hate campaigns. To retaliate with hate and bitterness would do nothing but intensify the hate in the world. Along the way of life, someone must have sense enough and morality enough to cut off the chain of hate. This can be done only by projecting the ethics of love to the center of our lives.

Civil rights movement

King described nonviolent resistance as "one of the most potent weapons available to oppressed people in their quest for social justice." The truth of this statement can be seen in the history of the civil rights movement, and the many social struggles that followed.

The civil rights movement was a campaign for legal enforcement of racial equality guaranteed by the Constitution (especially 1954–1968). It began as an attack on specific forms of segregation in the South, then grew into a massive challenge to all forms of racial discrimination. See Civil Rights timeline in Volume 1 Individual and Society, pages 34–35.

Summary

Disputes can be resolved in one of two ways, either through violent or nonviolent means. The two articles question if the ends justify the means. Can violent responses be justified when the goals are those of human freedom? Dr. Firoz Osman argues that violence is acceptable. He points to the difficult conditions under which Palestinians have lived in occupied territories of Israel, where fundamental rights are denied continually. He argues that only organized resistance to such treatment will give the Palestinian people their sense of human dignity. The Palestinian people will go to any lengths in their fight for freedom, including the use of human bombs. This form of struggle is intended to show the Israeli government that the cause of Palestine is greater than the individual. The ordinary Palestinian's resolve to live or even die for his or her rights should be admired not condemned, he claims.

The article by the Martin Luther King, Jr., Papers Project, however, denounces violence under any circumstances and tries to show the power of using nonviolent methods successfully against any campaign of injustice and inequality. The article discusses Martin Luther King's experiments with nonviolence, which were inspired by the social changes wrought in India by Mahatma Gandhi using passive resistance.

The article summarizes some of King's principles of nonviolence. It is, the author argues, a method that can be adopted only by the courageous, and its aim is not to humiliate the opponent but to win their friendship. Nonviolence, in the end, is not about individual but about the larger fight between good and evil. It is a method that avoids not only external violence but also violence to the spirit.

FURTHER INFORMATION:

Books:

Bass, Jonathan S., *Blessed Are the Peacemakers: Martin Luther King, Jr., Eight White Religious Leaders, and the "Letter from a Birmingham Jail."* Baton Rouge, LA: Louisiana State University Press, 2001.

Fischer, Louis (ed.), *The Essential Gandhi: His Life, Work and Ideas: An Anthology.* New York: Vintage Books, 1993.

Hitchens, Christopher, and Edward W. Said (eds.), *Blaming the Victims: Spurious Scholarship and the Palestinian Question.* New York: Verso, 1988.

Inbari, Pinhas, *The Palestinians between Terrorism and Statehood.* Brighton, Sussex: Academic Press, 1996.

Kumarappa, Bharatan (ed.), *Satyagraha (Non-Violent Resistance).* Ahmedabad, Gujarat: Navajivan, 1951.

Laqueur, Walter, *A History of Terrorism.* New Brunswick, NJ: Transactions, 2001.

Useful websites:

www.mahatma.org.in
The site of the official Gandhi archive.
www.standford.edu/group/king
The site for the Martin Luther King, Jr., Papers Project.
www.terrorismanswers.com
A site devoted to questions about world terrorism.

The following debates in the Pro/Con series may also be of interest:

In *Individual and Society*:
Topic 10 Is violent protest ever justified?

IS VIOLENCE ACCEPTABLE AS A MEANS TO ATTAIN HUMAN RIGHTS?

YES: Mahatma Gandhi and Dr. Martin Luther King, Jr., both showed that rights can be attained through peaceful means

YES: Although political and social groups have used violence to attain their ends, violent protest became increasingly more common in the 20th century

NONCOOPERATION
Is nonviolent protest the best way to achieve rights?

A MODERN PHENOMENON
Is violent protest a modern phenomenon?

NO: Nonviolent means often fail because they are easily ignored

NO: People have always used violent ends to attain their ends, which is one of the reasons that war is so common

IS VIOLENCE ACCEPTABLE AS A MEANS TO ATTAIN HUMAN RIGHTS?
KEY POINTS

YES: Sometimes terrorism is the only way that people can have a voice, especially under authoritarian regimes

YES: Everything is subjective, and one person's terrorism is another's legitimate fight for freedom

TERRORISM
Is terrorism ever justifiable?

NO: The eye-for-an-eye mentality never works

NO: When terrorist activity occurs, people listen less to the reasoning behind it and react more to stamping it out

PART 3
GENDER AND CHILDREN'S RIGHTS

INTRODUCTION

Although some human rights advocates agree that international codes of practice can protect the rights of women and children, they are in practice among the most vulnerable groups when it comes to abuse.

Millions of women around the world live in poverty, deprived of even the most basic of rights. Children are also extremely vulnerable to discrimination, poverty, abuse, and sexual exploitation among other things. The topics in this section examine important issues that affect gender and children's rights.

A "lack" of quality

For centuries women have been considered less important than men. The ancient Greek philosopher Aristotle wrote that a "female is a female by virtue of a certain lack of qualities," and "we should regard the female nature as afflicted with a certain defectiveness." Other writers and social commentators have observed that in most societies women are considered both the "second sex" and inferior to their male counterparts.

Women have traditionally been perceived as possessions that can be traded off by their parents, family, or by men in positions of power for political or economic gain. Many women's and human rights agencies, however, believed that the balance would be redressed by the adoption of the Universal Declaration of Human Rights (UDHR) in 1948. The UDHR defined human rights as "universal, inalienable, and indivisible"—they did not depend on gender or age. However, critics argue that women are still more likely than men to suffer economically and politically, even in western democracies. Wage inequality between genders, for example, is still a matter of heated debate, despite the introduction of legislation to protect women's rights in the workplace.

The fact that so many women live in poverty, are abused, and are exploited has led people to question if the idea of "human rights" is gender specific. The UDHR itself, they point out, uses male-biased language such as encouraging people to act "in the spirit of brotherhood." Topic 9 examines this issue further by looking at whether human rights and women's rights are the same thing.

Trophies of war

Women have historically been particularly vulnerable during wartime. There are many examples of women being kidnapped, captured, raped, or killed by opposing armies. Toward the end of the 20th century the incidence of women and young girls being raped during conflicts came to global attention with the discovery of "rape camps" in the former Yugoslavia when it was swept by ethnic violence in the 1980s and 1990s. At around the same time mass rapes were reported during the civil war in the African country of Rwanda. Pages 126–127 consider in more detail the treatment of women in wartime, particularly with regard to the crime of rape.

Marital arrangements

An issue that causes heated debate in current discussions of gender rights is that of arranged marriages. These are normal arranged marriages. Topic 10 examines the issue of human rights and arranged marriages.

Fetal and children's rights

Many people believe that women should have the right to choose whether or not to have children. If they do not want to have a child, such people argue, women have the right to choose to have an abortion. In many countries, however, abortions are still illegal. There has been a growing movement in the United States to pass legislation to protect the rights

> *"[H]umanity is male and man defines woman not in herself but as relative to him; she is not regarded as an autonomous being...."*
> —SIMONE DE BEAUVOIR, *THE SECOND SEX*

marriages that are arranged by families rather than simply the two individuals involved. They are common in numerous parts of Asia, such as India, for example, but are often criticized in western countries, which are dominated by the ideal of romantic love. Advocates argue that arranged marriages are an easy target for westerners who do not understand the motivating factors behind them. They argue that such arrangements are culturally specific and ensure that family relatives marry suitable people, and that such marriages are in fact more successful than many love marriages. They also emphasize that there is a distinction between "forced" marriages, which are abusive, and

of the fetus. But what impact, critics ask, do fetal rights have on women's reproductive rights? Topic 11 examines the issue of fetal rights further.

Most rights activists believe that children are a vulnerable group who need special protecting. For many people the United Nations has been the driving force in protecting children's rights, largely through the work of its Children's Fund (UNICEF), created in 1946. Since then international legislation has stipulated that children have the right to life, survival, and the right to hold and express an opinion. Critics argue that the existence of child labor and prostitution, for example, show how ineffective the UN has been. Topic 12 looks at this issue.

Topic 9

ARE HUMAN RIGHTS WOMEN'S RIGHTS?

YES

FROM "WOMEN'S HUMAN RIGHTS: AN INTRODUCTION"
INTERNATIONAL ENCYCLOPEDIA OF WOMEN: GLOBAL WOMEN'S ISSUES AND KNOWLEDGE IN 2000
CHARLOTTE BUNCH AND SAMANTHA FROST

NO

"ARE WOMEN HUMAN?"
REFLECTIONS ON THE UNIVERSAL DECLARATION OF HUMAN RIGHTS 171
CATHARINE MACKINNON

INTRODUCTION

In 1948 the General Assembly of the United Nations adopted the Universal Declaration of Human Rights (UDHR) in response to the atrocities of World War I (1914–1918) and World War II (1939–1945). The UDHR sets out what human rights people should have in the modern world regardless of sex, race, age, or other factors.

While it may seem natural to assume that women share the same human rights as men, many people argue that in reality the situation is far different and that women have far fewer rights than men.

In 2003 Human Rights Watch asserted that "Millions of women throughout the world live in conditions of abject deprivation of, and attacks against, their fundamental human rights for no other reason than they are women." Others also claim that bigotry, tradition, and economic, political, and social interests have helped deprive women of some basic rights.

Critics of current women's rights standards argue that the UDHR itself uses gender-specific language, such as *brotherhood, himself,* and *his.* They claim such language reinforces prevailing gender inequalities in society. While women continue to be treated as the subordinate sex, they argue, human rights will never be universal.

Other people state that existing abuses have arisen from the division of life into public and private affairs. The public sphere is the domain where citizens and state interact, where politicians formulate new policies, and where judges set legal precedent. Statistics have shown that men dominate public affairs, while traditionally women have been relegated to the private sphere of the home and the family, where they act primarily as child rearers and housekeepers.

The position of women changed greatly though during the 19th and

20th centuries, due mainly to political and economic developments that resulted in more women entering the work force, in what theorists have called the "feminization of the economy." Some critics argue that this change has led to more abuse, since women statistically earn less than their male peers in the same job and are more likely to be employed in menial work for a low wage.

Similarly they claim that the separation of public and private sphere has been detrimental to women's rights since many governments place more emphasis on protecting the rights of the individual in the public sphere, and only pay lip service to abuses that occur in the private sphere. Even though sexual violence, for example, is illegal in most liberal countries, in practice, they claim, such offenses are often ignored or go unpunished.

"Men have singled out women of outstanding merit and put them on a pedestal to avoid recognizing the capabilities of all women."
—HUDA SHAARAWI, EGYPTIAN WRITER AND WOMEN'S-RIGHTS CAMPAIGNER (1924)

Human rights activists also argue that in some countries women are viewed as the "second sex" and are often perceived as the property of their husband or male members of the family.

Different countries have laws and practices governing the personal status of a woman in the family. But others say that human rights are not universal and that factors like differences in culture, tradition, and religion, for example, must be taken into account when assessing human rights abuses.

Other commentators claim that the situation for women is not as bleak as it has been painted. Human and women rights groups have brought change, and women today have more rights than ever before, they argue. Most women are able to make their own reproductive decisions, and they are able to choose whether or not to marry. When abuses occur, human rights groups are quick to highlight problem areas, to campaign against them, and to mobilize governments to effect change.

The United Nations Decade for Women (1976–1985) and conferences in Mexico City in 1975, Copenhagen in 1980, and Nairobi in 1985, for example, have provided a framework for women to join forces and to advance women's rights as human rights. The United Nations World Conference on Human Rights in Vienna in 1993 became the launch-pad for a global campaign for women's human rights, highlighting problems such as rape in war, now recognized as a human rights abuse by international law courts.

In campaigning for women's human rights, women have also developed the skills needed to break down the gender barriers in politics and other public affairs. Such advances, supporters argue, show how far women's rights and human rights are indivisible.

The following articles by Charlotte Bunch and Samantha Frost and feminist academic Catharine MacKinnon show both sides of the debate.

WOMEN'S HUMAN RIGHTS: AN INTRODUCTION
Charlotte Bunch and Samantha Frost

YES

For further discussion of whether human rights can be applied to everyone see Topic 2 Can human rights be applied universally?

…The Universal Declaration of Human Rights defines human rights as universal, inalienable, and indivisible. In unison, these defining characteristics are tremendously important for women's human rights. The universality of human rights means that human rights apply to every single person by virtue of their humanity; this also means that human rights apply to everyone equally, for everyone is equal in simply being human. In many ways, this universality theme may seem patently obvious, but its egalitarian premise has a radical edge. By invoking the universality of human rights, women have demanded that their very humanity be acknowledged. That acknowledgement and the concomitant recognition of women as bearers of human rights mandates the incorporation of women and gender perspectives into all of the ideas and institutions that are already committed to the promotion and protection of human rights. The idea that human rights are universal also challenges the contention that the human rights of women can be limited by culturally specific definitions of what count as human rights and of women's role in society.

In 2003 the Justice Department estimated that around 50,000 women and children were trafficked into the United States each year. Go to http://www. usembassy.it/ file2003_02/ alia/a3022711.htm for more information on this topic.

The idea of human rights as inalienable means that it is impossible for anyone to abdicate her human rights, even if she wanted to, since every person is accorded those rights by virtue of being human. It also means that no person or group of persons can deprive another individual of her or his human rights. Thus, for example, debts incurred by migrant workers or by women caught up in sex trafficking can never justify indentured servitude (slavery), or the deprivation of food, of freedom of movement, or of compensation. The idea of inalienable rights means that human rights cannot be sold, ransomed, or forfeited for any reason. The idea of inalienability has also been important in negotiations over the priority given to social, religious and cultural practices in relation to human rights. For decades, work to transform practices which are physically or psychologically damaging to women and that have often been "protected" under the rubric of religion, tradition or culture has been particularly difficult, given both the integrity of culture guaranteed by the Universal Declaration and the history of Northern domination in much of the world. Thus it was important that both the Vienna Declaration and Programs of Action from the World Conference on Human Rights held in Vienna in 1993, and the United Nations Declaration Against Violence Against Women passed by the General Assembly the same year, affirmed that in cases of conflict between women's human rights and cultural or religious practices, the human rights of women must prevail.

The Vienna Declaration and Program of Action was adopted on June 26, 1993. The conference took historic new steps to promote and protect the rights of women by supporting a special rapporteur on violence against women.

The indivisibility of human rights means that none of the rights that are considered to be fundamental human rights is more important than any of the others more specifically, that they are inter-related. Human rights encompass civil, political, social, economic and cultural facets of human existence; the indivisibility premise highlights that the ability of people to live their lives in dignity and to exercise their human rights fully depends upon the recognition that these aspects are all interdependent. The fact that human rights are indivisible is important for women, since their civil and political rights historically have been compromised by their economic status, by social and cultural limitations placed on their activities, and by the ever-present threat of violence that often constitutes an insurmountable obstacle to women's participation in public and political life. The idea of indivisibility has provided women with a common framework through which to emphasize the complexity of the challenges they face, and to highlight the necessity of including women and gender conscious perspectives in the development and implementation of policy. By calling upon the indivisibility of women's human rights, women have rejected a human rights hierarchy, which places either political or civil rights or socio-economic rights as primary. Instead, women have charged that political stability cannot be realized unless women's social and economic rights are also addressed; that sustainable development is impossible without the simultaneous respect for, and incorporation into the policy process of women's cultural and social roles in the daily reproduction of life; and that social equity cannot be generated without economic justice and women's participation in all levels of political decision-making.

The movement for women's human rights

…While women have raised questions for a long time about why their rights are seen as ancillary to human rights, a coordinated effort to change this attitude using a human rights framework gained particular momentum in the early part of the 1990s. The opening of space for new debates afforded by the end of the Cold War facilitated the exchange of ideas and experiences among women around the world that led to strategizing about how to make women's human rights perspectives more visible. As women's activities developed globally during and following the United Nations' Decade for Women, more and more women raised the question of why "women's rights" and women's lives have been deemed secondary to the "human rights" and lives of men. Over the past decade, a movement around women's human rights has emerged to challenge limited notions of human rights, and it has focused particularly on violence against women as a prime example of the bias against women in human rights practice and theory.

Go to Volume 1, Individual and Society, Topic 3 Are women still the second sex? for more information on that subject.

Vienna

The United Nations World Conference on Human Rights held in Vienna in 1993 was the first such meeting since 1968, and it became a natural vehicle to highlight the new visions of human rights thinking and practice being developed by women. Its initial call did not mention women nor did it recognize any gender-specific aspects of human rights in its proposed agenda. Since the conference represented an historic reassessment of the status of human rights, it became the unifying public focus of a worldwide Global Campaign for Women's Human Rights—a broad and loose international collaborative effort to advance women's human rights. The campaign launched a petition calling upon the World Conference "to comprehensively address women's human rights at every level of its proceedings" and to recognize "gender violence, a universal phenomenon which takes many forms across culture, race, and class ... as a violation of human rights requiring immediate action." ...

By the time the World Conference convened, the idea that "women's rights are human rights" had become the rallying call of thousands of people all over the world and one of the most discussed "new" human rights debates. The Vienna Declaration and Program of Action, which is the product of the conference and is meant to signal the agreement of the international community on the status of human rights, states unequivocally that:

Is it necessary to quote from the UDHR to make this point? Is it stating the obvious?

> *The human rights of women and of the girl-child are an inalienable, integral and indivisible part of universal human rights. (I,18,1993).*

Women continued to lobby for and gain wider recognition of women's human rights at subsequent United Nations Conferences. So, for example, at the International Conference on Population and Development in Cairo in 1994, women's reproductive rights were explicitly recognized as human rights. A particularly significant development was the way in which the Platform for Action at the IV World Conference on Women in Beijing in 1995 became virtually an agenda about the human rights of women. This signaled the successful mainstreaming of women's rights as human rights.

United Nations conferences and women's rights

The agreements that are produced by such conferences are not legally binding; however, they do have ethical and political weight and can be used to pursue regional, national, or local objectives. Conference documents can also be used to reinforce and interpret international treaties such as the Covenant on Civil and Political Rights, or the Covenant of Social, Economic and Cultural Rights. These covenants, when signed by a country, do have the status of international law and have been used in courts by lawyers seeking redress for human rights violations. The most important international treaty specifically addressing women's human rights is the Convention on the Elimination of All Forms of Discrimination Against Women (CEDAW) which was initiated during the UN Decade for Women. ...

Women's human rights not only teaches women about the range of rights that their governments must honor; it also functions as a kind of gestalt by which to organize analyses of their experiences and plan action for change. The human rights framework creates a space in which the possibility for a different account of women's lives can be developed. ... it provides women with principles by which to develop alternative visions of their lives without suggesting the substance of those visions. The fundamental principles of human rights that accord to each and every person the entitlement to human dignity give women a vocabulary for describing both violations and impediments to the exercise of their human rights. The large body of international covenants, agreements and commitments about human rights gives women political leverage.... And finally, the idea of women's human rights enables women to define and articulate the specificity of the experiences in their lives at the same time that it provides a vocabulary for women to share the experiences of other women around the world and work collaboratively for change.

If conference agreements are not legally binding, do you think that conferences are still worthwhile?

The Convention on the Elimination of All Forms of Discrimination Against Women (CEDAW) was adopted in 1979 by the UN General Assembly. It has been described as an international bill of rights for women.

"Gestalt" means a structure, formation, or pattern. Is it a good word to use here, or would a more simple word be more effective?

ARE WOMEN HUMAN?
Catharine MacKinnon

Catharine MacKinnon wrote this article in 1998, on the 50th anniversary of the UDHR. MacKinnon is a lawyer, academic, and expert on sex equality.

NO

Fifty years ago the Universal Declaration of Human Rights defined what a human being is. It told the world what a person, as a person, is entitled to. Are women human yet?

If women were human, would we be a cash crop shipped from Thailand in containers into New York's brothels? Would we have our genitals sliced out to purify us (of what?) and to bid and define our cultures? Would we be used as breeders, made to work without pay our whole lives, burned when our dowry money wasn't enough or when men tired of us, starved as widows when our husbands died if we survived his funeral pyre, forced to sell ourselves sexually because men won't value us for anything else? Would we be sold into marriage to priests to atone for our family's sins or to improve our family's earthly prospects? Would be we sexually and reproductively enslaved? Would we, when allowed to work for pay, be made to work at the most menial jobs and exploited at barely starvation level? Would we be trafficked for sexual use and entertainment worldwide in whatever form current technology makes possible? Would we be kept from learning to read and write?

The author uses several very graphic images to capture the reader's attention. Would two or three of these examples have been enough?

Violence against women

If women were human, would we have little to no voice in public deliberations and in government? Would we be hidden behind veils and imprisoned in houses and stoned and shot for refusing? Would we be beaten nearly to death, and to death, by men with whom we are close? Would we be sexually molested in our families? Would we be raped in genocide to terrorize and destroy our ethnic communities, and raped again in that undeclared war that goes on every day in every country in the world in what is called peacetime? If women were human, would our violation be enjoyed by our violators? And, if we were human, when these things happened, would virtually nothing be done about it?

MacKinnon makes a convincing list of abuses against women. Can you make a list of abuses committed against men?

It takes a lot of imagination … to envision a real woman in the Universal Declaration's majestic guarantees of what 'everyone is entitled to'. After fifty years, just what part of 'everyone' doesn't mean us?

ELIMINATE FEMALE GENITAL MUTILATION

BAFROW YOUTH ADVOCACY GROUP
al : (220) 225270 / 223471 — Fax: (220) 223266

This poster, published by the Youth Advocacy Group, protests against female genital mutilation (FGM). MacKinnon discusses FGM as a women's rights abuse issue in this article. See the box on page 122 for more information.

The ringing language in Article 1 encourages us to 'act towards one another in a spirit of brotherhood.' Must we be men before its spirit includes us? Lest this be seen as too literal, if we were all enjoined to 'act towards one another in a spirit of sisterhood,' would men know it meant them, too?

Article 23 encouragingly provides for just pay to '[e]veryone who works.'…this ensures a life of human dignity for 'himself and his family.' Are women nowhere paid for the work we do in our own families because we are not 'everyone', or because what we do there is not 'work'? Don't women have families, or is what women have not a family without a 'himself'? If the someone who is not paid at all, far less the 'just and favorable remuneration' guaranteed, is also the same someone who in real life is often responsible for her family's sustenance, when she is deprived of providing for her family 'an existence worthy of human dignity,' is she not human? And now that 'everyone' has had a right 'to take part in the government of his country' for the past 50 years, why are most governments still run by men? Are women silent in the halls of state because we do not have a human voice? A document that could provide specifically for the formation of trade unions and 'periodic

> Article 23 states: "Everyone who works has the right to just and favorable remuneration ensuring for himself and his family an existence worthy of human dignity, and supplemented, if necessary, by other means of social protection."
> Go to: www.hrweb.org/legal/udhr.html for the full text of Article 23 and further information on the UDHR.

COMMENTARY: Female Genital Mutilation

Genital mutilation is any procedure involving the partial or total removal of the external female or male genitalia. It is performed for cultural, religious, and medical factors, and is most often associated with female genital mutilation (FGM), also known as female circumcision. There are several types of FGM. The most common, accounting for almost 80 percent of cases, involves the partial or total excision of the clitoris and labia minora; the most extreme type, which accounts for almost 15 percent of cases, is called infibulation (also known as pharaonic circumcision) and involves the excision of part or all of the external genitalia and the stitching or narrowing of the vaginal opening to allow a small hole for passing urine or menstrual blood. In some traditions a ceremony is held without actual genital mutilation occurring. Human rights and women's rights groups have campaigned against FGM for many years, arguing that it is inhumane and often a forced procedure. In response most democratic nations have banned the procedure, but FGM still occurs in many different cultures, including 28 African countries and some Asian nations.

The World Health Organization (WHO) conservatively estimates that around 135 million girls and women have undergone female circumcision and that a further two million procedures occur each year. It also estimates that most cases occur between the ages of four and eight, although there have been cases of FGM carried out on babies.

Girls undergoing the procedure have varying degrees of knowledge about what will happen to them. Sometimes FGM is explained as part of an initiation rite, and a group of women is allowed to attend to provide support. In many cases genital mutilation is carried out either without the permission of the girl or without her understanding exactly what is going on. For that reason many people argue that FGM is an outdated and inhumane practice—a violation of women's rights.

Pros and cons

Critics argue that apart from the pain and trauma caused by FGM, the patient risks infection from germs carried by unsterilized equipment, the insertion of herbs or other foreign matter during the operation, injury to other areas of the body, and hemorrhaging. Long-term problems may include cysts, incontinence, painful sexual activity, and severe difficulties in childbirth. Advocates claim, though, that FGM is essential for the preservation of traditional values, for initiating girls into womanhood, and also for defining their gender roles as adults. Cleanliness and hygiene are also cited as reasons for performing the surgery. Religion is also important, and FGM occurs in some Jewish, Islamic, and Christian communities around the world. Critics counter that FGM is just another way to control sexual and reproductive rights and that the practice is a human rights violation.

holiday with pay' might have mustered the specificity to mention women sometime, other than through 'motherhood', which is more bowed to than provided for. If women were human in this document, would domestic violence, sexual violation from birth to death including in prostitution and pornography, and systematic sexual objectification and denigration of women and girls simply be left out of the explicit language?

Women's right to equality

Granted, sex discrimination is prohibited. But how can it have been prohibited for fifty years, even aspirationally, and the end of these conditions still not be concretely imagined as part of what a human being, as human, is entitled to? Why is women's entitlement to an end of these conditions still openly debated based on cultural rights, speech rights, religious rights, sexual freedom, free market—as if women are social signifiers, pimps' speech, sacred or sexual fetishes, natural resources, chattel, everything but human beings?

The omissions in the Universal Declaration are not merely semantic. To be a woman is not yet a name for a way of being human, not even in this most visionary of human rights documents. If we measure the reality of women's situation in all its variety against the guarantees of the Universal Declaration, not only do women not have the rights it guarantees—most of the world's men don't either—it is hard to see, in its vision of humanity, a woman's face.

The world needs to see women as human. For this, the Universal Declaration of Human Rights must see the ways women distinctively are deprived of human rights as a deprivation of humanity. For the glorious dream of the Universal Declaration to come true, for human rights to be universal, both the reality it challenges and the standard it sets need to change.

When will women be human? When?

Sex discrimination is the unequal treatment of individuals based on their sex. Since 1960 the United States has adopted various measures to reduce sex discrimination. The Federal Equal Pay act of 1963 requires equal pay for men and women doing the same work. In the 1970s the Supreme Court required that women wage earners receive the same benefits for their families as male wage earners.

Would changing the language of the UDHR change anything? Do you think it would stop women from suffering violent or other abuses?

Summary

The Universal Declaration of Human Rights (UDHR) has both its supporters and its critics when it comes to the issue of women's human rights. The views expressed by Charlotte Bunch and Samantha Frost in the first article, "Women's Human Rights: An Introduction," generally support the charter in its aim to protect the rights of all human beings, including women. According to the UDHR, claim the authors, human rights are universal, inalienable, and indivisible.

Given those unequivocal definitions, the authors suggest that it is impossible to deny that women have the same rights as men. The authors go on to argue that women's issues are now at the very heart of human rights discussions. This success, say the authors, is thanks in large part to the coordinated efforts of women's rights campaigners worldwide and events such as the UN Decade for Women (1976–1985) and the World Conference on Human Rights held in Vienna in 1993.

But the UDHR has also come under a lot of criticism by women's rights campaigners such as Catharine MacKinnon—the author of the second article, "Are Women Human?" MacKinnon feels that women simply do not have the rights it guarantees. MacKinnon challenges the UDHR by identifying the "ringing language" it contains—gender-specific language such as *himself* and *him* that reinforces the inequality of the sexes.

More importantly, however, the author highlights experiences of violence, degradation, and exploitation to suggest that women are deprived of their human rights. Only when the UDHR is revised, says MacKinnon, will women start to enjoy the rights to which they are entitled.

FURTHER INFORMATION:

Books:

Agosin, Marjorie (ed.), *Women, Gender, and Human Rights: A Global Perspective*. Piscataway, NJ: Rutgers University Press, 2001.

Askin, Kelly D., and Dorean M. Koenig, *Women and International Human Rights Law*. Ardsley, NY: Transnational Publishers, 2000.

Fisher, Elizabeth, and Linda G. MacKay, *Gender Justice: Women's Rights Are Human Rights*. Washington, D.C.: Unitarian Universalist Service, 1997.

Human Rights Watch Women's Rights Division (eds.), *Women's Human Rights Step by Step: A Practical Guide to Using International Human Rights Law and Mechanisms to Defend Women's Human Rights*. Washington, D.C.: WLDI, 2003.

Wolper, Andrea, and J.S. Peters (eds.), *Women's Rights,*

Human Rights: International Feminist Perspectives. New York: Routledge, 1995.

Useful websites:

www.madre.org

Site for Madre, an International Women's Human Rights Organization.

The following debates in the Pro/Con series may also be of interest:

In this volume:
Topic 2: Can human rights be applied universally?

ARE HUMAN RIGHTS WOMEN'S RIGHTS?

YES: Women are often seen as the weaker sex and are more open to sexual and economic exploitation than men at home and in the work place

YES: All women should be able to enjoy certain basic human rights irrespective of culture, tradition, family, or other influences. A universal women's rights standard would protect every woman equally.

SECOND SEX
Are women treated differently than men?

UNIVERSAL RIGHTS
Can there be a universal women's rights standard?

NO: The women's rights movement, legislation, and the human rights movement mean that women often have the same rights as men

NO: Outside factors such as culture and tradition often mean that women are perceived differently in other cultures and are treated accordingly by society. Such behavior may be seen as abusive by other cultures even if it is acceptable within the more traditional one.

ARE HUMAN RIGHTS WOMEN'S RIGHTS?

KEY POINTS

YES: Men traditionally have dominated the public domain, and women have been relegated to the private sphere. Rights in the public sphere are better protected, and women inevitably lose out.

YES: The UDHR provides an international standard for human rights. It has benefited men and women alike.

PUBLIC VS. PRIVATE SPHERES
Has the separation of these domains contributed to women's rights abuses?

UNIVERSAL DECLARATION OF HUMAN RIGHTS
Has the UDHR done enough to protect women's rights?

NO: Women inhabit the public domain as much as the private one. They are protected by legislation that prevents abuses in both areas of life.

NO: The continuing abuses committed against women prove that the UDHR has let them down

RAPE AND WAR

"Rape and sexual violence are a form of genocide."
—DAVID J. SCHEFFER, AMBASSADOR-AT-LARGE
FOR WAR CRIMES, FORDHAM UNIVERSITY, NEW YORK (1999)

Sexual violence has been an element of war since history began.
For centuries civilians have been raped during war not only as an act of
violence but also as one of power. During the 20th century the world witnessed
many international conflicts. And the rape of women and children in particular,
documented by eyewitnesses, academics, and the media, occurred on
an unprecedented scale in such conflicts as the two world wars and as part
of the ethnic cleansing policies of the former Yugoslavia and Rwanda.
The use of rape in war has led people to question what can be done to
prevent such war crimes. This article examines the
relationship between rape and war.

A strategy of war?

In many communities women are still seen as the property of men. Throughout
history women, like other possessions—houses, land, and money, for example—
have been viewed as war trophies to be acquired by invading armies. Rape in war
is often an attack not only on the victim. Increasingly, rape has been used as a
weapon in wars to humiliate and disempower the enemy by breaking the bonds
of family and society. Mass rapes have become a weapon of war; there are many
examples of whole communities being herded into a public space, such as a school
or market place, so that they can watch as their women and children are
systematically raped by enemy soldiers.

In ethnic conflicts rape has been used as part of nationalistic policy and as a
military strategy to ethnically cleanse regions by deliberately impregnating women
of a different race. A 1993 United Nations (UN) report on human rights abuses in
the former Yugoslavia gave accounts of refugees who had witnessed the pubic
raping of women for that purpose. Similarly, a 1992 Asia Watch report recounted
how entire villages had fled from Burma to Bangladesh after Rohingya women
were raped by Burmese soldiers. The 1998 UN International Criminal Tribunal for
Rwanda (ICTR) heard how Hutu militia in Rwanda had targeted Tutsi women to
rape as part of their war strategy.

Human rights and women's rights

Although rape in war has been documented for many centuries, it was only in the
20th century that victims began to receive some sort of redress for the crimes

committed against them. International agreements, for the most part, have provided the basis on which perpetrators can be prosecuted.

The Nuremburg Trials, held after World War II in Germany to prosecute Nazis for war crimes, established rape as a crime against humanity. However, none of the defendants was prosecuted for the crime. The first real attempt to try men guilty of rape in war came during the Tokyo War Crime Trials, held from 1946 to 1948. Twenty-eight men were indicted for Class A war crimes, specifically promoting a method of conquest that included "mass murder, rape … and other barbaric cruelties" on the civilian populations of the countries Japan invaded. Since then, although crimes of sexual violence have been punishable under subsequent international codes—the 1949 Geneva Conventions, the 1948 Genocide Convention, and the 1984 Torture Convention among them—it was really only in the late 20th century that perpetrators were tried for war rape offenses.

The case of former Yugoslavia

In January 1993 the UN sent a medical team to investigate rape in the former Yugoslavia. They found evidence of rape used as an instrument of war on an unprecedented scale. Rape had been used as part of a Serbian campaign to ethnically cleanse the country, but also in the case of Bosnia, in a new and sinister way—through the forced impregnation of non-Serbian women by Serbian men to beget Serbian children.

Many mass rapes occurred in Bosnian "rape camps," found, for example, in Doboj, where 2,000 Muslim and Croatian women were held, and in the Vilina Vlas Hotel in Visegrad, where 300 girls were incarcerated specifically for the purpose of rape. The UN Commission on Human Rights subsequently passed a resolution making rape a war crime and calling for a special tribunal to try such offenses. The tribunals would make not only the rapist accountable but also those people who ordered him to commit the offense and those in authority who failed to prevent it. But many victims refused to come forward, traumatized by their experiences or scared of further reprisals. According to the U.S. National Center for Post-Traumatic Stress Disorder, the long-term emotional, mental, and physical effects of rape were found in around 60 percent of female survivors of rape in the United States, and similar symptoms were found in almost 75 percent of Bosnian rape victims.

The influence of the ICTY and ICTR

The International Criminal Tribunals for the Former Yugoslavia (ICTY) and Rwanda (ICTR) have provided the foundations on which rape and sexual violence crimes can be tried. The ICTR found former Mayor Jean-Paul Akayesu guilty of nine counts of genocide, crimes against humanity, and war crimes, including rape and sexual violence in 1998. That was significant since the ruling recognized rape as a method of ethnic cleansing. Similarly, in February 2001 the UN War Crimes Tribunal at The Hague in the Netherlands sentenced three Serbs to terms of up to 28 years for sexual crimes. Both cases show that the international community is taking seriously the issue of rape as an instrument of war.

Topic 10

ARE ARRANGED MARRIAGES AN ABUSE OF HUMAN RIGHTS?

YES

"LOVE, HONOUR AND OBEY?"

THE ALTERNATIVE, FEBRUARY 1997

JENNIE CHRISTIAN

NO

FROM "ARRANGED MARRIAGES: A TRUE FAMILY AFFAIR"

CAMPUS AND CULTURE, VOLUME 94, ISSUE 38, NOVEMBER 18, 2000

LEENA KAMAT

INTRODUCTION

An "arranged marriage" is normally one in which the parents or the immediate family, rather than prospective spouses themselves, select marital partners for their relatives, in most cases for their children. Arranged marriages have existed in the world for many centuries; many aristocratic families and political factions, for example, in Europe and Asia traded their sons and daughters for land and alliances. Marriages were also arranged to preserve bloodlines, to prevent tribes or races from dying out, and to maintain peace.

Sociologists accept that there are two main forms of marriage arrangement— "love marriages," the main method in democratic nations, and "arranged marriages." The notion of romantic love is a relatively new invention that was introduced by poets and singers in the 12th century in what is now southern France. Mass international migration, especially during the second half of the 20th century, has resulted in both

systems existing in many western democracies—the United States, the United Kingdom, and Australia among them. That has led some researchers to claim that as many as half the world's population are involved in some form of arranged marriage.

In 2003 arranged marriages could also be found in China, Japan, Pakistan, Bangladesh, Indonesia, Russia, and Nigeria. In India it is estimated that over 90 percent of all marriages are arranged, while in the United States arranged marriages among Indian Americans are not unusual.

Advocates of arranged marriages argue that they are the best way for parents and guardians to ensure that their children marry suitable partners and at the same time limit the likelihood of divorce (the divorce rate in India, where arranged marriages predominate, is about 2 percent). They assert that arranged marriages today take place in a modern context in which the prospective bride and groom meet each other several times and get a chance to find out if they are compatible. The Internet, they claim, has also made it possible for girls and boys to arrange meetings and get to know each other. Forced marriages, in which girls—and sometimes boys—are coerced into marriage against their will, are the exception and not the rule.

"If the consent be lacking in a marriage, all other celebrations, even should the union be consummated, are rendered void."

— POPE NICHOLAS I,

LETTER (866 A.D.)

Critics disagree, however, arguing that arranged marriages are archaic and outdated, and are often performed against the will of one or both of the marriage partners. They point out that Article 16 of the Universal Declaration of Human Rights states that "marriage shall be entered into only with the free and full consent of the intending spouses." Arranged marriages are thus, they argue, a violation of human rights.

Although arranged marriage has been a common practice for centuries, it has always had its critics. Some commentators in 19th- and early 20th-century British India criticized the fact that there seemed to be a high incidence of very young girls married off to elderly men; the girls were treated very much as slaves.

Critics also point to the numbers of "accidental" bride burnings in which girls, sometimes in cases in which they are unable to have children, are killed in domestic accidents, or to the numbers of girls who commit suicide rather than marry someone they do not know.

In 2003 academics Roger Penn and Paul Lambert examined arranged marriages in Britain in an article published in the *Pakistan Journal of Social Sciences.* They interviewed both Asians and non-Asians, finding for the most part that both were critical of the others' marriage system but very supportive of their own. They made a list of positive and negative attitudes associated with arranged marriages versus love marriages. Interviewees in favor of arranged marriages listed such positive attributes as the maintenance of strong family ties, a continuance of custom, discipline, and a clear enforcement of the delineation of gender roles. Opponents' claimed that arranged marriages were antiquated, were based in violence and coercion, and enforced the idea that women were chattels or objects. Advocates of love marriages listed as positives that they were a modern arrangement based on love in which gender roles were equal and a relationship based on mutual desire, personal choice, and fulfillment. However, the criticism listed were that they often ended in divorce, resulted in a high incidence of single parents, and led to undisciplined children.

The following two articles look at the debate in greater detail. In the first Jennie Christian looks at the case of an Asian girl forced into marriage in Australia. However, Leena Kamat argues that arranged marriages and love marriages are not so dissimilar after all, in the second extract.

LOVE, HONOUR AND OBEY?
Jennie Christian

YES

Rindi was 22 years old when she met Mark, a TAFE teacher in a western Sydney college where she studied laboratory techniques part-time.

They became friends, and she confided in him about her life at home with her Indian-born parents and close relatives in a north-western Sydney suburb. She was strictly supervised by her parents, brothers and in-laws, and her brothers often threatened to beat her for disobedience. One day she told him she was to be forced into marriage.

"I didn't believe they could do this, it scared Rindi very much," says Mark. Her family advertised for a husband, and had two replies with photographs. One man was known to the family in India. "He'd had a reasonable education and they thought he could solidify the family network."

An "arranged marriage" is a contract between families, not between individuals. The best interests of the family often govern the arrangements. Do you think marriage should be a family matter or just a matter for the couple concerned?

Escaping marriage

Rindi asked Mark if he could help her escape the marriage. They planned for her to fly to New Zealand where a brother lived whom she trusted to help her. "Rindi always talked about having her own freedom, because she never had it at home," says Mark. In several visits, she secretly transferred her belongings to Mark's flat. He lent her $400 for the airfare, as her earnings were paid into an account that only her mother could access. They said goodbye at the airport. "It was a sad parting, as if she had suddenly realised what it meant to be walking away from the life she knew."

But only a week later Rindi was back home: her brother tricked her into coming back by telling her that her father had suffered a stroke. When she next contacted Mark, she seemed to be have resigned herself to her fate.

If an individual does not want to enter into a marriage arranged by their family, should they have the right to say no? Do parents always have their children's best interests at heart?

"I'm sacrificing my life for my family," she told him in a brief phone call. Her family were keeping a close watch on her and would not allow her out of the house by herself. A week later Rindi was taken by her mother to India to be married.

Arranged marriages in Australia

This happened last year here in Australia. It is just one example of the many marriages arranged in Australia's ethnic

COMMENTARY: Marriage in Japan

In Japan there are two kinds of marriage: the love marriage and the arranged marriage. The love marriage is similar to the western tradition in which the couple meet independently without the assistance of a go-between. Arranged marriages were predominant up to the 19th century. Today the majority of marriages are love marriages. Estimates vary, placing the proportion of arranged marriages at between 25 and 50 percent.

Arranged marriages in the Meiji period

In the second half of the 19th century (the Meiji period) prospective partners were brought together in the presence of a go-between. The couple were allowed to meet, but the choice of partner rested in the hands of the relatives and those close to the affairs of the two families. The primary function of marriage was to ensure the continuation of the family and its assets. It was essential that the prospective spouse had compatible social status and family background. Whether or not the couple got on was a minor concern. That approach to marriage remained the norm in Japan until the end of World War II, in 1945.

Marriage after World War II

After World War II marriage underwent great change following amendments to the civil code. From the mid-1960s love matches replaced arranged marriages as the social norm, and dating became fashionable for young men and women looking for a partner. However, intimate contact outside of marriage was considered undesirable, in line with the teaching of Confucius that men and women should not mix after the age of seven. Young people who engaged in such intimacy were ostracized.

Modern arranged marriages

The modern system of arranged marriages is similar to blind dating in the United States. When a young woman reaches marriageable age (about 25), together with her parents she compiles a "packet" of information about her life. It includes a photograph of the girl dressed in a kimono, descriptions of her family background, education, accomplishments, and interests. Her parents ask their friends and acquaintances if they know of any suitable men. The person who does becomes the "go-between," showing the packet to the potential bridegroom and arranging a meeting between the man and the woman. The man provides a similar dossier of information about himself. The meeting is usually attended by the potential partners, the go-between, and representatives of both families. The couple make the final decision about the marriage, although they seek advice and approval from their parents and the go-between. Statistics show the divorce rate for arranged marriages is lower than for love marriages.

communities. Many marriages are arranged without the consent of the bride, or where she has little opportunity to go against the wishes of her parents.

The bride is likely to be still at school, and influenced by western values. But her parents are often immersed in a conflicting cultural and religious tradition in which arranged marriage is the norm. In some cases, their daughter's consent may also be subordinate to their desire to bring another member of the extended family from the home country into Australia.

Overseas marriages are being arranged for 14 and 15-year-old schoolgirls, and sometimes marriage is coerced with violence or the threat of violence, say social workers and sources in community groups.

Multiculturalism

"Multiculturalism" is a philosophical or political policy that promotes cultural diversity. Different cultural or ethnic groups within a nation keep their own identity and traditions.

Multiculturalism is about tolerating the differences between our rich mix of cultures, but it may also be an excuse for ignoring practices that would not be tolerated by most Australians.

Arranged marriages take place in Australia's Lebanese and other Arabic-speaking communities, as well as Turkish, Greek, Indian, Fijian, Bangladeshi, Sri Lankan and Filipino communities—within Muslim, Hindu and other religious groups.

Shadia Gedeon-Hajjar has lectured in Arabic culture at the Phillip Institute of Technology's Centre for Multicultural Studies. She is also the head of the community-based group, Voice of Arabic Women. She estimates that around one in three marriages in the Arabic community are arranged, among both Christian and Muslim families.

Without consent

The author states that no studies have been carried out on arranged marriages in Australia. Does the lack of statistics weaken her argument?

No studies have been done on arranged marriages in Australia, and it is not possible to say how many do not involve consent. However, there is strong evidence from welfare and community groups that many arranged marriages take place without the consent of the bride.

Under-age marriages

Robyn Auld, a social worker from Department of Community Services (DOCS), said that she was aware of arranged marriages taking place overseas among girls under 16 brought up in Australia—women in refuges who have left arranged marriages are often concerned for their sisters who await a similar fate.

"Generally the women contact the department after the marriage, saying it was arranged earlier at 14 or 16—now they are 19", says Auld. "An arranged marriage is taking away the rights of self-determination, it's taking away their freedom of choice to marry whom they wish. It's a power and control issue, but probably would not be considered abuse by DOC's guidelines."

Only limited action could be taken were DOCS to become aware of an under-age girl who was facing an arranged marriage, such as referring her to legal centres and counselling services. The need for confidentiality would prevent the department informing other authorities.

According to the Registry of Births, Marriages and Deaths, marriage in Australia under the age of 16 was no longer legal after 1991. However, an overseas marriage is valid in Australia provided it was legal in the overseas country, where the marriage age can be less than 16.

The minimum legal age for marriage varies from country to country, and in the United States from state to state. Can you think why different ages apply in different countries?

Irene Pearce, a Family Support coordinator based in the western suburbs of Sydney, believes it is common practice for girls to be taken by their family to their homeland to marry at 15 or 16. "Very often it appears they are using the arranged marriage to bring cousins into the country", Pearce says.

Immigration and arranged marriages

A spokesperson for the Department of Immigration said that a couple need not have met before marrying, although the overseas immigration office must believe that the sponsored spouse has consented to the marriage. "Marriages are quite often arranged, and that is accepted within the culture", he said.

Forced marriages

Whether we like it or not, forced marriages are a reality in Australia. It is important that we decide whether all women are entitled to the same basic human rights, regardless of background. Should these be watered down by concepts of multiculturalism or "ethnic sensitivity", or not discussed for fear of inciting racial hatred?

If we acknowledge that cultural practices do lead to the oppression of women in this country, this might also be used as an excuse to demand reduced migration and perpetuate racial intolerance.

Do you think that demanding an end to forced marriages in Australia would increase racial intolerance there?

It is a difficult dilemma, but the plight of women who are forced into marriages demands attention. How many women like Rindi are out there, awaiting the wedding from which she will have no escape?

ARRANGED MARRIAGES: A TRUE FAMILY AFFAIR
Leena Kamat

NO

For a discussion about marriage in general see Topic 3 Is marriage essential to the modern family unit? in Volume 11, Family and Society.

While many Western students assume they will marry someone of their own choice for love, there are some people who may not marry for these same reasons.

Arranged marriages are quite common in many faiths around the world. Marriages are often not only between the husband and the wife, but between both families. Therefore, the entire family is involved in the marriage preparation right from the beginning.

Muslim marriages in Canada

Love marriages are common in Canada among Islamic people, said Nina Karachi-Khaled, correspondence secretary for the National Executive of the Canadian Council of Muslim Women. Arranged marriages are more common in other countries, like Pakistan and India and in rural communities.

Karachi-Khaled said her parents had an arranged marriage, but her own was a love marriage. For many Muslim women living in Canada, the love aspect of marriage is paramount. Still, many people regard love as being the most important aspect [in marriage].

"People have a very stereotypical view on arranged marriages," said Fariha Tayyeb, a third-year honours economics student at Western. "What an arranged marriage is, is an introduction to a guy through your parents. It's like a blind date."

But the definition given to love today greatly differs from what is needed to keeping a marriage successful. "We're given the implication that love is all sex," Karachi-Khaled said. "Love is also working on communication skills and raising a family."

Some cultures accept arranged marriages because the family is involved in the decision Karachi-Khaled explained. "People say your parents know you the best," Karachi-Khaled said, adding parents may know their child's likes and dislikes, personal habits and preferences.

In the Islamic faith, the family's support is critical. "If family wants this marriage, then we're not alone," she said. "You need your family and friends' help."

Do you think fewer people would divorce if their families and friends were involved in their marriage choices?

A groom places the ring on his bride's finger during a Hindu marriage. Since gold lasts forever, rings made of gold are exchanged to represent a long married life. The bride wears her ring on the fourth finger, which is believed to have a vein leading directly to the heart.

COMMENTARY: Russian mail-order brides

Western men are turning to marriage agencies or introduction services to find spouses from the former Soviet Union. The mail-order bride industry was traditionally dominated by agencies on the Pacific rim, but with the spread of the Internet and the collapse of the Soviet Union Russian marriage agencies are expanding and taking over the market. The vast majority of those Internet sites are geared to U.S. men.

Mail-order brides

Various cultures around the world have advocated the arrangement of marriage between two individuals through the medium of a matchmaker or other third party. In America, for example, in the 18th and 19th centuries male settlers moving west traditionally outnumbered their female counterparts. Men would often find their future wives through friends, family, newspaper advertisements, and agencies. They would correspond with marriage-minded women, often becoming engaged to them without seeing them first, and would either marry their brides by proxy, or when the bride arrived at her new home.

This arrangement still continues today, especially in remote locations, such as Alaska, for example, where women are scarce, and among men who are both tired of the "dating game" and of independent women. They consider mail-order brides as the answer to their dreams, believing them to be less materialistic, more subservient, and more focused on meeting their husbands' every need. There are now new bride markets, and the collapse of the Soviet Union has provided a further good source of women.

According to some sources, for the former Soviet Union there are more than 600 agencies on the Internet that provide "introduction services." Some agencies have as many as 25,000 Russian women applying to them each year. Critics, however, argue that this system is not without risk for both partners. The bride is often isolated and lonely in her new country, especially if she does not speak English, and she may be subject to abuse; and the groom takes the chance that his wife is simply using him to obtain permanent residency status.

Alpna Patel was convicted of manslaughter in 2000 for killing her husband. She received a three-year sentence, but was released from prison in February 2002, after serving 13 months.

Being introduced by family members ensures parental approval of the husband. "I wouldn't mind marrying someone who my parents introduced me to," Tayyeb said.

Arranged marriages have become a topic of discussion with the recent trial of Saskatoon dentist Alpna Patel, who was found guilty of manslaughter in the stabbing to death of her husband. The couple had an arranged marriage and the unhappiness in their marriage was brought out as a defence during the trial.

Peter Chimbos, professor of sociology at Brescia College, said one case should not imply arranged marriages are more violent than others and the couples are more unhappy. "I cannot make that assumption on one or two cases.

"There is no data indicating arranged marriages are more lethal than individual mate selection," Chimbos said. "The majority of spousal killings occur among lower socio-economic classes."

In the Patel case, there could have been many incidents which led to the unhappy marriage and it cannot be assumed the arranged marriage played a significant role, he explained.

Arranged marriages have been criticized because most times the couple does not know each other well. However, Karachi-Khaled said she did not think people who marry for love always know each other really well before the wedding either. Even living together before marriage does not ensure a happy and successful union, she said. …

Other criticisms surrounding arranged marriages centres on the woman in the relationship having no say in her future. Karachi-Khaled said this is not a concern in Islamic marriages as the woman has to agree she wants to marry the man. During the wedding ceremony itself, the bride is asked three times for confirmation she wishes to marry her groom.

Tayyeb said not too many people have arranged marriages in which the couple has no say in whether they will finally marry or not. Those types of marriages are only found in small villages, amongst the lower class population, she explained. "There, it's a duty [for the parents] to get their daughters married off."

Non-arranged marriages

The freedom associated with non-arranged marriages should also be looked at more closely. "Even in non-arranged marriages, how much freedom is there?" Hsiung asked. "When people are dating, there is so much pressure to either continue or not continue the relationship. There is so much pressure after marriage."

Hsiung explained even in "love" marriages, people tend to marry within their background. The criteria used to find mates are generally the same in both types of marriages. "You cannot deny that people use criteria when finding their spouse."

"Even love marriages are arranged," Karachi-Khaled said. "Look at want ads." People specify everything they are looking for, including the possible mate's height, skin colour, religion, likes, education and job.

> The author uses quotations from acknowledged experts to back up her argument. Is this a convincing technique?

> Do you think there is any real difference between arranged Asian marriages and the western practices of blind dates or personal ads?

Summary

Are arranged marriages an abuse or an expression of love from parents who only want the best for their offspring? In the first article Jennie Christian argues that arranged marriages are abusive. She looks at the case of Rindi, a girl of Asian background who grew up in Australia in a Western environment with all its benefits, but was forced by her family to marry someone she had never met. She asked a male friend to help her escape to New Zealand to a brother, but ended up obeying her parents and marrying the man she had never met before.

Having stressed that Rindi grew up in a western environment, Christian questions why someone given the opportunity to be free thinking and who was given access to education was expected to put her family's expectations before her own. Christian also turns her attention to the authorities, whose limited resources were unable to protect Rindi and several other young women in similar circumstances.

Leena Kamat, on the other hand, questions the assumption made by westerners that there are vast differences between love marriages and arranged marriages. She argues that western intolerance to arranged marriages stems mainly from a lack of understanding, specifically of the importance of family and parental authority. She states that while she is aware of the problems attached to arranged marriages, she feels strongly that similar problems can occur within a variety of unions and that critics should not just oppose this form of marriage simply because it is based on duty rather than the individual choice.

FURTHER INFORMATION:

 Books:

Clayton, Richard R., *The Family, Marriage and Social Change*. 2nd edition. Lexington, MA: Heath, 1979.

Useful websites:

http://www.medusa2000.com/marriage.htmt
"Forced Marriages Are a Violation of Human Rights. End It!" Article that specifically looks at forced marriages.
http://marriage.about.com/cs/arrangedmarriages/
An about.com site that lists various articles in support of and against arranged marriages, including several on the system in Japan and articles in Southeast Asian women's magazines on the issue.
http://216.239.39.100/search?q=cache:8r5BovMQz68C:w
ww.geocities.com/jit_1pk/file1.pdf+In+support+of+
arranged+marriages+globally&hl=en&ie=UTF-8
An article specifically on the case of Southeast Asians in

Britain, which puts the topic in a global context and cites a lot of studies and statistical information.

The following debates in the Pro/Con series may also be of interest:

In this volume:
Part 3: Gender and children's rights

In Individual and Society:
Topic 3 Are women still the second sex?

ARE ARRANGED MARRIAGES AN ABUSE OF HUMAN RIGHTS?

YES: Historically many different societies used to allow arranged marriages, but today people are used to having choice and freedom

YES: It is barbaric to force young girls and women to marry someone whom, in some cases, they have not even seen before

ARCHAIC PRACTICE
Are arranged marriages an anachronism?

WOMEN'S RIGHTS
Should all women have the right to marry or not marry whom they please?

NO: Arranged marriages take place within specific cultural and religious contexts and often the young man and woman concerned have an opportunity to meet and see if they like each other

NO: Certain religions and cultures believe that arranged marriages are the best method of making sure that girls and women marry the right person

ARE ARRANGED MARRIAGES AN ABUSE OF HUMAN RIGHTS?

KEY POINTS

YES: There are reports of bride burnings, beatings, wife rape, and forced marriages each day in the media, and they show that arranged marriages are mostly abusive

YES: Arranged marriages promote the idea that women are just their husbands' possessions. As such, some men believe they can do anything they want with their wives.

ABUSE
Are arranged marriages more likely to be abusive?

NO: There is no evidence that proves that an arranged marriage would be more violent or abusive than a love marriage

NO: Statistics show that arranged marriages have as much chance of success as love marriages

Topic 11
DO FETUSES HAVE RIGHTS?

YES
"UNBORN VICTIMS ACT EXPOSES A LIE"
TOWNHALL.COM, MAY 4, 2001
DON FEDER
NO
FROM "WHAT'S WRONG WITH FETAL RIGHTS"
ACLU, JULY 31, 1996
AMERICAN CIVIL LIBERTIES UNION

INTRODUCTION

The question of whether a fetus has rights is a topical one in the United States today. At the heart of the debate on fetal rights is the question of whether a fetus is a human being from the moment of conception, or whether it is an "unborn child," as many critics of fetal rights claim.

If the fetus is a human being, it means that it can legally claim, among other things, both the right to a safe and healthy environment and the right to be born. Many civil liberties and women's rights groups argue that fetal rights threaten much-fought-for reproductive rights, placing the rights of the unborn before those of the mother. Advocates, however, counter that a fetus has the right to be protected from unlawful action.

In the United States fetal rights became a major issue during the intense debates around the legalization of abortion. Anti-abortion campaigners claimed that fetuses have the absolute right to life and that their right to life was more important than any concern for the pregnant mother. They argued

that the 1973 Supreme Court judgment on *Roe v. Wade*, which granted women the legal right to abortion, in principle limited a fetus's right to life from being absolute to being conditional.

The debate on fetal rights has, in recent years, moved beyond the context of abortion to highlight other situations that might endanger the life of a fetus. Acts of violence against pregnant women, exposure of women to unsafe working conditions, and substance use by pregnant women are among the circumstances that have led to a nationwide call for laws protecting fetuses from unlawful violent action while in their mothers' wombs.

The move to give legal protection to fetuses has evoked strong division of opinion. Those who favor fetal rights—anti-abortion groups among them—assert that the incidence of violence underscores the need for protective laws. Among those objecting to the idea that fetuses have rights are liberal-leaning politicians, civil rights groups such as the American Civil Liberties Union (ACLU), and prochoice groups.

Objectors are concerned that fetal rights conflict with reproductive rights. Once a fetus is granted the status of a human being, they assert, the mother may be forced to forfeit her right to make decisions about her body, especially that of abortion.

According to the *Journal of the American Medical Association,* in 1996 the prevalence of pregnancy-related violence in the general population in the United States was in the range of 4–8 percent—that translates to around 156,000–332,000 cases of battery against pregnant women each year. Advocates have campaigned for many years on the grounds that fetal rights legislation protects the mother as well as the fetus.

"However we may pity the mother whose health and even life [is] imperilled ... there yet remains no sufficient reason for condoning the ... murder of the innocent."

—POPE PIUS XI (1930)

Each state currently has the right to decide what action to take, if any, on fetal rights. Twenty-four states have enacted laws that recognize unborn children as human victims of violent crimes. Of those, 11 safeguard fetal rights throughout the period of pregnancy, while the rest recognize such rights only during specific periods of uterine development. In April 2001 the House of Representatives passed H.R. 503, S. 480, the Unborn Victims of Violence Act (see page 144), which seeks to make violent acts against the fetus a federal crime. The act protects fetal rights in the case of third-party violence, that is, when someone other than the mother causes harm to the child. Civil rights advocates, however, predict that this is the start of a slippery slope that will end in the revocation of some fundamental women's rights.

Fetal protection rights, they claim, could be used to discriminate against women and restrict their freedoms. A woman who is pregnant could, they argue, have every aspect of her life monitored, from what she eats or drinks to how she spends her recreation time. They argue that a number of states are introducing laws that penalize pregnant women for behavior deemed "unsuitable." South Carolina, for example, criminalizes prenatal substance abuse, while 13 states terminate parental rights in cases in which mothers are found to be using drugs. Eight other states require testing or reporting by health professionals of suspected cases of abuse.

The National Institute of Drug Abuse conducted a nationwide survey in 1992–93 and found that of the 4 million women who gave birth during the period, 221,000 women used illegal drugs during their pregnancies that year, of which 119,000 reported use of marijuana and 45,000 reported use of cocaine. That evidence proves, advocates claim, that such testing is necessary.

In the first of the two following articles journalist Don Feder examines the impact of the Unborn Victims of Violence Act. In the second article the ACLU examines recent reproductive rights cases and legislation.

UNBORN VICTIMS ACT EXPOSES A LIE
Don Feder

YES

At the heart of the abortion-rights battle lies a deadly
denial of reality.

The Unborn Victims of Violence Act, which passed the
House late last month, threatens a carefully constructed
worldview, hence the agitated opposition it has aroused.

H.R. 503, approved by a 252-to-172 vote, makes it a federal
offense to cause injury or death to a fetus (defined as
"a member of the species Homo sapiens, at any stage of
development, who is carried in the womb") in the course
of committing one of 68 other federal crimes. Abortion, or
harm caused by the mother, is exempted.

"The legislation is a deceptive and dangerous attack on a
woman's right to choose, disguised as an effort to protect
women from violence," charged the National Abortion and
Reproductive Rights Action League [NARAL]. Sponsors
of H.R. 503 are exploiting "unfortunate tragedies to
advance their anti-choice, anti-woman agenda," Planned
Parenthood snarled.

Now, let me see if I understand this. According to the
abortion lobby, if a woman is carrying a child she wants,
and someone deliberately causes its death, it is anti-woman
to punish the attacker for destroying the life in her womb.

Tracy Marciniak doesn't think so.

The case of Tracy Marciniak

On the evening of Feb. 8, 1992, Marciniak was four days
away from her due date. She had named her unborn child
Zachariah. The man who was then her husband beat her
brutally to cause a miscarriage.

Marciniak: "He punched me very hard twice in the
abdomen. Then he refused to call for help, and prevented
me from doing so."

When she finally made it to a hospital, her son was
delivered dead. Because Wisconsin had no fetal homicide
law at the time (it adopted one in 1998), her husband was
convicted of assaulting her, but did not receive so much
as a day in jail for murdering her child. In the face of
such horrors, 24 states have passed laws criminalizing
fetal homicide.

The photograph above shows a poster from a prolife protest outside Aitken High School,
South Carolina, March 5, 1996.

COMMENTARY: Recent legislation

The question of whether fetuses should have any rights under the law has long been the subject of serious contention in the United States. Supporters, including prolife groups such as the National Right to Life Committee (NRLC), claim that the fetus is a human being and should have the same rights as a living person. Conversely, civil rights groups, such as the American Civil Liberties Union (ACLU), counter that the recognition of fetus rights could adversely infringe on those of the mother.

State recognition

Many states have passed laws protecting the fetus. Possibly the most famous of them is the 2001 Unborn Victims of Violence Act (see below). Even before its passage 24 states had enacted some kind of legislation that recognized unborn children as victims of violent crimes, including 11 that provided protection throughout the period of in utero development. In 2002, 14 states, including Arizona, Louisiana, Pennsylvania, and Ohio, had homicide laws that recognized unborn children as victims throughout the whole period of prenatal development. A further 12, including Arkansas, California, Florida, and Washington, had homicide laws that recognized them as victims for only part of the prenatal development period.

The Unborn Victims of Violence Act (H.R. 503)

Sponsored by Representative Lindsey Graham (R–SC), the bill was passed in April 2001 by 254 votes to 172 in the House of Representatives. The act states that if an unborn child is injured or killed by an assailant committing a violent federal offense against a pregnant woman, the attacker will be charged with the crime on behalf of the unborn child.

The act was not passed without opposition. During the 106th Congress prochoice groups proposed alternative legislation known as the Lofgren substitute amendment or "Motherhood Protection Act," which defined an "offense" as an "interruption to the normal course of the pregnancy." This terminology suggested that in the case of a violent attack against a pregnant women there was only one victim not two, as advocates of fetal rights suggested. The House of Representatives rejected the proposal, however, on September 30, 1999.

Advocates of the Unborn Victims of Violence Act (UVVA), such as Clarke Forsythe of Americans United for Life, an anti-abortion rights group, argue that UVVA's passage was inevitable given the growing incidents of violence against pregnant women and the need to seek justice for all the victims. Opponents, however, disagree, claiming that the UVVA will hurt women's reproductive rights. As Professor Rachel Roth states quite clearly, "The [federal] bill ... gives fetuses their own rights. Inevitably it will erode or come head-to-head with abortion rights."

Marciniak has a message for opponents of H.R. 503: "Please hear me on this. On the night of Feb. 8, 1992, there were two victims. I was nearly killed—but I survived. Little Zachariah died."

The bill has nothing—and everything—to do with abortion. Opponents are intimidated by seven words ("a member of the species Homo sapiens"). In the House, they offered a substitute with neutral language, providing a stiffer penalty for harm done to the mother which also "interferes with the normal course of the pregnancy."

It's instructive to witness the mental gymnastics of abortion advocates. Under the substitute, someone who killed a pregnant woman would have been punished for one murder and one act of interfering with ... what—a process, a condition? Opponents of H.R. 503 can't be specific because to do so would imply that the fetus is something other than a thing.

A fetus by any other name?

"A member of the species Homo sapiens?" But what else could it be? It has that species' genetic code. At 10 to 12 weeks of development, it has a beating human heart, as well as other human organs, formed but not fully developed. If nature is allowed to take its course (in Marciniak's case, in a matter of hours), it will emerge from the womb with an identity apparent even to the most myopic.

When we know that a woman is pregnant, we instinctively identify the life she's carrying as human. Have you ever heard an officeworker greeting a pregnant colleague at the water cooler with, "Well, how's the fetus doing?" Still, one side of the debate is forced to play semantic games.

In 1994, NARAL President Kate Michelman was put in an uncomfortable position, after she told an interviewer, "We think abortion is a bad thing." Michelman at first denied making the statement, then explained she had misspoken.

What else could she do? Bad is a moral judgment. It suggests there's something wrong with the act under scrutiny, which implies that someone's rights have been violated. But whose? Surely not the woman who voluntarily seeks an abortion or the abortionist.

With the support of President George Bush, the legislative battle now moves to the Senate. The Unborn Victims of Violence Act addresses one aspect of a far-reaching tragedy.

There are 1.2 million unborn victims of violence in this country each year. Some die in the course of a crime. Most are killed by a lie.

By using the emotional example of Tracy Marciniak, Feder makes his point forcibly. Could he have been equally effective using a different technique?

This is the core of the argument about fetal rights. At what stage does a fetus become a human being? Do you think the argument is convincing?

George W. Bush supports the Unborn Victims of Violence Act, yet his government also supports the use of fetal tissue in scientific experiments. Are the two mutually exclusive?

WHAT'S WRONG WITH FETAL RIGHTS
American Civil Liberties Union

…In the past two years, a number of states have considered or enacted legislation designed to protect fetuses and punish individuals who injure them or cause their death. The ACLU recognizes that a woman may suffer a serious physical and emotional injury if her pregnancy is ended by an assault, a drunk driving accident, or other criminal or negligent acts. But we have serious reservations about legislation designed to protect fetuses, because it can endanger women's rights by reinforcing claims of "fetal rights" in the law.…

The ACLU fully supports a woman's right to obtain redress under civil law for an injury to her fetus, and we support society's right to punish criminal conduct. But we urge legislators and advocates of choice to take a careful look at bills designed to protect fetuses. They must be alert to the pitfalls in such bills and refrain from supporting statutes that endanger civil liberties.

A. The varieties of fetal protection legislation

Legislation to protect fetuses can take many different forms. The extent to which such a bill may endanger reproductive rights depends on its specific terms and implications. For example, states may: 1) amend existing homicide statutes to include the fetus as a possible victim; 2) pass statutes defining the fetus as a person or human being, thereby making the fetus fall within the compass of other statutes applicable to all persons or human beings; 3) enact freestanding statutes to define and penalize a new crime of injury to a fetus, fetal homicide, or "feticide"; 4) extend wrongful death statutes to permit civil suits against individuals who cause the death of a fetus; or 5) enact new statutes to penalize injury to a pregnant woman that causes her fetus to die or be injured. In some instances, two or more of these approaches to fetal protection may be combined in a single bill.

B. Fetal protection legislation can infringe on the right to abortion

To conform with the constitutional right to choose established in *Roe v. Wade*, fetal protection legislation must

---

Is the ACLU's position weakened by its desire to balance everyone's rights: women, society, and the unborn child?

By listing issues in a point-by-point fashion, the ACLU makes sure that its argument is clearly put across to the reader.

Roe v. Wade *(1973) was a landmark case in abortion history. In writing his decision on the case, Justice Harry Blackmun stated that current laws infringed on a woman's right to privacy—thus her right to abortion—under the Fourteenth Amendment. For further information on this case go to volume 1,* Individual and Society, *page 196.*

exempt abortion from punishment. The exemption should explicitly cover: 1) abortions performed by health care workers with the consent of the woman or in medical emergencies; and 2) self-abortions....

C. Fetal protection statutes may encourage the "policing" of pregnancy

Fetal protection bills must also exempt conduct of the pregnant woman herself. If they do not, they will encourage the "policing" of pregnancy by those attempting to control the conduct of pregnant women.... We could also expect to see still more criminal prosecutions or child abuse or neglect proceedings brought against women who make childbirth choices of which doctors or judges disapprove....

D. Fetal protection bills may violate other constitutional rights

Some fetal protection bills disregard the Constitution's promise that citizens are entitled to due process of law. They violate due process guarantees if they lack a scienter requirement or are unacceptably vague.

A scienter requirement specifies that the perpetrator of a crime must have intended to commit the crime. Such a requirement is usually necessary for a person to be convicted of an offense in criminal law. When legislation fails to address intent, as some fetal protection bills do, a person may be prosecuted and punished for a crime that he or she did not intend to commit, when a lesser charge would be more just. Fetal protection bills also run the risk of being unconstitutionally vague if they do not define all of their terms and spell out precisely what conduct is prohibited. A fetal protection statute that leaves the public, health care workers, and law enforcement authorities uncertain as to its meaning is especially dangerous because it threatens to chill the exercise of constitutionally protected reproductive rights.

E. Factors to evaluate

Fetal protection bills must be analyzed very carefully.... Here is a checklist of some important factors that you should evaluate in the bills and discuss with us:

- Does the bill cast the fetus, the woman, or both as the victim?...
- Does the bill have an exemption for abortions performed by health care workers with the consent of the woman

On October 4, 2002, the Supreme Court heard the oral arguments for Ferguson v. City of Charleston, a case brought by 10 women who had secretly been tested for cocaine use during a routine prenatal care visit at a South Carolina public hospital. The women who tested positive argued that the tests violated their Fourth Amendment right to be free from unreasonable searches. The jury ruled in their favor, but the United States Court of Appeals for the Fourth Circuit found the searches reasonable as a matter of law under the United States Supreme Court's "line of cases recognizing that 'special needs' may, in certain exceptional circumstances, [justify] a search policy designed to serve non-law enforcement ends."

or in medical emergencies, as well as an exemption for self-abortions?…

- Does the bill exempt conduct of the pregnant woman herself?…
- What language does the bill employ to describe the fetus?…
- Does the bill create criminal or civil liability?…
- Does a bill proposing a criminal penalty include a scienter requirement?…
- Does the bill define all of its terms and spell out precisely what conduct is prohibited?…
- In a bill proposing a criminal penalty for causing the death of a fetus, how does that penalty compare to the penalty for causing the death of a live person?…

Do you think the ACLU is going overboard in listing these questions, or are they helpful?

II. Wrongful death actions on behalf of fetuses

Many states have "wrongful death" statutes, which allow someone acting on behalf of a deceased person—usually a surviving relative or an administrator of the estate—to recover damages for a wrongful or negligent act that caused the person's death. The state courts are divided on whether or not stillborn fetuses may be regarded as "persons" for the purpose of bringing wrongful death actions on their behalf.

The ACLU takes the position that when a prospective parent's plans to continue a pregnancy to term have been frustrated by others, that individual should be compensated for the loss of the pregnancy and the harm suffered. The prospective parent should bring a cause of action and be compensated under tort law, the area of the law concerned with compelling wrongdoers to compensate those whom they have injured.…

Does action such as the ACLU recommends mean that there is no need for fetal rights legislation?

Legal claims made on behalf of stillborn fetuses risk intruding upon women's constitutionally protected privacy rights. A recent Florida case in which we participated, *Young v. St. Vincent's Medical Center*, demonstrates the important issues at stake when a wrongful death action is brought on behalf of a fetus. In April 1995, the Florida District Court of Appeals asked the Florida Supreme Court to decide whether a stillborn fetus has a right of recovery under Florida's Wrongful Death Act. This question arose because a woman had brought a wrongful death action on behalf of her stillborn fetus to seek damages for a hospital's alleged negligence. The state court of appeals, as well as the district court, dismissed the plaintiff's claim on the ground that Florida law permits a cause of action for wrongful death only for those born alive.…

The plaintiff's claim was dismissed on the grounds that Florida law permits wrongful death actions only in cases in which the victim is alive. Do you think that is right?

Is *Young v. St. Vincent's Medical Center* important?

The central question posed by *Young v. St. Vincent's Medical Center* was not whether the prospective parent's loss should be compensated, but rather, how it should be compensated. The Project and the ACLU of Florida urged that any money damages should go to the prospective parent, who should be compensated for the loss of her child and the harm she suffered when her choice to continue a pregnancy to term was frustrated. The understandable impulse to compensate the loss of a fetus, we argued, should not lead to an award of damages to the stillborn fetus. Instead, the prospective parent's loss could and should be compensated within the existing tort law framework, which recognizes a unified legal interest between the pregnant woman and her fetus. Moreover, the ACLU brief argued that according independent legal rights to fetuses opens the door to causes of action against pregnant women in violation of their autonomy and privacy. Any equating of a fetus with a "person" or "child" in the wrongful death context would have ramifications in other realms of the law. It might, for example, spur claims for "prenatal negligence" by children suing their own mothers, like *Grodin v. Grodin*, the Michigan case mentioned earlier in which a child alleged that his mother's conduct during pregnancy had discolored his teeth. Recognition of independent "fetal rights" would encourage prosecutors and medical personnel to punish women for drug use during pregnancy or other conduct that could potentially harm a fetus....

On March 14, 1996, the Florida Supreme Court upheld the lower court's decision in *Young v. St. Vincent's Medical Center* and dismissed the wrongful death claim on behalf of the fetus....

III. Conclusion

While acknowledging the deep emotions that fetuses may evoke for millions of Americans, the ACLU opposes the creation of theories of "fetal rights." Permitting legal actions on behalf of stillborn fetuses or enacting laws to protect fetuses opens a Pandora's box in terms of how the law treats pregnancy and childbirth.

However great our compassion and concern for bereaved prospective parents, we must examine such lawsuits and legislation with a critical eye. If they pose a real threat to reproductive rights, as they often do, then we must intervene and oppose them.

> If the ACLU is right that action violates the right to autonomy and privacy, is it unconstitutional?

> According to Greek mythology, Pandora was created by Hephestus as the first woman (the equivalent of Eve). Her companion Epimetheus had a large box in his house, which he told Pandora not to touch. One day, though, Pandora heard a voice beckoning to her from the box; she opened the lid and released all the plagues of the world on man. When she realized what she had done, Pandora tried to close the box; but it was too late, although at the very bottom lay Hope, which sprang out to join the plagues. Is that a fair analogy in this case?

Summary

The question of whether fetal rights should exist is a contentious one. Should a human embryo still within the womb of its mother have the same rights as other living members of society? And if that is the case, how does that affect the reproductive rights of women?

In the first article Don Feder supports the passing of the Unborn Victims of Violence Act in the House of Representatives. He argues that it is a fallacy to pretend that a fetus in the womb is anything but an unborn child. As such, any violent act that harms the fetus must be treated as a crime. He is critical of abortion advocates who choose not to refer to the fetus as a "member of the species homo sapiens." His article implies that the act will go a long way in highlighting abortion as one among the many crimes of violence that an unborn child endures. The ACLU article, on the other hand, highlights some of the pitfalls in granting protective legal rights to fetuses. It points out that in the long run many of those laws will have an adverse effect on women's hard-earned reproductive rights, especially that of abortion. The article sets down a checklist to evaluate if a particular fetal-protection law is likely to discriminate against women's rights. The ACLU position is that reparation for any damage to a fetus should be claimed under tort law, not wrongful death statutes. The tort statute sees a unified legal interest between the pregnant woman and fetus instead of separating them. A wrongful death claim allows anyone to ask for reparations on behalf of a fetus against anyone, including the mother. The ACLU article, in the end, argues that the interest of the fetus cannot supersede the rights of the mother.

FURTHER INFORMATION:

Books:
Purdy, Laura M., *Reproducing Persons: Issues in Feminist Bioethics*. Ithaca, NY: Cornell University Press, 1996.

Useful websites:
www.religioustolerance.org/abo_feta.htm
"Balancing the Rights of the Woman and Her Fetus."
http://www.users.bigpond.com/russellblackford/fetus.htm
"The Supposed Rights of the Fetus," an article by Russell Blackford that looks at the main issues in the debate.
http://abcnews.go.com/sections/us/DailyNews/fetal010625.html
Article that looks specifically at the legal protections available in drug cases and third-party violence in the fetal rights debate.

The following debates in the Pro/Con series may also be of interest:

In this volume:
Part 3: Gender and children's rights

Topic 9 Are human rights women's rights?

In *Individual and Society*:
Topic 15 Is abortion a right?

Abortion in the United States, pages 200–201

DO FETUSES
HAVE RIGHTS?

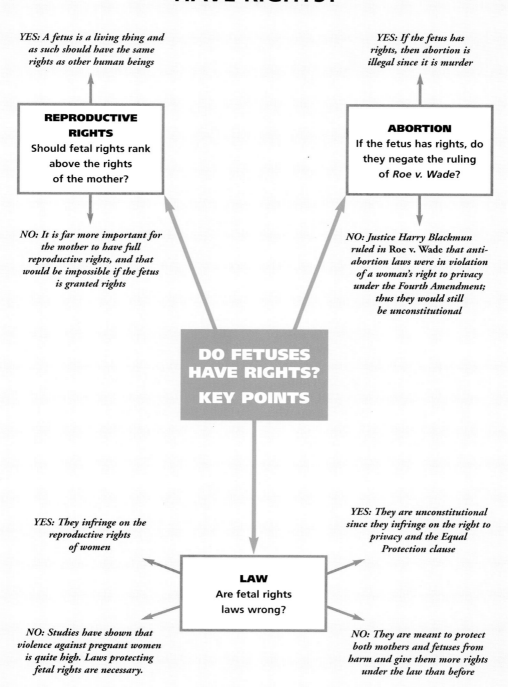

YES: A fetus is a living thing and as such should have the same rights as other human beings

REPRODUCTIVE RIGHTS
Should fetal rights rank above the rights of the mother?

NO: It is far more important for the mother to have full reproductive rights, and that would be impossible if the fetus is granted rights

YES: If the fetus has rights, then abortion is illegal since it is murder

ABORTION
If the fetus has rights, do they negate the ruling of *Roe v. Wade*?

NO: Justice Harry Blackmun ruled in Roe v. Wade *that anti-abortion laws were in violation of a woman's right to privacy under the Fourth Amendment; thus they would still be unconstitutional*

DO FETUSES HAVE RIGHTS? KEY POINTS

YES: They infringe on the reproductive rights of women

YES: They are unconstitutional since they infringe on the right to privacy and the Equal Protection clause

LAW
Are fetal rights laws wrong?

NO: Studies have shown that violence against pregnant women is quite high. Laws protecting fetal rights are necessary.

NO: They are meant to protect both mothers and fetuses from harm and give them more rights under the law than before

Topic 12

IS THE UN AN EFFECTIVE ADVOCATE FOR CHILDREN'S RIGHTS?

YES

FROM "CHILDREN'S RIGHTS"
UNITED NATIONS, BACKGROUND NOTE
UNITED NATIONS

NO

"BUSH TO UN–U.S. IS PRO-FAMILY: A REPORT FROM THE FRONT"
ISSUE ANALYSIS, MARCH 2001
NATIONAL CENTER FOR HOME EDUCATION

INTRODUCTION

Many of the world's children suffer from human rights abuses, whether as a result of extreme poverty or because of exploitation in the form of child labor, child abuse, child prostitution, or the forced conscription of children into armies. Most people agree that children are an especially vulnerable group who may have difficulty making themselves heard and that it is therefore especially important to try to protect their rights.

Nevertheless, there is much debate about the best way to protect children's rights. Human rights organizations, like Amnesty International, together with charities, educators, and parents, are among those who have contributed to this debate. Some argue that the organization better equipped to help is the United Nations (UN)—the voluntary association of countries formed after World War II (1939-1945) to promote global peace and security. However, others argue that children's interests are better served by the actions of individual governments, not those of a single, worldwide authority.

The idea that children have rights at all is a relatively new one. In the west children were for many centuries considered merely miniature adults who needed no special protection, which often meant that they were treated extremely harshly. In the 19th century, for example, most of the poor worked long hours, for very little money, in extremely bad conditions. The labor laws did not protect children, and they were severely exploited in factories and mines. Pressure from social reformers eventually forced western governments to pass laws limiting the hours children worked and stipulating that they should receive a minimum amount of education.

During the 20th century this process continued, and the international community recognized in a series of international codes that children had a basic right to exist free from exploitation and fear. Many people claim the UN was crucial in this process and that the Universal Declaration of Human Rights provided a basic code of human rights. Critics, however, believe that while the UN has talked a lot about rights, in practice it has achieved relatively little for the majority of children in the world.

One example of the UN's work for children is its International Children's Emergency Fund (UNICEF), set up in 1946 to help children affected by the war. Over the years UNICEF has grown and now helps children from many parts of the world obtain food, medicine, clean water, sanitation, education, and emergency assistance.

The UN has also worked to produce international agreements on children's rights. In 1959 the UN Declaration on the Rights of the Child set out a list of agreed international aspirations, which were eventually followed by a legally binding treaty: the International Convention on the Rights of the Child, (CRC), which the UN adopted in 1989.

> *"Adults go to war, but they don't realize the damage they are doing to children."*
> —NICARAGUAN CHILD

The CRC affirms the right of all children to life, survival, and personal development, as well as the right to hold and express their own opinion. It states that they have the right to be free from discrimination and stipulates that all decisions relating to them by states or nonstate organizations will be taken in their best interests. It demands that countries identify their most vulnerable children and act to protect their rights. It also establishes an elected committee to check that the convention is being adhered to internationally.

The CRC quickly gained wide acceptance, and by 2003 it had been ratified by every country in the world except Somalia and the United States. According to its advocates, the CRC helps all children receive the respect they deserve without infringing on the rights and responsibilities of others. However, opponents argue that the treaty is intrusive and misguided. Some critics state that is the main reason behind the U.S. failure to ratify the CRC, even though it has signed it. They state that the U.S. government believes that domestic laws do enough to protect children's rights.

Critics of the CRC also argue that it may actually harm children by undermining the role of the family— the most suitable framework, they feel, for protecting children. They claim that the CRC conflicts with the fundamental right of parents to bring up their children in the way that they think best.

Although most people believe that agreements like the CRC show that the UN is trying to improve children's rights around the world, the consistent violation of children's rights around the world demonstrates that there is still a long way to go before every child attains its basic human rights.

In the first of the following articles a UN background paper outlines some of ways the UN promotes children's rights. The second article looks at U.S. opposition to the UN's views on children's rights.

CHILDREN'S RIGHTS
United Nations

YES

✓ …While victims of injustice and poverty have always had trouble being heard, none have had more trouble, historically, than children. Whether exploited as child labourers or prostitutes, drafted as young teenagers into armed forces, forced as young girls into a lonely life as domestic workers, deprived of an education to work on the family farm, or denied adequate nutrition and health care, children need help and protection from an adult world that perpetrates most of the abuse.

The Special Rapporteur's role

To highlight the existence of the most egregious [conspicuous] violations of international human rights law and encourage Governments to investigate particular cases, the United Nations [High] Commission on Human Rights has appointed a Special Rapporteur [person who makes reports] on the sale of children, child prostitution and child pornography. The Special Rapporteur, an expert in the field, works to gather and analyse facts for the Commission.…

Solving a complex dilemma

A number of those working on behalf of child rights have come to realize that in many of the poorer countries, if children are to stop working, some form of financial compensation must be found for their families.…

In July 1995, after negotiations with non-governmental organizations (NGOs), as well as UNICEF [United Nations Children's Fund] and the International Labour Organization (ILO), the Bangladesh Garment Manufacturers and Exporters Association (BGMEA) signed a Memorandum of Understanding stipulating that BGMEA would ask "that no underaged worker will be terminated until the appropriate school programmes for the workers can be put in place".

UNICEF has committed itself to supporting the education of the children, and the ILO has pledged to contribute money and technical assistance to the establishment of a labour inspection system to monitor implementation of the Memorandum of Understanding. Under the agreement, stipends [payments] will be provided to child workers

Do you think a Special Rapporteur can play a significant part in stopping the exploitation of children? Go to www.unhchr.ch/html/menu2/7/b/mchildsra.htm for reports and articles relating to the work of this Special Rapporteur.

The ILO is an agency of the UN that works for social justice and international labor rights. Go to www.ilo.org/public/english/ for more information.

The BGMEA is a nongovernmental body that promotes the Bangladeshi garment trade. See www.bgmea.com/social.htm for more about its actions against child labor. How successful have those actions been?

attending the school programmes. All parties also agreed to take steps "to create positive public awareness" with respect to issues of child labour and education....

Development of child policy

...Prior to the 20th century, children were for the most part regarded as inferior and subordinate to adults, and childhood was a period of life that was often brief and regarded as a stage of passage to adulthood. Now ... childhood is regarded as a relatively sacred part of life among many of the more affluent. But it is still a period of great struggle and deprivation for children in most of the rest of the world. Children have been included, either directly or indirectly, in most of the nearly 80 treaties and decrees on human rights in this century. The first major step on behalf of children taken by the United Nations was UNICEF's creation in December 1946. Two years later, the Universal Declaration of Human Rights was adopted by the General Assembly. The provisions of that Declaration and its two International Covenants on human rights, adopted in 1966, recognized that child rights need protection.

Do you agree that only richer societies can afford to see childhood as a special time?

See page 66 for more information about both the International Covenant on Civil and Political Rights (ICCPR) and the International Covenant on Economic, Social, and Cultural Rights (ICESCR).

The 1959 Declaration on the Rights of the Child was the first United Nations statement devoted exclusively to the rights of children, but served more as a moral rather than legally binding framework. The special plight of girls was addressed in part by the Convention on the Elimination of All Forms of Discrimination Against Women ...[1979]. The Working Group on Contemporary Forms of Slavery ... addresses such issues as child labour and debt bondage.

See Topic 9 Are human rights women's rights? Do you think there is too much emphasis on women's rights? Are male rights adequately covered?

A global pact on children's rights

It took until the 1990s, however, for all of the pieces to come together in the form of the Convention on the Rights of the Child, which was adopted by the General Assembly in 1989. The Convention's 54 articles cover everything from a child's right to be free from sexual and economic exploitation, to the right to his or her own opinion, and to the right to education, health care, and economic opportunity.

By September 1995, 178 countries had ratified the Convention. A dozen more, some of which had been created since the Convention was adopted six years earlier, were considering it. As a result of this growing support, according to Ms Albenez of UNICEF, childhood is coming to be widely seen not as "some kind of probation period before becoming an adult". Instead, she said, "the child emerges as an individual with dignity who has all the rights of a full human being."

Radda Barnen is the Swedish Save the Children charity. It is a member of the International Save the Children Alliance. Defense for Children International is based in Geneva, Switzerland. Do you think that too many competing children's organizations are counterproductive? Would one organization be more effective?

See page 66 for more information about the 1993 Vienna Conference.

James P. Grant (1922–1995) served as UNICEF's third executive director (1980–1995). Go to www.unicef.org/about/bio-grant.html to find out more about him.

Go to www.cesr.org to find out more about the the connections between human rights and social and economic development.

The initiative for the Convention came from the Government of Poland, which submitted a Draft Convention to the Commission on Human Rights in 1978, prior to celebration of the 20th anniversary of the Declaration on the Rights of the Child during the International Year of the Child in 1979. That led to a decade of collaboration between a small group of non-governmental organizations, including Radda Barnen of Sweden, the International Catholic Child Bureau, and Defense for Children International, and United Nations human rights experts.

After a lengthy period of careful negotiations, the Convention on the Rights of the Child was adopted in November 1989 by a vote of the General Assembly. By September of the following year, the Convention had obtained the 20 ratifications required for its entry into force as international law. Its importance as a foundation of modern human rights law was later underscored at the 1993 World Conference on Human Rights in Vienna.

Human rights and development

By the late 1980s, progress in attracting support for the Convention had drawn the attention of UNICEF. While the organization has always devoted itself to the improvement of social and economic conditions for children, primarily in the fields of health and education, it was not until then that it saw the potential for integrating human rights objectives with more traditional development programmes.

While UNICEF originally included the Convention as one of a number of its programme and advocacy concerns, by late 1994 UNICEF's Executive Director, James P. Grant, announced that the Convention would become the framework for all of UNICEF's programming. In May 1995, UNICEF announced a new procurement policy on child labour, pledging to purchase materials and supplies only from companies that do not exploit child labour. The UNICEF Representative in each country is required to assess the local situation and evaluate the child labour practices of local companies.

Historically there had been a conceptual divide between those who acted as advocates on behalf of human rights and those who pursued the development of economic and social policies and social welfare programmes. Because the Convention … covers so much ground, it has provided a conceptual and legislative umbrella for both traditions. The child-protection issues normally associated with human rights are included—among them those of sexual and economic exploitation, of refugee status, and of juvenile justice….

A catalyst for national action

"The Convention is our essential framework," says Mrs. [Soussan] Raadi-Azarakhchi of the Centre for Human Rights who serves as the Secretary of the Committee on the Rights the Child, a United Nations body. "It's really a catalyst for action at national level. It provides universal standards— but there are ways it can be interpreted that can be suited to various cultural situations."

The Committee on the Rights of the Child was established by the Convention as a means of monitoring and aiding Governments in bringing their national laws and practices into conformity with the treaty. By late 1995, the Committee, which consists of 10 international members with backgrounds in law, education and social work, had reviewed some 40 reports on implementation plans since 1993 from countries that had ratified the Convention. Reports are required within two years of ratification, and are used as a means of opening a dialogue between members of the Committee, the Government of a ratifying state, and the public in that country....

> The Centre for Human Rights is part of the UN Office of the High Commissioner for Human Rights, based at Geneva, in Switzerland.

The power of moral [per]suasion

Much of the power of the Convention comes from mutual example and pressure from the public and from donor countries rather than any real enforcement power. Those that fail to take action or do not take it seriously enough can be admonished by Governments that have taken steps to abide by the Convention. But more persuasive pressure may come from those countries that ratify the Convention and, in turn, receive donor funding for various national initiatives, or assistance with the drafting of laws or establishment of child-advocacy bureaus....

> The author concedes that the CRC lacks "any real enforcement power." Do you think that matters?

Listening to children's voices

Even in countries where both the legality and morality of human rights covenants have been abandoned or repeatedly violated, efforts are being made in the name of the Convention.... The hope is that the Convention will continue to stimulate the kind of debate that often leads to attitudinal change. Child rights need to be actively respected rather than simply acknowledged, and advocates admit that more than the passage of laws and publicizing of the Convention will be required....

"We believe the Convention is a wonderful instrument," says Ricardo Domenici, secretary-general of the NGO group Defense for Children International....

> Why is there such a big gap between acknowledgment of children's rights and "active respect" for them? Do you think that the gap is bigger in the case of children's rights than for human rights in general?

BUSH TO UN—U.S. IS PRO-FAMILY: A REPORT FROM THE FRONT
National Center for Home Education

NO

Why do you think conservatives and profamily groups would vote against United Nations' proposals for protecting the rights of children?

UNITED NATIONS–NEW YORK, NY

With little fanfare, on February 1, 2001, the Bush State Department, in one of its first international statements, delivered a major win for conservatives and the pro-family movement.

UN Summit for Children

The occasion was the second in a series of three scheduled meetings held at the United Nations in New York in preparation for the UN World Summit for Children. Scheduled in September 2001, the Summit is an unprecedented meeting of the UN General Assembly dedicated to the children and adolescents of the world. It will bring together government leaders and Heads of State, Non-Governmental Organizations (NGOs), so-called children's advocates, and young people themselves.

The purpose of the meeting in February was to negotiate the outcome document, *A World Fit for Children* for the Summit. The UN says the Summit will present a great opportunity to "change the way the world views and treats children."

Of course that is the problem.

Reasons to be suspicious

See page 159, and go to www.unicef.org for more information on UNICEF. What reasons can you think of to explain why the author claims that UNICEF has worked to undermine the UN?

There are many reasons to be suspicious of the UN. In spite of their 1948 Universal Declaration of Human Rights which declared "The family is the natural and fundamental group unit of society and is entitled to protection by society and the State" (Article 16–3), various interest groups including UNICEF have worked to undermine this position.

In 1990, world leaders gathered at the UN for the first World Summit for Children. The Summit adopted a Declaration on the Survival, Protection and Development of Children and a plan of action for implementing the Declaration during the 1990's which included a call for ratification and implementation of the UN Convention on the Rights of the Child (CRC).

COMMENTARY: UNICEF

UNICEF is an acronym of the United Nations International Children's Emergency Fund, the original name of the agency. It was established on December 11, 1946, by the United Nations.

The organization was set up to help children damaged by the devastation caused by World War II (1939–1945), but it was conceived as a temporary agency and was not intended to last beyond the postwar emergency period. In practice, however, UNICEF's work was needed far beyond that time. The founding resolution contained the phrase "for child health purposes generally," and that allowed UNICEF to continue to help control and prevent diseases affecting children.

In 1950 the United Nations General Assembly extended UNICEF's mandate to include work with children and families throughout the developing world. Three years later UNICEF became a permanent part of the UN, and its name was changed to the United Nations Children's Fund, although it kept the acronym by which it had become known. In 1965 it was awarded the Nobel Peace Prize for "promotion of brotherhood among nations."

Its purpose

Throughout its history UNICEF has campaigned on a wide range of issues, including the fight to eradicate epidemic diseases and poverty, reducing preventable deaths from conditions like measles, and supporting teacher training in developing countries. Many people believe that UNICEF has helped improve children's conditions around the world, and as a result of its work several declarations have been adopted by the international community to protect children's rights globally. In 1959 the UN General Assembly adopted the Declaration of the Rights of the Child, which highlighted the right of children to good nutrition, health care, and education. Similarly in 1989 the UN General Assembly passed the Convention on the Rights of the Child, which became law in 1990.

UNICEF has also promoted children's rights through events such as the 1979 International Year of the Child, during which people and organizations reaffirmed their commitment to children's rights. Programs to control dehydration and diarrhea in children, and to support breastfeeding and nutrition have similarly helped save millions of children's lives.

Some critics, however, believe that UNICEF is not doing enough to help children in need since so many still live in degradation and poverty or suffer abuse on a daily basis. Others argue that UNICEF actually works against children by taking away the rights of the parent and undermining family values. But supporters claim that UNICEF has changed children's lives; they assert that reports like the 1996 "Impact of Armed Conflict on Children," which drew international attention to the plight of millions of children in war, show just how important UNICEF is in protecting children's rights.

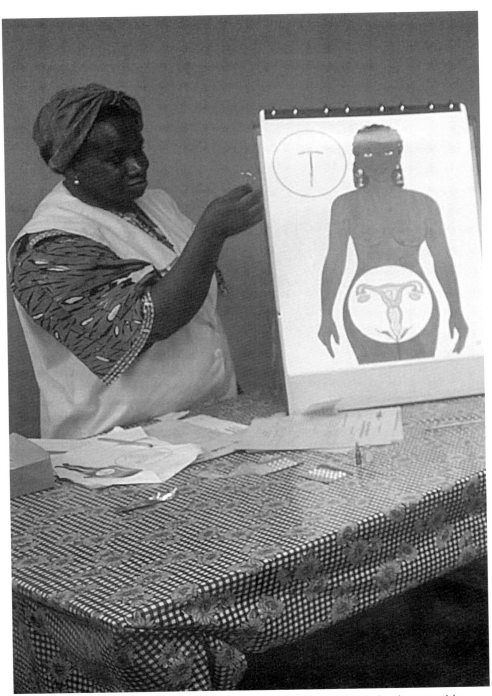

An African aid worker teaches reproduction issues and contraception to local young girls and women.

These documents reflect a globalist approach to family planning, giving a government the ultimate power to control citizens in the name of children's rights. For this reason many pro-family groups, including HSLDA, have long opposed the UN Convention on the Rights of the Child...

Go to www.hslda.org to find out about the HSLDA (Home School Legal Defense Association).

The United States and the convention

Since 1992, the U.S. government itself supported the general goals of the Convention but opposition from American citizens and members of Congress (especially Senator Jesse Helms) prevented the treaty from being ratified.

So on February 1 when Ambassador Michael Southwick, Deputy Secretary of State for International Organization Affairs took the microphone to deliver the U.S. response to the outcome document, the General Assembly hall was packed as the international community waited to hear what the new Administration would say. The message was simple—there is a new sheriff in town.

Southwick delivered a strong but respectful statement on protecting children and the humanitarian tradition of American generosity. Then he said:

Senator Jesse Helms (1921–), a former journalist and broadcaster, began his first term in the Senate (Republican, North Carolina) in January 1973 and was reelected four times. Go to www. jessehelmscenter.org for more information about his views.

Finally, I would like to say a few words about the...Convention on the Rights of the Child and other international instruments in the current text. States may be encouraged to consider ratification of these instruments, but it is wrong to assert an obligation to ratify them. We also believe it is misleading and inappropriate to use the Convention as a litmus test to measure a nation's commitment to children. As a non-party to the Convention, the United States does not accept obligations based on it, nor do we accept that it is the best or only framework for developing programs and policies to benefit children. The Convention on the Rights of the Child may be a positive tool in promoting child welfare for those countries that have adopted it. But we believe the text goes too far when it asserts entitlements based on the economic, social and cultural rights contained in the Convention and other instruments. The human rights-based approach, while laudable in its objectives, poses significant problems as used in this text. This demonstrates the impact one election can make. Although the UN will keep pushing and the Conventions are not dead, it is clear that President [George W.] Bush has placed himself squarely on our side of this fight.

Do you agree with Southwick? Does the text go too far in asserting that the rights of the child should be based on economic, social, and cultural rights?

161

Summary

Has the United Nations (UN) been effective in protecting children's rights? The first article—a background note from the UN itself—claims that the UN gives children much help and protection. It highlights, for example, the role of the Special Rapporteur who gathers evidence on cases in which the rights of children are abused. The article summarizes the history of the UN's work on behalf of children, from the establishment of the United Nations Children's Fund (UNICEF) in 1946 up to the 1989 Convention on the Rights of the Child (CRC). The CRC, it argues, is a vital instrument for establishing respect for children's rights, though it admits that there is a long way to go before all the rights outlined in it are universally enjoyed.

The second article is a report from the United Nations meeting held in New York in February 2001 prior to the UN World Summit. The meeting was held to work out a document entitled *A World Fit for Children*. The report details the U.S. government's position and explains that while the UN is seen by the government to do good work for children, there are other methods. The report points out that U.S. citizens and members of Congress have opposed the CRC because they do not approve of the globalist approach adopted by the UN. It asserts that organizations like UNICEF sometimes work to undermine family values and parental rights and, as such, are not necessarily acting in the best interest of the child.

FURTHER INFORMATION:

Books:

Andrews, Arlene Bowers, and Natalie Hevener Kaufman (eds.), *Implementing the UN Convention on the Rights of the Child*. New York: Praeger, 1999.

Clark, Christian, *UNICEF for Beginners*. New York: Writers and Readers Publishing, 1996.

UNICEF, *The State of the World's Children, 2002*. New York: UNICEF, 2002.

Useful websites:

www.ausmcgill.com/idssa/latitudes/pdf/children-Dawes.pdf
Article in *Latitudes* by Andrea Dawes, "The Universalization of Children's Rights: An Analysis of the United Nations Convention on the Rights of the Child."
www.heritage.org/Research/InternationalOrganizations/BG1407es.cfm
A Heritage background paper by Patrick F. Fagan on women's and children's rights.

www.hrw.org/children/
Children's rights section of Human Rights Watch site.
www.unicef.org
United Nations Children's Fund (UNICEF) site.
www.unhchr.ch/html/intlinst.htm
UN Office of the High Commissioner for Human Rights site. Archive containing texts of the 1959 Declaration and the 1989 Convention on the Rights of the Child.

The following debates in the Pro/Con series may also be of interest:

In this volume:

 Topic 4 Should human rights come before national sovereignty?

Part 3: Gender and children's rights

IS THE UN AN EFFECTIVE ADVOCATE FOR CHILDREN'S RIGHTS?

YES: Children have rights, like everyone else. It is especially important to protect their rights since they are vulnerable and often have difficulty making themselves heard.

YES: Since establishing UNICEF in 1946, the UN has helped millions of children in need all over the world

CHILDREN'S RIGHTS
Do children have rights?

THE UNITED NATIONS
Has the UN helped the plight of children in need?

NO: Children have no rights in reality. They are always being told what to do, either by a parent or some other adult. Statistics show that children are among the most oppressed groups in the world.

NO: The UN is always talking about children's rights, but in practice it is often powerless to fight the root causes of abuse

IS THE UN AN EFFECTIVE ADVOCATE FOR CHILDREN'S RIGHTS?
KEY POINTS

YES: The CRC is a legally binding treaty, and international adherence to its terms is closely monitored by an elected committee

YES: The CRC shows the international community's commitment to improving the lives of many children in distress around the world

CHILDREN'S CONVENTION
Is the Convention on the Rights of the Child really effective?

NO: The CRC undermines the authority of elected governments, and the committee has too much power to impose its own agenda, which may even be harmful to children

NO: Some countries, including the United States, have not ratified the CRC

PART 4
HUMAN RIGHTS AND THE UNITED STATES

INTRODUCTION

On September 11, 2001, the United States experienced the worst terrorist attacks the world has ever seen. Images of the 9/11 attack in New York, Washington, D.C., and Pennsylvania were played and replayed on news networks around the world. At least 3,000 people from more than 60 countries were killed in the events of that day. From the beginning people sought to make sense of what had happened. Who was responsible and why? And what should be the U.S. response to such atrocity?

President George W. Bush soon blamed the attacks on the Muslim leader Osama Bin Laden and his terrorist group Al Qaeda. The president found international agreement when he declared that 9/11 was an attack on the very ideals of the United States. For some commentators, however, the events were also a response to America's political intervention in the affairs of other countries.

Many people disagree profoundly. They argue that the United States has historically been a staunch defender of human rights, with a Constitution that protects the inherent rights of individuals. They claim that the country has one of the best human rights records in the world. It has also led the international community in creating influential legislation like the Universal Declaration of Human Rights to ensure that people around the world are equally protected.

U.S. record

On September 20, 2001, George W. Bush announced the beginning of a War against Terrorism. Most Americans saw this as a necessary action. But while human rights organizations like Amnesty International called for governments to bring to justice those responsible for the 9/11 attacks, most also insisted that any action taken be in accordance with international human rights standards.

On October 7, 2001, the United States and its coalition allies began a sustained bombing campaign in Afghanistan. Afghanistan's radical Muslim Taliban government had given sanctuary to Osama Bin Laden and members of Al Qaeda. The Bush administration argued that its campaign was not only an attack on terrorism but would also liberate the millions of Afghans whose rights had been abused under the Taliban regime.

Members of the international community and human rights groups in the United States and abroad expressed concern about the way the attacks were carried out and their impact on Afghan civilians. By December the Taliban had been driven from power and a new interim administration formed in

Afghanistan. The treatment of prisoners taken from Afghanistan to the U.S. military base at Guantanamo Bay in Cuba has brought more international criticism on the United States. Human rights campaigners argue that the prisoners should be protected under the Geneva Conventions, which regulate the treatment of prisoners of war. The United States argues that its prisoners are not soldiers and so are not protected by the code. Some of indigenous people, critics claim, often reflect a desire to exploit their valuable natural resources. Topic 14 looks at the protection of indigenous rights by the U.S. government.

International human rights

Some commentators argue that America is inconsistent in its human rights policy both at home and abroad. Topic 15 examines the United States' economic relationship with countries

"As with all victims of violent crime, human rights violations and abuses, the suffering of victims, survivors and the bereaved demands compassion and justice. We urge you to ... to take every necessary human rights precaution in pursuit of justice, rather than revenge...."
—LETTER FROM IRENE KHAN, SECRETARY GENERAL OF AMNESTY INTERNATIONAL, TO PRESIDENT GEORGE W. BUSH, SEPTEMBER 2001

commentators believe that the refusal to grant the prisoners' rights undermines the United States' moral authority. Many Americans, however, believe that the actions undertaken by the Bush administration have promoted human rights and freed previously suppressed people. Topic 13 examines whether the United States has a good human rights record.

Human rights apply at home as well as overseas. The treatment of Native Americans, for example, has always caused much heated debate. Many critics argue that the native population is as exploited in the 21st century as it was in the early 16th century when European colonists first arrived. Even treaties drawn up to protect the rights

with poor human rights records. It placed economic sanctions against some offending countries such as Pakistan but continued to trade with China, which, critics argue, also has a poor human rights record but is potentially more valuable as a trading partner.

Some critics also argue that the U.S. failure to recognize international initiatives brings America's human rights policy into conflict with that of the international community. Topic 16 questions whether the United States should recognize the International Criminal Court (ICC) set up by the Rome Statute in 1998. Iraq and the United States are among seven countries who voted against the ICC.

Topic 13
DOES THE UNITED STATES HAVE A GOOD HUMAN RIGHTS RECORD?

YES
FROM "THE ROLE OF HUMAN RIGHTS IN FOREIGN POLICY"
REMARKS TO THE HERITAGE FOUNDATION, WASHINGTON, D.C., OCTOBER 31, 2001
WWW.STATE.GOV/G/DRL/RLS/RM/2001/6378.HTM
LORNE W. CRANER

NO
FROM "UNITED STATES OF AMERICA: HUMAN RIGHTS VS. PUBLIC RELATIONS"
WWW.AMNESTY.ORG, AUGUST 24, 2002
AMNESTY INTERNATIONAL

INTRODUCTION

Since World War II (1939–1945) the concerted efforts of a number of governments, individuals, pressure groups, and other organizations have placed human rights issues firmly in the spotlight. These people and groups have worked very hard to create internationally approved human rights standards. Many of these standards were born out of the widespread condemnation of the human rights abuses people, such as Jews and Gypsies, faced during World War II, as well as of an increased public awareness of human rights issues.

It did not take very long for the hard work to pay off. In 1948 the General Assembly of the United Nations unanimously approved the Universal Declaration of Human Rights (UDHR). This landmark ruling states that human rights are universal and that countries do not have the sole right to determine their domestic human rights standards.

Many American citizens consider the United States to be a leader in the field of human rights. Since the signing of the Declaration of Independence in 1789, the United States has had its values deeply rooted in the principles of democracy and individual liberty.

The 1791 Bill of Rights (the first 10 amendments to the Constitution) established fundamental rights and freedoms for all American citizens. Many people feel that the United States has set the human rights agenda ever since. For example, U.S. representatives played a central role in drafting the content and subsequent amendments of the UDHR, and the United States championed freedom and democracy throughout the uncertainties of the Cold War. The monitoring of human rights conditions worldwide through regular Country Reports on Human Rights Practices, available to millions on the Internet, also demonstrates commitment to the human rights agenda.

While the United States considers itself to be a leader in establishing international human rights protection, critics suggest that U.S. domestic policies do not always measure up to international standards of human rights protection. For example, the United States is one of the few countries in the world where the death penalty can be given to juvenile offenders. Defenders of the U.S. position argue that the legal system already has rights guarantees based on the Constitution and the decisions of the Supreme Court, and that it therefore does not need the additional protection of international standards.

"The United States cannot expect to reap the benefits of internationally recognized human rights—in the form of greater worldwide stability and respect for people—without being willing to adhere to them itself."
—SENIOR DISTRICT JUDGE JACK WEINSTEIN, JANUARY 2002

On September 20, 2001, President George W. Bush announced the start of an international "War on Terror" in response to the terrorist attacks in the United States on September 11, 2001. Most people agree that acts of terrorism

cannot be allowed to undermine freedom and democracy, but many have also expressed genuine concern that human rights are being compromised in the name of the War on Terror. The treatment of prisoners at Guantánamo Bay in Cuba, where Al Qaeda detainees have been subjected to interrogation and not been permitted legal representation, is one example of a situation in which the United States may be falling far short of its commitment to human rights.

Critics also suggest that the United States may be operating double standards in its attitude toward human rights. While government officials are quick to criticize the action of countries not considered to be allies, they refuse to take appropriate action when abuses are committed by U.S. allies or when action would run counter to domestic political and economic interests. For example, the United States refuses to criticize widely condemned human rights violations by allies such as Israel and Saudi Arabia. It also seems to distrust the United Nations. Indeed, the United States has failed to ratify more than half of the important UN covenants and treaties.

In the first article, "The Role of Human Rights in Foreign Policy," Lorne W. Craner argues that the United States has been a leader in the field of human rights since World War II, so its own human rights record must be good. Craner believes that human rights are central to government policy. In the second article the author of the Amnesty International report believes that the United States has a poor human rights reputation abroad, citing examples in which the United States shows a lack of respect for international law.

THE ROLE OF HUMAN RIGHTS IN FOREIGN POLICY
Lorne W. Craner

YES

… This country is not the cause of all the problems of this world—quite the contrary. We spend a great deal of time and effort trying to solve them. But still, we cannot be everywhere at once. We cannot solve every regional dispute and ethnic conflict. And yet, we are the sole superpower. Our reach is global and unprecedented. People look to us. Our power and our potential are immense. We have interests and we have obligations to our friends and allies.

As the head of the bureau charged with advising the President and Secretary of State on human rights, I have to worry about the causes and consequences of conflicts wherever they take place, for all of them involve human rights in one way or another—whether in Sudan or Sierra Leone, Indonesia, Macedonia, or the Middle East.

I suspect most of you are looking to hear something about this administration's priorities within the field of human rights, especially after the September 11th attacks. Let me begin by outlining the general principles that I think will guide us.

First, over the past 20 years, both political parties— Republicans and Democrats—have firmly embraced the belief that America has an obligation to advance fundamental freedoms around the world. Thus human rights have the deep and strong backing of both parties, all branches of government, and, most importantly, the American people. This will not change.

In a multilateral sense, the United States has been the unquestioned leader of the movement to expand human rights since the Second World War. We pushed it in the UN Charter, the Universal Declaration of Human Rights and into the conventions and treaty bodies that have ensued. And when I say "we," I do not just mean the U.S. government. For it was our people, Americans from every walk of life, who gave the international non-governmental organization (NGO) movement so much of its intellectual force, its financial muscle, and its firm commitment to civil society.

Lorne Whitney Craner was sworn in as assistant secretary of state for democracy, human rights, and labor on June 4, 2001. The secretary of state coordinates U.S. foreign policy with a view to promoting democracy and human rights worldwide.

The Yahoo! directory http://dir.yahoo.com/Society_and_Culture/Issues_and_Causes/Human_Rights/Organizations/ lists the website addresses for some of the most popular NGOs involved in human rights.

This, too, will not change. We in this administration are conscious of our history and are proud to bear the mantle of leadership in international human rights into this new century.

While my first point is the continuity of our policy, the second is the way our approach to human rights policy will shift.

Our policy in this administration, and it is certainly true after September 11th, is to focus on U.S. national interests. Lest that sound bloodless to my colleagues in the human rights community, it should be understood that the definition of national interests can never be as narrow as it was through the late 1970s. Indeed, those at high levels of this administration watched during those years as a narrow definition of national interests led us to back the Shah of Iran, Somoza, and others. As Colin Powell writes in his autobiography, "In the end, in Iran, all our investment in an individual, rather than a country, came to naught. When the Shah fell, our Iran policy fell with him. All the billions we spent there only exacerbated conditions and contributed to the rise of a fundamentalist regime implacably opposed to us...."

Our focus on national interests will come by concentration on advancing human rights and democracy in countries important to the United States. Some are obvious—nations of the former Soviet Union, Indonesia, Colombia and Cuba—but others come to mind, including nations in Africa with a high demonstration value in their respective regions, such as Zimbabwe, Kenya, and Nigeria.

A third characteristic of our democracy policy will be a willingness to take on tough jobs, long term projects in countries and regions that today appear inhospitable to human rights and democracy. We are working every day to end human rights violations in China, but beneath the surface are developments in terms of rule of law, basic elections at the village level, nascent legislative oversight, and some journalistic independence. These changes are necessitated by economic development, but they are also important blocks in building a democratic society.

Similarly, in the Persian Gulf, Oman is experimenting with an increasingly independent legislature and Qatar will hold local elections, with women voting, in 2003. No one, least of all me, would claim that any of these countries are democracies, and it may be that the end result, many years from now, is not precisely comparable to our democratic system. The point is that the United States is now willing

Some countries continue to see U.S. leadership in human rights as interference in their affairs. Can both viewpoints be right?

In 1979 the U.S.-backed Shah Muhammad Reza Pahlavi of Iran was overthrown by the Muslim cleric Ayatollah Ruhollah Khomeini, who fiercely opposed U.S. involvement in Iran's affairs. Khomeini's accession to power marked a period of intense hostility between the two countries.

You can find out more about human rights violations in China by visiting the Human Rights Watch website www.hrw.org. Click on "Asia" under the "Information by country," and follow the link for "China and Tibet."

A pluralist society is one in which many different cultural, ethnic, or religious groups are represented. How pluralistic is the United States?

The fall of the apartheid regime heralded a new political era in South Africa, but many black South Africans became disillusioned when democracy failed to make an immediate difference to their standard of life.

What sort of things do you think companies and corporations could do to show more responsibility toward the community? Would the businesses themselves benefit?

to assist those working to bring pluralism to their countries, even if it may only occur over the long term.

In countries that have already made democratic breakthroughs, a fourth tenet of our policy will be to increase governance assistance. In the 1980s, many believed that elections made a democracy. In the 1990s, we concentrated on the demand side of governance, civil society. We cannot lose our proficiency in helping advance balloting, political parties and non-governmental organizations abroad. But the challenge of the third decade of democracy assistance must be helping new democratic rulers govern their countries in a manner that advances democratic practices, an end to the corruption that often afflicts authoritarian nations, and economic well being. The latter is especially important; if those who have lived with tyranny associate democracy with economic dislocation—in other words, losing their jobs— they could well choose to revert to stable authoritarianism.

A component of this effort will be an emphasis on labor rights. This administration does not see globalism as the enemy, just the opposite. Globalism can promote democratic ideas as well as economic growth, but we do believe that it can be made kinder and gentler. Indeed, as I just outlined, an absence of attention to worker rights would lead to dissatisfaction in a developing democracy, and therefore take us back in time.

In a similar vein, one of the areas where I think we in the human rights community can gain some important new leverage is with this country's companies and corporations. In the first place, they are laboratories of innovation, repositories of experience, talent, and, yes, resources. They have relationships that go beyond those we have in government. But more than that, an increasing number of businesses share some of our interest in advancing human rights. Why? Because countries that respect human rights have more open and transparent laws and financial systems, less corruption, better educated workforces, and more stability and security.

I don't want to oversell the idea. Business runs on profits, not on human rights. But more and more companies are beginning to see that they can help themselves by paying close attention to giving back to the communities in which they operate. Companies are also anxious to protect their corporate image and reputations.

That's why my bureau is giving a high priority to working with many companies on issues of corporate responsibility, building on the good work the previous administration did in this domain. We are especially proud of the beginnings of progress made with oil and gas and mining companies, who often operate in very difficult situations in countries riven with conflict and internal tension. By working together with governments and NGOs, companies can strengthen the business and human rights environment that is needed for their success. Changing the face of globalization may require us to change the way that we as members of the global community do business.

An additional area of emphasis for the administration will be in the area of religious freedom, tolerance and understanding. Our nation was founded on this ideal. I will work to ensure, to a greater degree than has been the case, and particularly in light of the events of September 11th, that it receives due consideration in our foreign policy. We will also seek allies abroad in our efforts, for other countries and the United Nations are working to integrate considerations of religious freedom into their diplomacy.

The first principles set out by the Framers of the 1791 Bill of Rights concerned religious freedom, because many of the early settlers had escaped religious persecution in Europe. The Framers decided that the best way to protect religious freedom would be to exclude the government from matters of religion.

Finally, our core function in DRL … is monitoring and reporting on human rights conditions throughout the world. This process, I believe, is of great value to our country. The monitoring we do, in conjunction with our human rights officers in the field, the media and the growing human rights NGO community, ensures a steady stream of information will flow throughout our government.

No other country produces anything like our annual reports on country situations, international religious freedom, and now trafficking in human beings. Even the NGOs, who often have occasion to criticize us, have for some time acknowledged their accuracy, integrity, and comprehensive nature. That is a tribute to my predecessors, most notably Harold Koh. The policy of making honest, comprehensive reports on every country is the world is one that both Republicans and Democrats embrace. And because they are available to everyone, via the Internet, they can now reach millions of people across the globe. This reinforces the seriousness with which the United States takes human rights. And so our dedication to the quality, integrity, and inclusiveness of our reporting will not change, even as the number we are asked to prepare keeps growing.…

Visit the website of the U.S. Bureau of Democracy, Human Rights, and Labor at http://www.state. gov/g/drl/ to access an archive of reports on a range of issues.

UNITED STATES OF AMERICA: HUMAN RIGHTS VS. PUBLIC RELATIONS
Amnesty International

NO

The CFR-sponsored report "Public Diplomacy: A Strategy for Reform" was published by the Independent Task Force on Public Diplomacy on July 30, 2002.

A recent report sponsored by the non-partisan US think tank, the Council on Foreign Relations (CFR), concluded that the US government is failing to counter the fact that "around the world, from Western Europe to the Far East, many see the United States as arrogant, hypocritical, self-absorbed, self-indulgent, and contemptuous of others." On the day of publication, the White House responded that it will set up an Office of Global Communications to play a coordinating role in countering such perceptions. As the President's spokesman put it, "better coordination of international communications will help America to explain what we do and why we do it around the world."

George W. Bush, 43rd President of the United States, established the new Office of Global Communications by executive order on January 21, 2003.

In the area of human rights, at least, the USA will need to move beyond public relations and into substantive change if it wishes to improve its reputation abroad. There are some immediate ways in which it could begin to do this, while at the same time promoting and upholding international law.

In 2002 the U.S. military detained suspected Al Qaeda terrorists at Guantánamo Bay. Since the base is not strictly part of U.S. territory, the detainees have been denied certain rights, such as a trial by jury, guaranteed to prisoners on U.S. soil. The detainees have not been classified as prisoners of war, so they are also not subject to the provisions of the Geneva Conventions.

Almost 600 foreign nationals from over 30 countries are being held at the US Naval Base in Guantánamo Bay, Cuba. The US Government has paid lip service to the Geneva Conventions—the principal and almost universally ratified instruments of international humanitarian law—but refused either to grant any of the detainees prisoner of war status or to have any disputed status determined by a "competent tribunal" as the Conventions require. The prisoners are held in cells smaller than the minimum recommended by the American Correctional Association. The use of shackles appears to have been excessive, the out-of-cell time minimal. Some of the detainees have now been held without charge or trial for seven months. Senior government officials, including President Bush, have been less than respectful for the fundamental rule of the presumption of innocence, collectively labelling the group as hard-core "terrorists." Interrogations, with a view to possible prosecutions as well as for intelligence-gathering purposes, have been ongoing for months. Yet none of the detainees has had access to legal counsel. Meanwhile, still looming is the prospect of trial by military commission, executive bodies with the power to hand down death sentences; in violation of international law, the commission's decisions cannot be appealed to a higher court.

Foreign nationals held at Guantánamo Bay have thus far been kept out of the reach of the US courts....

Given the US government's unchanged stance on the Guantánamo detainees, the conclusion of the Council on Foreign Relations that, in the Middle East, Europe, Asia and Latin America many people "do not trust what we say because they feel our words are contradicted by our policies," is given further relevance. As is Secretary of State Powell's assertion in March that the US "will not relax our commitment to advancing the cause of human rights." Assistant Secretary for Democracy, Human Rights and Labor, Lorne Craner, joined him and gave assurances that the "US Government is deeply committed to the promotion of universal human rights." In similar vein, in his State of the Union Address in January, President Bush promised that "America will always stand firm for the non-negotiable demands of human dignity," including the rule of law....

The concerns of other human rights bodies have also not been acted upon. On 23 July 2002, the Inter-American Commission on Human Rights of the Organization of American States repeated the request it first made to the USA on 12 March, to "take the urgent measures necessary to have the legal status of the detainees at Guantánamo Bay determined by a competent tribunal." The Commission stressed that "it is not sufficient for a detaining power to simply assert its view as to the status of a detainee to the exclusion of any proper or effectual procedure for remedying that status." The government has so far refused to comply with the Commission's request.

Double standards?

There are other, equally urgent, matters for the USA to consider. Recent and forthcoming executions in violation of international law are cases in point. The USA has, of course, frequently been criticized in international fora for its continuing resort to judicial killing in an increasingly abolitionist world, and has responded that the death penalty is an internal matter to be determined by public opinion and constitutional constraints. It is noteworthy, then, that the CFR report says: "The United States must feel free to criticize undemocratic or corrupt regimes, especially on human rights abuses.... This is admittedly delicate because blunt criticism

Do you think the suspected terrorists at Guantánamo Bay represent a threat to the national security of the United States? How should they be dealt with? See Topic 6 Do threats to national security ever justify restrictions on human rights?

Visit the website of the Organization of American States at www.oas.org to find out more information about the work of the Inter-American Commission on Human Rights.

Most American citizens support the death penalty. Visit the American Civil Liberties Union website at www.aclu.org to find out the views of an organization that lobbies against the death penalty.

of regimes—especially those we directly or indirectly support—are likely to be resented as "interference in domestic affairs." "Quiet diplomacy," the CFR report says, "is essential in pointing out to foreign leaders that abuses of human rights and other undemocratic actions will undermine bilateral relations." This is no less true when the violator is the United States.

The execution of Mexican national Javier Suárez Medina in Texas on 14 August has damaged US relations with Mexico.... Like most of the other 100 or so foreign nationals on death row in the USA, Javier Suárez was never informed of his right, under the Vienna Convention on Consular Relations, to contact his consulate for assistance. It is not difficult to imagine the outrage that would be expressed by the USA in the event of the same thing happening to one of its own nationals abroad....

*Visit http://www.
ccadp.org/
javiermedina.htm
to find out more
about Javier
Medina's case and
the international
condemnation of
his execution.*

*Argentina, Brazil,
Chile, Colombia,
Costa Rica,
El Salvador,
Guatemala,
Honduras, Panama,
Paraguay, Poland,
Slovenia, Spain,
Switzerland,
Uruguay,
and Venezuela also
formally opposed
the execution
by sending appeals
for clemency or by
intervening at the
Supreme Court in
support of a
judicial review.*

Joining Mexico's interventions on behalf of Javier Suárez were the governments of 16 other countries.... No amount of public relations can gloss over the fact that the USA's refusal to heed their appeals resulted in an irrevocable violation of international law.

The report of the Council on Foreign Relations noted that many people are critical of "what they see as a unilateral approach to international affairs" on the part of the United States. T.J. Jones recently paid the ultimate price for such an approach, when he was put to death in the USA on 8 August for a crime committed when he was 17 years old. Toronto Patterson is due to be put to death on 28 August for a crime committed at the same age. There is almost no other country in the world where he would be facing this prospect. For the international community has agreed that the use of the death penalty against child offenders, people who were under 18 at the time of the crime, is unacceptable and an unequivocal violation of international law. One hundred and ninety one countries have ratified the Convention on the Rights of the Child, one of the treaties which contains this non-derogable prohibition. The USA—which although not a state party to the Convention is a signatory to it, and thereby obliged not to do anything which would undermine its provisions—has executed 11 child offenders since 1998, more than two thirds of the known world total in that period....

*To back up the
argument, Amnesty
International lists a
number of cases in
which the United
States has opposed
or failed to ratify
or comply with
international
agreements
concerning human
rights issues.*

International agreements

• International Court of Justice. Apart from so far failing to take the necessary measures to comply with the

ICJ decision on the issue of consular rights and capital defendants, the USA was already one of only two countries to have ignored an ICJ ruling(18) (the other being Iran);
● Inter-American Commission on Human Rights.
Aside from ignoring the Commission in relation to the Guantánamo detainees, the USA continues to disregard its call for individual executions to be halted while it examines the prisoners' claims....
● American Convention on Human Rights, which the USA has failed to ratify 25 years after signing it;
● Geneva Conventions, as outlined above with respect to the Guantánamo detainees;
● Vienna Convention on Consular Relations, as it impacts on foreign nationals in the USA accused of capital crimes;
● Convention on the Elimination of All Forms of Discrimination Against Women. The USA is one of only 23 countries not to have ratified this Convention;
● International Covenant on Civil and Political Rights, which the USA has ratified, but agreed to be bound by only to the extent that its restrictions on the death penalty and its prohibition on torture or other cruel, inhuman degrading treatment or punishment match its own constitutional constraints;
● International Covenant on Economic, Social and Cultural Rights. While 145 countries have ratified this treaty, the USA has not, 25 years after signing it;
● Convention Against Torture and Other Cruel, Inhuman and Degrading Treatment or Punishment, to which the USA attached a number of "reservations" and other conditions upon ratification. The Committee Against Torture, the expert body established by the Convention to oversee its implementation, has asked the US Government to withdraw these reservations. The US Government has failed to do so and has ignored other recommendations by the Committee, such as to prohibit the remote-controlled electro-shock stun belt, widely used in the USA;
● Optional Protocol to the Convention Against Torture. This Protocol aimed at providing a system of unannounced visits to places of detention such as police stations and prisons was approved by the UN Economic and Social Council on 24 July 2002 despite US opposition;
● Convention on the Rights of the Child. In May 2002, Somalia signed the Convention, and indicated its intention to ratify it. Once it does so, becoming the 192nd state party to the Convention, the USA will be the only country not to have ratified this fundamental treaty....

What might make the United States reluctant to ratify such positive-sounding agreements? Does this mean, for example, that the United States supports discrimination against women?

Prison authorities in the United States approve the use of electroshock stun belts to incapacitate difficult prisoners. Many human rights organizations think that the use of such belts constitutes a violation of human rights standards, which prohibit cruel, inhuman, or degrading treatment or punishment.

Summary

In the first article, "The Role of Human Rights in Foreign Policy," Lorne W. Craner suggests that the United States has been the world leader in human rights since World War II. Craner points out that the United States was born out of the ideals of freedom and democracy, so it has an obligation to advance these ideals around the world. The U.S. government publishes more accurate and comprehensive reports on human rights issues than any other country. Current policies focus on national interests by supporting human rights in countries that are important to the United States. Globalism can promote democracy as well as economic growth, says Craner, and future human rights efforts will center on labor issues. Craner suggests that the U.S. commitment to human rights is even greater since the terrorist attacks of September 11, 2001, but he concedes that there is much more work that can be done.

In the second article, "United States of America: Human Rights vs. Public Relations," Amnesty International suggests that the United States has violated international humanitarian law. It cites as an example the treatment of the Guantánamo Bay prisoners, who were held without trial for over a year with no access to legal counsel. Another example given is the execution of juvenile offenders despite overwhelming international objection. The article details a 2002 report by the Council on Foreign Relations, which indicates that many people around the world do not trust what the United States says because they feel that its words are often contradicted by its policies. Amnesty International believes that the United States should move beyond lip service into genuine respect for international humanitarian law.

FURTHER INFORMATION:

Books:

Dunne, Tim, and Nicholas J. Wheeler (eds.), *Human Rights in Global Politics.* New York: Cambridge University Press, 1999.

Donnelly, Jack, *Universal Human Rights in Theory and Practice.* Ithaca, NY: Cornell University Press, 2002.

Donnelly, Jack, *International Human Rights (Dilemmas in World Politics).* Boulder, CO: Westview Press, 1998.

Forsythe, David P., *Human Rights in International Relations (Themes in International Relations).* New York: Cambridge University Press, 2000.

Forsythe, David P. (ed.), *The United States and Human Rights: Looking Inward and Outward (Human Rights in International Perspective).* Lincoln, NE: University of Nebraska Press, 2000.

Steiner, Henry, and Philip Alston, *International Human Rights in Context.* New York: Oxford University Press, 2000.

 Useful websites:

http://www.amnesty.org
Amnesty International monitors human-rights violations worldwide, reporting on cases within specific countries.
http://www.whitehouse.gov/ogc
Find out about the new Office of Global Communications, set up to convey U.S. policies and values to the world.

The following debates in the Pro/Con series may also be of interest:

In this volume:
Topic 6 Do threats to national security ever justify restrictions on human rights?

DOES THE UNITED STATES HAVE A GOOD HUMAN RIGHTS RECORD?

YES: *The United States has signed many important international treaties and agreements concerning human rights issues*

YES: *The United States was founded on the ideals of liberty and tolerance. Human rights are guaranteed by the Constitution.*

INTERNATIONAL LAW
Does the United States meet its obligation under international law?

PRINCIPLES
Does the United States support the objectives of human rights?

NO: *The United States consistently violates international humanitarian law, for example, by its policy of giving the death penalty to juveniles*

NO: *The U.S. reluctance to sign international human rights agreements shows that it is reluctant to protect the rights of Americans and others*

DOES THE UNITED STATES HAVE A GOOD HUMAN RIGHTS RECORD?

KEY POINTS

YES: *U.S. reporting is extremely important in keeping the world informed of human rights violations around the world*

YES: *The United States has always been prepared to fight for freedom and democracy*

INTERNATIONAL REPUTATION
Does the United States have a good reputation for human rights?

NO: *Many foreign governments do not trust what the U.S. government says because its policies often contradict its words*

NO: *U.S. foreign policy is in keeping with the interests of the United States. For example, it would never criticize human rights abuses of an ally such as Israel.*

Topic 14

IS THE GOVERNMENT DOING ENOUGH TO PROTECT THE RIGHTS OF INDIGENOUS PEOPLES?

YES

FROM "THE RIGHT TO FREEDOM"
INTERNATIONAL BROTHERHOOD OF TEAMSTERS
CONFERENCE ON HUMAN RIGHTS, JANUARY 16, 2002
TARA M. SWEENEY

NO

"NO CARIBOU FOR OIL: AN ARCTIC TRIBE STRUGGLES FOR SURVIVAL"
WWW.ALTERNATIVES.CA, AUGUST 2001
NADINE PEDERSEN

INTRODUCTION

The native peoples of the modern United States can be considered as belonging to three distinct groups on the basis of their geographic dispersion. First there are the nations of the contiguous mainland—the Hopi, Navajo (or Dine), Shoshone, and many others. Second there are the 90,000 people who are indigenous to Alaska. Third there are the native Hawaiians—Polynesians who today make up 2 percent of Hawaii's population.

The three groups of native peoples have very different backgrounds both in terms of their origins and in their relationships, past and present, with the government of the United States. However, in terms of their rights today and where those rights might come into conflict with those of non-Native Americans or U.S. policy, they have much in common.

Most scholars agree that the government did not do enough in the past to protect the rights of its indigenous peoples.

The first permanent European settlers in North America arrived about 400 years ago. As first traders and trappers, and later settlers, railroaders, cattlemen, and farmers crossed from east to west, indigenous hunters and farmers were driven from their homelands. Initially the young United States made treaties with hundreds of indigenous nations, recognizing them as separate, sovereign entities. The treaties established distinct boundaries between native territories and those of the settlers. Native Americans governed their own internal affairs. As time went on and more land was needed for settlement, however, the government switched to a policy first of removing indigenous peoples to areas west of the Mississippi River and then to one of moving them onto reservations. Those who resisted forced resettlement were killed. By the late 1800s the reservations were also coming under pressure.

In addition, the government set out to assimilate native peoples to the norms of a European-based society, such as by forcing Native American children to attend English-speaking schools. It was not until 1961 that political and legislative policies moved toward self-determination for Native American nations as well as individuals. The premise from that time on has been that indigenous nations possess certain sovereign powers to exercise government, enter into agreements, and to develop and protect natural resources on their land.

> *"The meek shall inherit the earth, but not the mineral rights."*
> —JOHN PAUL GETTY (1892–1976), OIL EXECUTIVE

Self-determination has caused, and continues to cause, clashes as Native Americans seek to control property rights, water rights, and fish and wildlife resources—often referring them back to their nation's original treaties with the United States. That sometimes brings them into conflict with the rights of state and federal governments to exercise power over their citizens.

The situation is somewhat different in Alaska and Hawaii. These regions did not come under U.S. jurisdiction until 1867 in the case of Alaska and 1898 in the case of Hawaii. Rather than reservations, Congress mandated in Alaska that regional corporations based on tribal, ethnic, and linguistic boundaries be established. Nor were the native peoples of these regions pressured to move from their land, although in some cases control of its use was taken away from them.

The question, then, is whether or not the U.S. government is doing enough now to protect the rights of its indigenous population—in mainland America, in Alaska, and in Hawaii. Those arguing "yes" point to the policy of self-determination that exists for indigenous peoples in the United States today. The rights of Native American nations have been afforded both respect and protection since the early 1960s, whereby they have been allowed a degree of self-government and the freedom to protect and develop natural resources on their own land.

Those arguing that the government is doing little, if anything, to protect the rights of indigenous peoples say that government and industry often pressure people to give up their land for exploitation when it is discovered to be economically valuable. While local people may make short-term economic gains, they stand to lose their heritage and their traditional ways of life.

The two articles that follow are both written by Native Alaskans. Tara Sweeney, in the first extract, and Nadine Pedersen, in the second one, give directly opposing views of whether or not the U.S. government should allow oil drilling in the Arctic National Wildlife Refuge (ANWR), and how that decision will affect the rights of those indigenous to the region.

THE RIGHT TO FREEDOM
Tara M. Sweeney

YES

Alaska became part of the United States in 1867. The author states that it did not have "Indian reservations." There was little or no pressure for native peoples to be restricted to reservations since few outsiders wanted to settle in Alaska. Go to www.usdoj.gov/crt/ indian/broch.html to see if that affected indigenous human rights.

✓ ...I am a lifelong Alaskan, raised in the Arctic region of Alaska.... My people are Inupiat Eskimos. We comprise 8,000 of the over 90,000 Alaska Natives that are indigenous to the State. ...I work for the Arctic Slope Regional Corporation, or ASRC, as its shareholder and government relations manager. ASRC is an Alaska Native corporation established through federal legislation in 1971. Instead of the commonly known Indian reservations prevalent throughout what we Alaskans call the lower 48 states, Congress mandated that Alaska establish regional corporations based on aboriginal, ethnic and linguistic boundaries.

The Inupiat

My people, the Inupiat, comprise the membership of ASRC. We hold title to 92,000 acres of privately owned land in the middle of the controversial Coastal Plain of the Arctic National Wildlife Refuge, also known as ANWR. We believe that responsible development of this area is our fundamental human right to economic self-determination....

Freedom means recognition of certain rights: the right to choose religion, free speech, to bear arms, even the right to organize. These rights and others are embodied in our country's declaration of independence, constitution and bill of rights.... Who in here can think of freedom, of America's great history, without thinking of the great westward expansion that accompanied the birth of our nation?...

Dee Brown (1908–2002) was a historian and librarian. He wrote Bury My Heart at Wounded Knee (1971), which viewed the conquest of the American West from the Native American perspective.

For America's indigenous people, the Indians of North America however, the same image [evokes] far different feelings. To the Indians of the Lower 48, America's westward expansion represents—to paraphrase author Dee Brown—not how the west was won, but how it was lost. Where other Americans see the birth of the nation, the Indians see the taking of the land, broken treaties and the establishment of reservations.

For my people, the Inupiat, the effects of America's westward expansion are far different. We've had no wars against expansion, and we have no treaties. We do not have reservations. Our land has never been ceded ... in battle.

Truly our history was different. Yet we still struggled for freedom. Our struggle was not on the battlefield or on the ripped pages of broken treaties. Our struggle was in courtrooms and capitol buildings and it continues to this day. It is not a struggle of Eskimos against the world. Our struggle, happening as we speak … is between the informed and the uninformed, and it is happening in the halls of Congress.

Within those halls there is a debate on the most controversial element of the President's national energy plan. This element is the responsible development of oil and gas on a tiny parcel of land within my region; it is the Coastal Plain of ANWR. Again, my people hold title to 92,000 acres of land within the Coastal Plain. We cannot develop our privately owned land unless Congress authorizes development within the Coastal Plain.

The uninformed will tell you that the Coastal Plain is untouched by man; that it is America's Serengeti; the last great wilderness on earth; or that it cannot be developed responsibly. I am here to tell you the truth. In short, the Coastal Plain of ANWR is not untouched by man, nor is it the last great wilderness on earth. Finally, we believe that ANWR can be developed responsibly.

Kaktovik

For thousands of years the Inupiat people have occupied the Arctic region of Alaska called the North Slope. This area is 89,000 square miles in size, equivalent to the size of the state of Minnesota. We have eight villages scattered throughout the North Slope. One of our villages is Kaktovik, the only village within the recognized boundaries of the entire 19.6 million acres of ANWR.

Kaktovik is situated within the 1.5 million acres of the Coastal Plain. To put this in perspective for you, Kaktovik is the only village within the boundaries of an area the size of the state of South Carolina. The Inupiat people of Kaktovik own the surface rights to the 92,000 acres while ASRC owns the subsurface rights to that land.

Kaktovik residents support responsible ANWR development, as do 75% of all Alaskans and the Alaska Federation of Natives, an organization that represents all Alaska Natives. To allege the Coastal Plain, or ANWR as a whole, is untouched by man is incorrect. Kaktovik has a population of roughly 260 people…. This area is not the last great wilderness on earth. ANWR, especially the Coastal Plain, was utilized by my ancestors and it is currently inhabited by only my people; the U.S. government even

President George W. Bush unveiled his National Energy Plan on May 17, 2001. It focused on increasing the supply of fossil fuels, such as oil, and increasing the use of nuclear power. Go to www.whitehouse.gov/energy/ to view the text.

For centuries before white settlers came to Africa, the Masai grazed their cattle on the Serengeti or "Siringitu," "the place where the land moves on forever," south of Nairobi, Kenya. In 1913 an American hunter, Stewart Edward White, came across it and called it paradise.

Ownership of land is rarely absolute for any group or individual. One owner may have the right to use the land on the surface, another to use minerals found underneath. Do you think that is right?

established DEW line radar sites within the Coastal Plain; and, in the southern portion of ANWR where development is strictly prohibited, nor desired, America's wealthy and elite disrupt wildlife when they charter their helicopters in to hike the mountains or float the river. An average of 100 Americans a year visits the southern portion of ANWR that will never be open to development.

The decision of my people to support development was not made in haste, nor were we pressured by the industry. Our decision is rooted in our knowledge of the environment, stewardship of the animals and history with the Prudhoe Bay development. The Prudhoe Bay oil fields lie within our regional boundaries. When oil was discovered in our region in the late 1960's, we were fearful of development. It represented the abolishment of our traditional way of life; we feared development would drive out the caribou that we depended on for sustenance. Concerns of the care for the environment were raised, and the industry was viewed as an incompetent steward of our homeland.

Those issues were and still are very important to my people. The land and sea bear the fruits of our garden. We depend on both to provide us with food, to carry on our ancient traditions, to live, to exist. Safeway, Wegmans or Kroger stores are not present in our region. Therefore, we feared development threatened our very existence. To exist without the bounties of both land and sea was to not be Inupiaq at all. So, we opposed development.

What impact?

Over thirty years later we have changed our opinion. Development has not adversely impacted our ancient traditions or our food supply. The caribou population that we feared would be abolished as a result of development has thrived since the Prudhoe Bay discovery. What was once a meager population of 3,000 caribou in the late 1960's, is now flourishing to numbers over 27,000. The population increase is a result of our careful stewardship over the land.... Our regulatory powers over the oil industry safeguard our wildlife and protect the environment.

When oil was first discovered our great leader Eben Hopson, Sr., had some foresight to organize our people and form a home-rule government called the North Slope Borough.... The North Slope Borough has broad powers of permitting, taxation, zoning and education. It is the country's farthest north municipality, all in a land with no agriculture, no commercial fishing, minimal tourism, no road system, and

Prudhoe Bay, on the north coast of Alaska, contains one of the largest oil deposits in North America. Since oil production began in 1977, it has yielded more than 12 billion barrels. Oil is pumped to southern Alaska through the 800-mile (1,300-km) Trans-Alaska Pipeline.

Eben Hopson (1922–1980) was an important political leader of the Inupiat. He founded the Inuit Circumpolar Conference, an international organization. See www. ebenhopson.com for further information.

weak federal and state programs. The industry was moving into our region, despite our objections. We chose to organize a government to help our people.

From the outset, the North Slope Borough took strong local control of the growing development industry. The goal was to protect the environment and our traditional lifestyles while balancing the nation's need for energy. The North Slope Borough allowed development within the region, but had the power to regulate when and how. Today, development activity occurs only in the winter, when few animals are present. To minimize impact on the land, the industry is required to create ice roads. When the ice melts in the spring, all activity ceases. The pipeline was built to accommodate the migration of the caribou, high enough for them to cross under and ramps for those who feared the pipeline overhead. The same restrictions, if not more, would apply to ANWR....

> The author lists the measures used to regulate development. Do they seem comprehensive enough to preserve the "wilderness character" of the area?

Development and environment

We believe ... that development and wildlife can co-exist. It is with that belief that we are fighting for our human right to survive. Responsible ANWR development means energy for America, roughly 750,000 jobs for Americans and a healthy existence for my people.... The taxation powers exercised by the North Slope Borough over the oil industry created a revenue base for our people. As a result of Prudhoe Bay development, we now have heat in our homes, most villages have running water and some even flush toilets. The water and sewer project in Kaktovik will be the last for our region but the project start date is not scheduled for another two years. All villages now have local health clinics, with one hospital in the entire 89,000 square miles of our region. Fortunately, each village has both an elementary and high school to educate our children. However, as the production in the Prudhoe Bay fields decline so do our financial resources to maintain our infrastructure and social programs. Responsible development of the Coastal Plain of ANWR is our only hope in sustaining the luxuries ... in our homes ... health care facilities, schools, police and fire protection, as well as social programs needed for a healthy, thriving society.

> The author argues for oil development because the revenue is necessary for the Inupiat to support their standard of living. Should all groups who are affected share that income?

As Inupiat people we are proud and hard working. We want to become productive members of society, independent of state and federal programs.... We are fighting for our human right to economic self-determination. This is our image of freedom. This freedom was not ... written down on paper. It was inscribed in the hearts of my Inupiaq people....

> Is the Inupiat desire for economic self-determination more important than any considerations about protecting the environment? Who should decide?

NO CARIBOU FOR OIL...
Nadine Pedersen

Since the ANWR is protected land, a change in the law is required to allow drilling for oil there. This change was introduced as a clause of the bill that aimed to put the president's national energy plan into effect. Although the clause was approved by the House of Representatives, it was later rejected by the Senate.

NO

In early August [2001], the U.S. House of Representatives passed an energy bill that included a provision to open the coastal plain of the Arctic National Wildlife Refuge to oil drilling. If the bill passes in the U.S. Senate in September, multinational oil and gas corporations stand to make billions of dollars in profit, while the Gwitch'in people stand to lose their livelihood and their culture.

For over 10,000 years the Gwitch'in, Athabaskans who live north of the Arctic circle, have relied on the Porcupine Caribou herd for clothing, medicine and their primary food source. Every year the herd migrates from its wintering grounds in the North West Territories to its calving grounds in Alaska, passing through nineteen Gwitch'in villages along the way.

The real cost of drilling

"The life of the Gwitch'in is at stake here" said Lorraine Peter, a member of the Vuntut Gwitch'in First Nation and the MLA for the village of Old Crow in the Yukon Territory.

Compare this with the account of the development of Prudhoe Bay on page 182. How do the accounts differ?

"If they (the oil companies) get in there with any kind of development they'll ruin that land. They can tell us all they want about their environmentally-friendly, new technology, but any time you go in to that type of area you're playing with nature and no matter what you do to bring nature back to the state that was before, it's never going to happen."

As a calving area, the area known as the '10-02' lands on the coastal plain of the Arctic National Wildlife refuge (ANWR) is ideal. Winds off the Arctic Ocean give nursing mothers and new-born calves some relief from mosquitoes, its flatness allows the herd to spot predators from far away and the vegetation there is full of nutrients the caribou need to survive through the long arctic winter.

Nobody yet knows how much oil is in the ANWR, and the highest estimate is six times more than the lowest. Go to www.usgs.gov/ public/press/ public_affairs/ press_releases/ pr1183m.html for information on the assumptions behind estimates of oil reserves.

The land is also rich in oil. In 1987, the U.S. Department of the Interior estimated that there is anywhere from 4.8 billion to 29.4 billion barrels of oil under the coastal plain. Since then, companies such as Exxon, Chevron and BP Amoco have been pushing to allow drilling in the ANWR.

"If there's full-blown developing in the 10-02 lands, there'll be displacement from calving areas to the east, the calf

An indigenous woman in the Arctic uses caribou to pull her sled. People such as the Gwitch'in also rely on caribou for food and clothing.

mortality rate will increase, and we'll see further displacement to get food and body reserve in insect season and we'll see a herd that's already in decline in more rapid decline," said Don Russell, a caribou biologist and the manager for the Canadian Wildlife Service in Whitehorse.

Russell explained that unlike other caribou in the North American arctic the Porcupine Caribou herd has been declining since 1989. In the last two years, as a result of climate change affecting snow conditions , the herd calved before reaching the 10-02 lands and the rate of calf mortality doubled to over 40 per cent.

A way of life worth protecting

Having long ago figured out that oil drilling in the calving grounds would cause the Porcupine Caribou population to plummet, the Gwitch'in began mounting a public education campaign in the late 1980s. Since then they have travelled annually to the lower 48 states to teach Americans about their culture and urge them to pressure their elected representatives to protect 10–02 lands. They have also met directly with politicians in Washington to try to educate them on the issue. In recent years their campaign has picked up steam and conservation groups such as the Sierra Club, the Audubon society and Greenpeace have mounted campaigns of their own to protect the coastal plain.

Pro-development groups, such as Arctic Power, an Alaskan "grassroots organisation" that receives 85 per cent of its funding (approximately $3.75 million) from the state of Alaska and $50,000 annually from oil giant BP Amoco alone, have also stepped up their campaign. Aside from minimising environmental consequences, they argue that given the current "energy crisis" drilling for oil in Alaska makes economic sense and that the United States is too reliant on importing gas from other countries; thereby transforming the issue into one of public security.

The Audubon Society [a New York-based wildlife and conservation society] points out that "ruining the wilderness character of the Arctic Refuge forever would equate to less than a 180-day supply of oil, and it would take a full 10 years before any oil began to flow. These truths, however, did not sway a sufficient number of House Members."

In the recent [2000] US election, George W. Bush made opening ANWR to oil and gas development a major part of his election campaign, whereas Al Gore campaigned to have the land preserved. Not surprisingly, Bush also received 10 times as much funding from the oil and gas industry for his

The Canadian Wildlife Service is the wildlife protection agency of the Canadian government. See www.cws-scf.ec. gc.ca/index_e.cfm for more information.

Could the measures taken to help caribou at Prudhoe Bay help prevent the caribou population dropping here too?

The Sierra Club, founded in 1892, is an organization that seeks to preserve wilderness areas. See www.sierraclub.org for more information.

What other measures might be taken to reduce U.S. dependence on imported oil?

campaign. Despite the Republican victory, the Gwitch'in thought they had successfully convinced enough Congressman to vote against drilling in the 10–02 lands. So it came as a surprise when the amendment that would have stripped the ANWR section from the Republican energy bill was narrowly rejected by a 223–206 vote.

"I was shocked and frightened," said Sandra Newman, a member of the Vuntut Gwitch'in First Nation chief and council. "I didn't think it would pass at all because many of my people have been travelling to the United States for years trying to educate Americans on how we live with the caribou and how important it [is] for us"

Lorraine Peter was in Alaska visiting relatives when she learned about the vote. She said the Gwitch'in she spoke with on the U.S. side of the border took the news even harder.

"I had to offer them some encouragement and support that even though this bill had gone through Congress, there's still hope in the (Democrat-controlled) Senate. This is something we still have: hope. It comes from our ancestors and elders.

In September Peter and other members of the Gwitch'in Nation will be travelling to Washington, D.C., where she plans to meet with Senators as part of her peoples' continuing campaign to protect their rights, land and way of life.

Most of the Gwitch'in protesting ANWR oil development live in Canada. Does the U.S. government have a responsibility to take their views into account?

Before the midterm elections of November 2002, the Democrats held a slim majority in the Senate. On April 18, 2002, the Senate voted against allowing drilling to take place in the ANWR.

Summary

In the first article Tara Sweeney an Alaska native of the Inupiat people, argues that it is her people's right to support the "responsible development of oil and gas" on land within the Arctic National Wildlife Refuge (ANWR). In her view development of the Prudhoe Bay oil fields—an area also within the Inupiat regional boundaries—30 years previously did not adversely affect their way of life nor their food supply. The caribou population continues to thrive in that region, while at the same time Inupiat villages have benefited from central heating, running water, sewerage, health-care facilities, schools, and social programs as a direct result of that development. In Sweeney's view the U.S. government is actually protecting the rights of indigenous people in the region by allowing oil and gas exploitation to take place in a way that allows those people to share in the wealth that is generated. In particular, it is protecting her people's right to economic self-determination.

In the second article Nadine Pedersen argues the case of the Gwitch'in, who oppose the provision in the U.S. government's energy bill that will allow drilling within the ANWR. In their view such exploitation will destroy the Gwitch'in traditional way of life and culture. This nation is worried about the environmental impact the drilling will have, particularly on the Porcupine caribou herd, on which they rely for food, clothing, and medicine. In Pedersen's view the U.S. government, by rejecting an amendment that would have stripped the ANWR from the energy bill, is not doing enough (or indeed anything) to protect the rights of indigenous people in the region. Their rights, land, and way of life are under threat as a direct result of the government's prioritizing oil and the rights of industry over the environment.

FURTHER INFORMATION:

 Books:

Case, David S., and David A. Voluck, *Alaska Natives and American Laws*, Fairbanks, AK: University of Alaska Press, 2001.

Johnson, Troy R. (ed.), *Contemporary Native American Political Issues*, Walnut Creek, CA: AltaMira, 1999.

Wunder, John R. (ed.), *Native American Cultural and Religious Freedoms*, New York: Garland, 1999.

 Useful websites:

www.lectlaw.com/files/env21.htm
The 'Lectric Law Library's page on "Environmental Regulations on Indian Lands—A Question of Jurisdiction."
www.fw.umn.edu/indigenous/history.htm
University of Minnesota page giving historical background on U.S. government policy toward Native Americans.

www.usdoj.gov/crt/indian/broch.html
U.S. Department of Justice page on "Protecting the Civil Rights of American Indians and Alaska Natives."
www.heritage.org/Research/PoliticalPhilosophy/EM432.cfm
Heritage Foundation's page making the case for drilling in the ANWR.

The following debates in the Pro/Con series may also be of interest:

In this volume:
 Part 4: Human rights and the United States, pages 164–165

IS THE GOVERNMENT DOING ENOUGH TO PROTECT THE RIGHTS OF INDIGENOUS PEOPLES?

YES: *The government has set up organizations and provided funding to make sure that rights are observed*

YES: *There are numerous laws that protect the rights of indigenous people*

EXPLOITATION
Does the government do enough to protect indigenous people from exploitation?

LAW
Do laws adequately protect the rights of indigenous people?

NO: *The government is more interested in economic development than protecting indigenous people's rights*

NO: *Laws are insufficient to protect indigenous people when business interests take priority*

IS THE GOVERNMENT DOING ENOUGH TO PROTECT THE RIGHTS OF INDIGENOUS PEOPLES?

KEY POINTS

YES: *History has shown how little regard corporations have for indigenous people and the environment*

YES: *As economies develop, people begin to assimilate, and the traditional ways are quickly lost*

DEVELOPMENT
Are development and the maintenance of a traditional culture mutually exclusive?

NO: *Development offers indigenous people a chance for economic self-determination*

NO: *Development has already occurred in Alaska without negative effects on the environment*

Topic 15

SHOULD THE UNITED STATES HAVE RELATIONS WITH COUNTRIES THAT ABUSE HUMAN RIGHTS?

YES

FROM "DEFENDING LIBERTY IN A GLOBAL ECONOMY"
COLLATERAL DAMAGE CONFERENCE, CATO INSTITUTE, JUNE 23, 1998
RICHARD B. CHENEY

NO

FROM "STRATEGIES FOR TRANSNATIONAL CIVIL SOCIETY: BUSINESS:
TARGET OR PARTNER IN PROMOTING POSITIVE ECONOMIC POLITICAL CHANGE"
FOREIGN RELATIONS CONFERENCE ON NIGERIA, JANUARY 30, 1998
JENNIFER DAVIS

INTRODUCTION

The debate about whether governments should have relations with countries that abuse human rights is a heated one. Any U.S. administration faces difficult choices when confronting a country that is violating human rights. Should it adopt a "softly-softly" approach and register its disapproval through established diplomatic channels, or should it take punitive measures? Does the breaking off of diplomatic relations or the imposition of sanctions work to force a country to change its ways? Or is the maintenance of relations and negotiation a better way forward?

The United Nations is considered by many to be the best arbiter of when and how any protest against an abusing government should be made and applied, ensuring that it is both fair and effective. However, a large number of the UN's constituent states are abusers themselves. The United States itself flouts several articles of the UN's human rights charter, for example, by retaining the death penalty in some states. How, then, can the United States avoid double standards when making a protest against another government?

Protest can take many forms, such as a refusal to allow the offending state to participate in sporting events, an end to diplomatic relations, a ban on foreign investment, a moratorium on arms sales, and a complete embargo on trade and investment. The best-known examples of U.S. sanctions and withdrawal of relations have been the cases of South Africa in opposition to its apartheid policies, the former Soviet Union as a protest against the invasion of Afghanistan, and Iraq in response to its human rights abuses under the regime of Saddam Hussein.

Sanctions and other protests may be unilateral—when one country decides to make a stand regardless of the attitude of other states—or multilateral, when several or many states make a united protest. A multilateral response is generally more effective, though as the world's dominant economic and military power, the United States is in a position to be effective unilaterally.

"Not only will we survive [sanctions], we will emerge stronger on the other side."
—P. W. BOTHA, SOUTH AFRICAN PRESIDENT, SEPTEMBER 28, 1986

Critics of punitive measures such as sanctions claim they do not work. After the Soviet invasion of Afghanistan in 1979 the United States refused to supply grain to the former Soviet Union. This unilateral measure failed because the Soviet Union went elsewhere for its grain—and American farmers suffered as a result. The policy was abandoned in spring 1981.

Another argument against sanctions is that they do not hit the right people. Sanctions were imposed on Iraq in 1990, but the ruling elite kept itself in power until the overthrow of the regime in April 2003. During that time it enjoyed wealth and privilege while most of the Iraqi people, including children, suffered severe privation.

Nonetheless, there is some precedent for the imposition of measures such as the withdrawal of diplomatic relations and trade sanctions to bring about change. For many years the United

States chose to maintain business links with South Africa and attempted diplomacy to persuade the government to abandon apartheid. However, a lack of progress and mounting pressure from the international community and human rights groups caused a switch in policy. More effective economic sanctions were imposed in 1985, and eventually apartheid was dismantled.

Still there remains the question of whether or not human rights are really the issue when a government breaks off relations with another country. In contrast to its late withdrawal from South Africa, the United States imposed severe measures against Cuba in the wake of Fidel Castro's revolution of 1959, banning all trade and tourism. While few doubt there have been abuses in Cuba, critics point out that the speed and severity of sanctions were likely inspired by the nationalization of U.S. business interests following the revolution.

Critics point out that the United States supplied arms to Saddam Hussein before he ordered the invasion of Kuwait in 1990—despite the fact that Iraq's human rights record was just as bad at that time. China is another country where human rights are abused—summary executions are not uncommon. However, as a potentially huge trading partner, the United States is eager not to upset the Chinese regime. Is it hypocrisy or pragmatism that is at work in cases such as these?

In the first of the following articles Richard B. Cheney contends that sanctions do not work, and that maintaining business and other links is the best way forward. Jennifer Davis, by contrast, argues that those countries that can should impose sanctions on states guilty of human rights violations.

DEFENDING LIBERTY IN A GLOBAL ECONOMY
Richard B. Cheney

Richard, or Dick, Cheney became the vice president in 2001. This paper was written several years before he took office. Cheney bases his argument on the belief that human rights abuses overseas can best be addressed via economic engagement. Do you agree?

YES

☑ ...I think it is a false dichotomy to be told that we have to choose between "commercial" interests and other interests that the United States might have in a particular country or region around the world. Oftentimes the absolute best way to advance human rights and the cause of freedom or the development of democratic institutions is through the active involvement of American businesses. Investment and trade can oftentimes do more to open up a society and to create opportunity for a society's citizens than reams of diplomatic cables from our State Department....

"Sanctions happy"

I want to spend a few minutes this afternoon on my favorite hobbyhorse, the question of unilateral economic sanctions. Let me emphasize at the outset that I am not automatically, absolutely opposed to all sanctions. I think there are occasions when an appropriate policy response by the United States is to impose sanctions on some foreign government. But those occasions are relatively few. I think in most cases they are appropriate only where we can think in terms of multilateral sanctions, when there is something of an international consensus willing to follow U.S. leadership. Under those circumstances it may make sense to pursue a sanctions policy. I would cite, for example, what the international community has done with respect to Iraq in the period since the Gulf War as an appropriate use of multilateral economic sanctions.

Iraq was not allowed to legally export or import any goods, including oil, outside the UN sanctions system. In 1996 the Oil for Food program was introduced whereby Iraq was allowed to sell a limited amount of oil to buy humanitarian goods.

But my concern today is primarily with unilateral economic sanctions imposed by the United States.... Unfortunately ... our government has become "sanctions happy." I don't mean to be partisan here. I think there's plenty of blame to go around for both parties with respect to this question.... But let me cite a couple of facts from a recent issue of *U.S. News & World Report*. In the last 80 years, the United States has imposed economic sanctions some 120 times. More than half of those 120 instances have occurred in the last five years, since the Clinton administration came to power....

Currently, again according to *U.S. News*, we've got some 70 countries around the world affected by sanctions of one kind or another imposed by the United States. Those 70 countries are home to almost two-thirds of the world's population.

Unilateral sanctions do not work

Now, again, I might be willing to listen to arguments for the imposition of all those unilateral economic sanctions if somebody can produce significant evidence that they work. At a minimum, I would think such evidence ought to illustrate that we achieved the desired change that was used as the rationale when we adopted these sanctions in the first place. Typically, some government is pursuing a policy we don't like or we disagree with and we impose sanctions with the expectation that they will then understand we don't like that particular policy and they'll change it. As a practical matter, it's almost impossible to find examples where in fact that has happened....

It makes one wonder why the United States, on purpose, would want to consistently pursue policies that don't work. But that is what we do every time we fall back on the use of unilateral economic sanctions. They don't produce the desired result, in part because most of the time such policies are motivated primarily by domestic political considerations, by a desire to respond to pressure from some group or other here at home. They are rarely adopted with respect to whether or not they make sense in terms of overall U.S. foreign policy goals and objectives....

Right now there are sanctions on Azerbaijan. We're not allowed to spend any U.S. government dollars in that country. That's not a response to what we perceive to be sound foreign policy in that part of the world. It's more specifically a reflection of a desire by Congress to respond to the concerns voiced by the Armenian–American community, which is bigger than the Azerbaijani–American community. As a result we currently have a prohibition against U.S. government money being spent in Azerbaijan.

The problem in part stems from the view by my former colleagues on Capitol Hill that sanctions are the low-cost option.... You don't have to appropriate any taxpayer's money. You don't send any young Americans into combat. We're able to take a firm, aggressive action and do something about the outrageous behavior of the offending government, and ... it does not cost a thing. But that's a shaky premise, at best. Even though that is the view you will hear bandied about in the cloakroom, it is a false notion that has serious

Is the author correct? Can you think of any examples in which a government has fallen or changed its policies as a direct result of another country imposing unilateral sanctions?

Sanctions were used on Azerbaijan in 1992 after the Azerbaijan government imposed a railway blockade against Armenia during their conflict over the enclave of Nagorno-Karabakh. Sanctions were waived by President George W. Bush in 2002.

Do you agree that policymakers may see sanctions as an easy option?

consequences, in part because our sanctions policy oftentimes generates unanticipated consequences. It puts us in a position where a part of our government is pursuing objectives that are at odds with other objectives that the United States has with respect to a particular region.

Against American interests

An example that comes immediately to mind has to do with efforts to develop the resources of the former Soviet Union in the Caspian Sea area. It is a region rich in oil and gas. Unfortunately, Iran is sitting right in the middle of the area and the United States has declared unilateral economic sanctions against that country. As a result, American firms are prohibited from dealing with Iran and find themselves cut out of the action, both in terms of opportunities that develop with respect to Iran itself, and also with respect to our ability to gain access to Caspian resources. Iran is not punished by this decision. There are numerous oil and gas development companies from other countries that are now aggressively pursuing opportunities to develop those resources.... The most striking result of the government's use of unilateral sanctions in the region is that only American companies are prohibited from operating there.

Should U.S. business interests take precedence in foreign affairs? Go to the Middle East Economic Survey at http://www. mafhoum. com/press3/ 108E16.htm to read about this issue.

Another good example of how our sanctions policy oftentimes gets in the way of our other interests occurred in the fall of 1997 when Saddam Hussein was resisting UN weapons inspections. I happened to be in the Gulf region during that period of time. Administration officials in the area were trying to get Arab members of the coalition that executed operation Desert Shield/Desert Storm in 1991 to allow U.S. military forces to be based on their territory. They wanted that capability in the event it was necessary to take military action against Iraq in order to get them to honor the UN resolutions. Our friends in the region cited a number of reasons for not complying with our request. They were concerned with the fragile nature of the peace process between Israel and the Palestinians, which was stalled. But they also had fundamental concerns about our policy toward Iran. We had been trying to force the governments in the region to adhere to an anti-Iranian policy, and our views raised questions in their mind about the wisdom of U.S. leadership. They cited it as an example of something they thought was unwise, and that they should not do.

Does it matter what international opinion thinks about the actions of the United States? If so, why?

So, what effect does this have on our standing in the region? I take note of the fact that all of the Arab countries we approached, with the single exception of Kuwait, rejected our request to base forces on their soil in the event military action was required against Iraq. As if that weren't enough, most of them boycotted the economic conference that the United States supported in connection with the peace process that was hosted in Qatar during that period of time. Then, having rejected participation in that conference, they all went to Tehran and attended the Islamic summit hosted by the Iranians. The nation that's isolated in terms of our sanctions policy in that part of the globe is not Iran. It is the United States. And the fact that we have tried to pressure governments in the region to adopt a sanctions policy that they clearly are not interested in pursuing has raised doubts in the minds of many of our friends about the overall wisdom and judgement of U.S. policy in the area....

Business encourages democracy

...There is a whole long, separate speech I could give on the difficulties U.S. firms encounter as a result of the use of unilateral economic sanctions and on the subsequent commercial and economic consequences to the U.S. economy. What I've tried to do today is make the policy case against sanctions. They don't work. And as long as they don't work I think it is important for us to continue to remind people that we need to have some concern for the efficacy of policy before we advocate it as something the United States ought to pursue. I think it is important for us to recognize as a nation the enormous value of having American businesses engaged around the world. To recognize that engagement does more to encourage democracy and freedom, to open up societies, to create opportunities for millions of people ... than just about anything else we can do. We should look upon the capacities and capabilities and the desire of American businesses to be involved around the world as a valuable asset and not as a club that we can use to punish those who disagree with policies or goals or objectives of the United States.

According to this argument, the United States is doing no good to anyone, least of all itself, when it takes a moral stance against a government with whose policies it disagrees with. Are there any circumstances under which the United States should cease to have relations with another country?

STRATEGIES FOR TRANSNATIONAL CIVIL SOCIETY...
Jennifer Davis

NO

X ...Since the early 1970s the production and export of crude oil has come to totally dominate Nigeria's economy, most reserves being found along the country's coastal Niger River Delta. Oil revenues are vital to the survival of the military dictatorship, accounting for 95 percent of hard currency earnings and at least 80 percent of government revenue. Nigeria is among the largest producers of oil in the world ... currently producing at least two and one quarter million barrels of high grade "sweet light" crude a day.

The U.S. is by far the single largest market for Nigerian oil, purchasing between 35 and 45 percent of total production annually. Figures for 1996 ... place U.S. purchases of Nigerian crude at over $4 billion dollars (595,000 barrels per day...).

1998 [the year of this article] marks the 40th year of oil production operations in Nigeria, initiated by Shell in 1958. In that time the company has pumped $30 billion worth of oil from Ogoniland alone and well over $100 billion worth of oil from the whole country. Nigeria's oil wealth has financed decades of military dictatorships ... but it has brought only oppression, poverty and pollution to the Nigerian people.

Indeed, between 1983 and 1994, a period of dramatic growth in Nigerian oil production, per capita income plunged from nearly $1200 to less than $250 in an unbroken period of dictatorship that continues to this day.

Despite the immense cash flow generated by oil sales, the Nigerian military regime is severely squeezed for capital and has failed to meet payments on its huge foreign debt. It is also about $1 billion dollars in arrears to the oil companies on its share of production and maintenance costs....

Corporate/state partnerships

Under Nigerian law all oil production operations are structured as joint ventures between the multinationals and the State oil company—with the foreign firms as minority partners. This means that Shell, Mobil, Chevron and the other foreign producers are literally business partners with the Nigerian military government....

"Hard" currency is a currency in which investors have confidence, such as that of an economically stable country.

The Ogoni are an ethnic minority of about half a million people living on part of the Niger Delta (Ogoniland), where oil reserves are particularly abundant.

Are companies responsible for trying to influence the policies of governments with which they deal? Is it any of their business?

All the oil companies are deeply and structurally connected to the repressive apparatus of the state. All oil companies are required to pay the salaries and expenses of a special armed and uniformed national police force tasked with guarding oil industry facilities. These are not company security guards but national security forces answerable to the dictatorship. In addition, after years of public denials, Shell was finally forced to admit that it purchased thousands of guns and millions of rounds of ammunition for its police contingent, known among the people as the "Shell Police." (There are also "Mobil police", etc.) According to the [U.S.] State Department's 1996 country human rights report ALL Nigerian security forces engaged in widespread and systematic human rights abuses, though MOSOP has charged that the Shell Police have been particularly brutal....

Ken Saro Wiwa's trial and execution in 1995 focused world attention on what were longstanding acute tensions between Shell and the Ogoni people; millions saw grim pictures of environmental devastation and brutal military occupation....

The debate

Given the regime's dependence on oil exports for its economic survival, the Nigerian human rights and democracy movements have called for international oil sanctions to secure the release of political prisoners, return the military to barracks and implement the 1993 election results.

But sanctions have been dismissed by the private sector, the Clinton Administration and many policy analysts as, variously, unwise (companies), politically impractical and functionally ineffective. The private sector position can be understood as self interest. The policy establishment argues that sanctions cannot work because: i) Nigeria could, over the medium term, find new markets, in, the most current, Asia, to replace lost sales in the U.S. and Europe; ii) only multi-lateral sanctions could be effective and there is no consensus among the great powers; iii) enforcement would require a naval blockade of Nigerian ports.

They argue instead for the maintenance of the largely ineffective diplomatic sanctions currently in place in the U.S. and Europe, with the addition of a freeze on the personal assets of members of the regime....

These measures would be further weakened by "constructive engagement" i.e. normalized and ... expanded diplomatic contact, including direct military to military contacts with the regime and at least tacit support for Abacha's transparently fraudulent 1998 transition exercise.

MOSOP (the Movement for the Survival of the Ogoni People) has been campaigning since 1990. Issues include resource control, governance in the region, and protests against the environmental degradation that has resulted from oil exploitation.

Ken Saro Wiwa was a Nigerian writer and campaigner on behalf of the Ogoni people. In 1995 he and eight fellow MOSOP activists were sentenced to death by the Nigerian government on what most agree were false charges of murder. Despite an international outcry, Saro Wiwa and the other campaigners were executed on November 10, 1995.

General Sani Abacha, Nigeria's military head of state at the time of the article, died in 1998. He was succeeded by General Abdulsalam Abubakar, who pushed ahead with state and national elections. President Olusegun Obasanjo was elected in 1999.

Nigeria is not South Africa, the argument goes, and sanctions cannot and will not work as they did against apartheid. They are correct, Nigeria is not South Africa. The [Nigerian] regime's absolute dependence on oil exports for survival and U.S. dominance of the Nigerian petro-economy as both producer and consumer make a much stronger case for sanctions than South Africa's relatively diversified economy ever did....

Sanctions can work

[I]t is only with hindsight that many argue that sanctions on South Africa were a good idea. The are as wrong about Nigeria now as they were about South Africa, when the battle for sanctions started in the 1960s.

At the heart of the case for sanctions is the understanding that Abacha does not have a "medium term" in which to re-route his markets. Asia in an economic crisis of vast proportions has already dramatically reduced its energy demands. China, often pointed to as a likely replacement market for Nigerian oil, is, as the *New York Times* reported last year, heavily committed to coal for energy production and lacks both the capital and the will to convert to oil.

Moreover, there are significant retooling costs associated with converting refineries geared for heavier middle eastern crude to Nigeria's lighter premium grades. Adding to Abacha's difficulties in locating new markets is the large and growing glut of crude on the world market—an oversupply likely to grow with the return of Iraq to the market, the coming online of the Caspian Sea fields and the ready abundance of North Sea and other crude grades comparable in quality to Nigeria's sweet light exports.

At best Abacha would have to market his oil at a sharp discount to attract buyers, further weakening his ability to finance his corrupt and reactionary regime and imposing real costs for his repressive policies.

Fewer dollars to spend and increased international diplomatic support for democracy, can force Abacha to release prisoners and open a dialogue with the democratic movement to resolve the crisis.

Abacha is clearly feeling increasing domestic pressures, as evidenced by his mass arrests of "coup plotters" ... and the outpouring of people in Abacha's northern political stronghold to mark the death in prison of popular democracy leader Shehu Yar-A'dua in December. At the point where he is unable to pay off the Nigerian military and civilian ruling elites his regime is doomed.

When did the United States finally break off relations with South Africa? How important was this and its adoption of sanctions in the eventual downfall of the apartheid regime?

"Retooling costs" are the costs that a factory (or in this case a refinery) has to bear in order to equip itself with new or adapted tools to deal with a different production process.

Arguments that only military action can effect sanctions miss the point. The real goal of oil sanctions is to raise the costs of repression past the point that the regime can bear.

The case for going it alone

American diplomacy combined with determined American action can build multi-lateral support for sanctions. But given the extraordinary U.S. dominance of the Nigerian economy, the U.S. can act unilaterally and should do so if necessary.

While the U.S. market is vitally important—and we believe irreplaceable—to the dictatorship, Nigeria accounts for less than 7 percent of American oil imports. The U.S. can easily and cheaply find new sources of Nigerian oil—a view confirmed by a 1994 GAO report. But Abacha cannot find ready markets for half of his exports.

…[T]wo U.S. companies, Mobil and Chevron, produce nearly half of Nigeria's oil, while the single largest producer, Shell, is also vulnerable to U.S. pressure because the U.S. is its single largest profit center. The U.S. therefore has the capacity to act effectively and unilaterally against Nigeria.

The companies argue that others would replace them should they withdraw, but only a handful of corporations have the capital and the technical capacity to maintain Nigeria's huge production and they too are American.

What seems lacking is not an analysis to support sanctions, but rather the will to act to support democracy in Nigeria.

The White House has avoided involving human rights and environmental groups in the current review process and Congress seems paralyzed by a combination of corporate lobbying and Nigerian influence buying.

Recent reports raise concerns about whether illegal Nigerian campaign contributions to President Clinton's re-election campaign have touched the review process; there is certainly growing evidence of Nigerian payoffs to U.S. religious and political leaders, though grassroots support for sanctions is growing.

World leaders from Nelson Mandela to Bill Clinton to John Major and other Commonwealth heads of state have engaged in protracted diplomacy to resolve the crisis in Nigeria and avert a bloody repetition of the Biafran civil war. But without sanctions diplomacy has been disarmed and [is] ineffective.

It is past time for America and the West to arm diplomacy with power. There must be real consequences for the regime if it continues its bloody war on its own people and real consequences for the oil companies if they continue to finance military dictatorship in Nigeria.

Would sanctions really hurt the elite of Nigeria? Critics argue that such elites make sure that ordinary people suffer while continuing to enjoy luxury themselves. Go to www.cnn.com and see if you can find other examples of that type of behavior.

Does the United States have an obligation to support democracy in the world?

Do you agree with the author? Were the U.S. and other western governments more concerned with oil than human rights in Nigeria? Would sanctions have made any difference even if they had been applied?

Summary

In the first article Richard B. Cheney argues that there were around 120 instances of U.S.-imposed economic sanctions between 1918 and 1998, but that, with a handful of exceptions, such punitive measures did not bring about the changes desired by the government and should never have been applied. Cheney believes maintaining links through investment and trade is more likely to open up an undemocratic state to democratic influences than boycotts. Such boycotts, in any case, might serve to drive local opinion away from the United States and toward the undemocratic ruler. In the aftermath of the Gulf War in 1991 attempts to build stronger economic and military links in the Middle East were damaged by an anti-Iranian sanctions policy. If the U.S. government is serious about achieving democracy and respect for human rights worldwide, Cheney believes it should maintain relations, encouraging more—not less—business with and investment in recalcitrant states, so opening them up to democratic influences.

Commenting on the human rights record of Nigeria in 1998, Jennifer Davis describes how the Nigerian military regime consistently ignored appeals to improve its human rights record. In the 1990s the undemocratic military caste ruling Nigeria was responsible for what Davis describes as "a bloody war on its own people," perhaps demonstrated most clearly by the execution of prodemocracy activist Ken Saro Wiwa in 1995. Oil production dominates the Nigerian economy, and the revenues from the industry long financed its military dictatorship. Davis claims the United States was in a strong position to bring about change by withdrawing from its business partnership with Nigeria and imposing sanctions. Given that it was the largest market for Nigerian oil, sanctions could have been successful even if applied unilaterally.

FURTHER INFORMATION:

Books:

Brysk, Alison (ed.), *Globalization and Human Rights*. Berkeley, CA: University of California Press, 2002.

Haass, Richard N., and Meghan L. O'Sullivan (eds.), *Honey and Vinegar: Incentives, Sanctions and Foreign Policy*. Washington, D.C.: Brookings Institution, 2000.

Schwab, Peter, *Cuba: Confronting the U.S. Embargo*. New York: Palgrave Macmillan, 1999.

Tomasevski, Katarina, *Responding to Human Rights Violations: 1946–1999*. Cambridge, MA: Kluwer Law International, 2000.

Useful websites:

www.humanrightsforum.com
The Human Rights Forum features stories and human-rights related links from around the world.

www.amnesty.org
Site for Amnesty International, a charity that campaigns on behalf of human rights worldwide.

The following debates in the Pro/Con series may also be of interest:

In this volume:
Topic 4 Should human rights come before national sovereignty?

Topic 13 Does the United States have a good human rights record?

SHOULD THE UNITED STATES HAVE RELATIONS WITH COUNTRIES THAT ABUSE HUMAN RIGHTS?

YES: Nigeria, China, Iraq, and others show that the United States' relations with undemocratic governments is driven by economic interests rather than concerns about human rights

YES: Trade and sports sanctions have helped improve human rights globally

SANCTIONS
Do sanctions work?

ECONOMICS
Is government human rights policy driven by economics?

NO: Sanctions do not work; they just make conditions worse for the majority of people already suffering in countries that commit human rights abuses

SHOULD THE UNITED STATES HAVE RELATIONS WITH COUNTRIES THAT ABUSE HUMAN RIGHTS?

KEY POINTS

NO: The United States is a leading human rights advocate; it has helped promote human rights and stop human rights abuses in countries where it has investment and trade links

YES: Countries as important and influential as the United States have a duty to comment on the affairs of other countries

UNIVERSAL HUMAN RIGHTS
Does the United States have the right to interfere in the human rights issues of other nations?

YES: The United States is one of the most privileged nations in the world and as such should help people in other countries achieve the same freedom and rights that its citizens enjoy

NO: The United States behaves as a sovereign state in its own affairs; it cannot comment if other countries are to do the same

NO: The United States commits human rights violations itself, for example, in its continuance of the death penalty in many states

Topic 16

SHOULD THE UNITED STATES RECOGNIZE THE JURISDICTION OF THE INTERNATIONAL CRIMINAL COURT?

YES

"THE ICC CAN SERVE THE U.S."
WALL STREET JOURNAL, JULY 10, 2002
SAMANTHA POWER

NO

"NOT-SO-SUPREME COURT:
THE PROBLEM OF AN INTERNATIONAL CRIMINAL COURT"
NATIONAL REVIEW ONLINE, APRIL 9, 2002
GARY DEMPSEY

INTRODUCTION

On July 17, 1998, the Rome Statute was passed at a diplomatic meeting in Rome. The treaty created an International Criminal Court (ICC). The ICC's function was made both explicit and limited: to hold individuals accountable for war crimes, genocide, and crimes against humanity. The court would only be able to act when the national justice system of the person or persons charged refused or was unable to do so.

While 120 nations voted for the Statute, 21 countries abstained, and 7, including Iraq and the United States, voted against it. Then-president Bill Clinton consequently signed the treaty on December 31, 2000, thus allowing the United States to have some say in the shaping of the ICC. His successor, President George W. Bush, opposed it, however, and the United States was

not one of the 66 countries whose ratifications brought the court into being on July 1, 2002.

Supporters of Bush's decision argue that the ICC might possibly hinder the actions of military personnel engaged in legitimate operations and thus could undermine U.S. national security.

Many people have, however, criticized the U.S. position. They argue that it reflects the country's lack of commitment to universal human rights. But is that really the case? Should the United States accept the jurisdiction of the ICC?

The idea that there should be some kind of code of conduct and ethics during war dates back centuries, but it was really in the late 19th century that various international agreements came into effect governing behavior during war and the treatment of prisoners. It is, however, debatable how effective such measures were, since it was left to each individual country to deal with their soldiers' conduct. The laws did at least indicate a widespread belief that some moral code was necessary.

After World War II (1939–1945) the Allies, horrified by the brutalities carried out by German and Japanese forces, set up international tribunals to prosecute war crimes. The Nuremberg Trials (1945–1949) and the Tokyo Tribunals (1946–1948) established the basic principle that all individuals could be held accountable for actions that were in violation of international humanitarian law, and that "obeying orders" was no defense. Those two tribunals, however, were specific to World War II and did not lead to the establishment of a permanent court.

"[T]he most serious crimes of concern to the international community as a whole must not go unpunished...."

—PREAMBLE TO THE ROME STATUTE, 1998

In the 1990s the United Nations (UN) set up two further specialized war crimes tribunals. One dealt with genocide perpetrated during the civil war in the Central African state of Rwanda in 1994, and the other with atrocities committed during civil wars in former Yugoslavia in the 1990s (see page 206). While those tribunals have resulted in the prosecution of many war criminals, some critics suggested that a permanent international criminal court would be a much better option.

Many allies were shocked by the decision of Bill Clinton's administration not to back the Rome Statute in 1998. The United States had been a leading player in the criminal tribunals of the 1940s and 1990s, although some cynics have argued that was only because the pursuit of international justice was at the time in harmony with U.S. security interests. Clinton's administration was reluctant to subject its citizens (and by extension the U.S. government) to the jurisdiction of a court outside its control. Clinton subsequently signed the treaty in 2000; but he made it clear that although he was giving his approval in theory, he would not forward the treaty to the Senate for ratification since he considered it seriously flawed. His successor, George W. Bush, subsequently, on May 6, 2001, notified the UN that the United States was "unsigning" the treaty.

The ICC held its first assembly at the UN headquarters in New York in September 2002. By February 2003, 89 countries, but without the United States, had ratified the ICC. Many people still believed America would have to accept the ICC, since it claims jurisdiction over all individuals, even if their government is not a party to the treaty. In 2002, however, Bush won a one-year exemption from ICC prosecutions for U.S. citizens by threatening to withdraw support for international peacekeeping.

In the first of the following articles Samantha Power argues that it is in the interests of the United States to support the ICC. In the second piece Gary Dempsey argues that U.S. opposition to the ICC is justifiable.

THE ICC CAN SERVE THE U.S.
Samantha Power

This article first appeared in the Wall Street Journal, July 10, 2002. On July 12 the United Nations agreed to a one-year exemption from prosecution by the ICC for U.S. citizens involved in UN missions. In return, the United States withdrew its controversial threat to end its support for the UN peacekeeping mission in Bosnia.

YES

U.S. officials and United Nations diplomats this week resumed their high-stakes game of chicken over the future of the newly-minted International Criminal Court. With a July 15 deadline fast approaching for extending the UN mission in Bosnia, [President George W. Bush's] administration is threatening to yank U.S. support from this and all peacekeeping operations around the world if U.S. soldiers are not granted immunity from the ICC. The administration fears that, absent such immunity, anti-American judges will haul our soldiers into the dock.

Court supporters argue these worries are unfounded. For an American to be tried, a panel of eminent international judges would have to charge that he or she had carried out genocide, "systematic and widespread" crimes against humanity or war crimes. Only if the U.S. justice system itself then refused to investigate these alleged attacks would the ICC be able to proceed.

Until the court becomes functional and proves itself, neither side will be able to prove its point. But while the Bush administration focuses on the risks posed by the court, it has devoted virtually no time considering the ways the ICC could benefit the U.S.

In fact, as is illustrated by two recent cases of genocide—Iraq's brutal campaign against the Kurds in 1988 and the Serb assault against the Bosnian Muslims in 1992-1995—U.S. interests are greatly undermined by policies antithetical to American values. And U.S. security will best be advanced if genocide and crimes against humanity are suppressed and their perpetrators punished. The ICC can be an important tool in achieving that end.

Iraq

Saddam Hussein (1937–) became president of Iraq in 1979. He has crushed a number of rebellions by the ethnic Kurds in the north of Iraq. President George H.W. Bush (1989–1993) at first saw Iran as the main threat to U.S. interests in the Middle East. The United States helped both countries in the long and bitter Iran–Iraq War (1980–1988), giving financial aid to Iraq and military intelligence to Iran.

In a six-month campaign in 1988, Iraqi dictator Saddam Hussein systematically gassed and machine-gunned Kurds in northern Iraq, killing 100,000 Kurds and bulldozing some 1,000 villages. The first Bush administration viewed Iraq as a bulwark against Iran, and reasoned that the way Saddam acted inside his own borders was his own business. In 1988, while Saddam was carrying out the gas attacks, the

U.S. provided Baghdad some $500 million in credits to buy American farm products. The year after the genocidal campaign, the U.S. doubled its contribution to Saddam's coffers, offering $1 billion in credits.

"Human rights and chemical weapons use aside," one shockingly misguided secret State Department assessment said, "in many respects our political and economic interests run parallel with those of Iraq."

Chemical weapons use aside?

In 1990, emboldened by his ability to get away with literal murder, Saddam invaded Kuwait. Because the occupation threatened U.S. oil supplies, the Bush administration of course changed course. Mr. Bush detailed the horrors that he had previously ignored and threatened Nuremberg-style trials. "Saddam Hussein must know the stakes are high, the cause is just, and today more than ever, the determination is real," the president declared.

There was just one problem: No such court existed. But suppose the ICC had already been established. Saddam's genocide against the Kurds would certainly have earned him and his top officials indictments. If U.S. forces had ventured to Baghdad in 1991—or if they were to reach the Iraqi capital this year—they would carry a list of indictees prepared by a panel of independent judges. The arrests and the subsequent ICC trials would have far greater credibility internationally than any that might be carried out at U.S. bidding. The trials would also rid postwar Iraq of many of its most ruthless officials, a purge that would spur the development of the rule of law. The U.S. role in law enforcement would have all the more standing because the U.S., too, had accepted court jurisdiction.

Bosnia

In the case of Bosnia, while militant Serbs ethnically cleansed and murdered their way through 70% of the country in 1992, the Bush administration concluded it had "no dog" in the fight. But eventually editorial and elite pressure at home convinced George H.W. Bush that he could not do nothing. In December 1992 Secretary of State Lawrence Eagleburger named leading war crimes suspects in the Balkans, and publicly warned that a "second Nuremberg" awaited them. But again there was a catch: No court existed. Thus, the most noxious, bloodthirsty thugs in the region continued to prosper, hijacking the negotiation process, murdering U.N. peacekeepers and humanitarian aid workers, and dragging on the bloody war.

Iraq invaded its southern neighbor Kuwait on August 2, 1990, seizing its oil fields and gaining access to the Persian Gulf. In January and February 1991 a U.S.-led coalition army drove Iraqi forces out of Kuwait. Critics claimed that the Persian Gulf War occurred only to safeguard western oil supplies. See Volume 13, U.S. History, Topic 15 Was the Persian Gulf War a war about oil?

This article was written before the U.S.-led invasion of Iraq in 2003. The invasion was part of President George W. Bush's War on Terror to both enforce Iraq's compliance with the United Nations' repeated demands for disarmament and also to depose Saddam Hussein.

Muslim-dominated Bosnia-Herzegovina seceded from Serb-dominated Yugoslavia in 1992, but the Serbian minority in Bosnia, backed by Serbia itself, violently opposed this. In the ensuing civil war (1992–1995) many war crimes were committed —see page 206.

COMMENTARY: The Slobodan Milosevic case

In May 1993 the International Criminal Tribunal for the Former Yugoslavia (ICTY) was established in the Netherlands. Dealing with war crimes in former Yugoslavia since 1991, it is the first international war crimes tribunal since the Nuremberg and Tokyo trials. The ICTY trial of Slobodan Milosevic (1941–), former president of Serbia (1989–1997) and Yugoslavia (1997–2000), began in February 2002. Nicknamed the "Butcher of the Balkans," he is accused of genocide, war crimes, and crimes against humanity in Croatia (1991–1992), Bosnia-Herzegovina (1992–1995), and Kosovo (1998–1999). Milosevic, a trained lawyer, rejects the legality of the ICTY, calling it a "lynching." The trial is expected to be long and drawn out.

Milosevic and Serb nationalism

Yugoslavia—formed in 1918 from the union of several states with distinct identities but mixed ethnic populations—has a history of ethnic tension. After World War II (1939–1945) the resistance leader Josip Tito (1892–1980) turned Yugoslavia into a federal communist state made up of six republics: Slovenia, Croatia, Bosnia-Herzegovina, Macedonia, Montenegro, and Serbia (including the autonomous province of Kosovo). Tito's iron rule ensured stability until his death in 1980. In the following decade, however, as communism declined throughout Eastern Europe, ethnic and nationalist tensions grew.

Milosevic, born in Serbia in 1941, climbed through the ranks of the Serbian Communist Party to become its leader in 1987. Exploiting existing Serb–Albanian tensions in Kosovo, he rose to prominence after he promised to protect Serbs from alleged abuse by the Albanian majority. He was elected president of Serbia in 1989, stripping Kosovo of its autonomy. Increasing Serbian power within Yugoslavia prompted Croatia, Slovenia, and Macedonia to claim independence in 1991. The Serb minority in Croatia opposed those moves and turned to Milosevic for military aid. His forces allegedly murdered thousands of civilians in the ensuing war (1991–1992), and 170,000 Croats and non-Serbs were forced out of the region. In 1992 Bosnia declared independence, igniting another civil war (1992–1995). Milosevic backed the Serb minority again; they massacred thousands of Bosnian Muslims to "ethnically cleanse" the region of non-Serbs. In 1997 Milosevic became president of Yugoslavia (Serbia and Montenegro). A year later he ordered his troops to crush Albanian separatists in Kosovo. Fearing further massacres, western leaders and Russia insisted that the Serbs and Kosovar Albanians reached a peace settlement. Milosevic rejected the idea, and NATO (North Atlantic Treaty Alliance) began a bombing campaign. Milosevic became the first acting head of state to be indicted for war crimes. He was finally ousted from power in 2000. In 2001 he was handed over by the Serbian authorities to the ICTY to face trial.

President Clinton proved no more willing than his predecessor to confront the Serbs. Walking away from his campaign pledge to bomb the Serbs and lift an arms embargo against the outgunned Bosnian Muslims, Mr Clinton instead pressed for the establishment of a war crimes tribunal. But when the ad hoc UN court came into existence in 1994 [sic], two years into the Bosnian war, it deterred no one. How could it? Ad hoc tribunals are slapdash creations that have to raise money, hire staff, establish rules, and earn credibility. All of this takes time—time that murderers exploit. While the court issued indictments during the war, the Serbs knew that Western troops were unwilling to risk casualties by making arrests. The massacres continued, the war criminals were feted at peace talks in Western capitals, and the toothless U.N. court came to symbolize Western apathy.

As in Iraq, however, allowing genocide in the Balkans proved costly to the U.S. As the clock ticked, some of the desperate Bosnian Muslims began to radicalize, as they deduced that their only hope of rescue lay with Islamic extremists. For the last two years of the Bosnian war, while the indicted war criminals roamed free, Osama Bin Laden's Al Qaeda and other radical Islamic groups used Bosnia as a training base. While the U.S. and its allies were bystanders to genocide, Bin Laden traveled on a Bosnian passport.

The U.N. court gradually earned its keep. Once NATO troops proved themselves willing to stage daring arrest raids, beginning in 1997, panicked indictees began turning themselves in. Forty-seven of the most dangerous men in southeastern Europe are currently behind U.N. bars. Hundreds, perhaps even thousands, who have blood on their hands have been driven underground, afraid that they may have been secretly indicted....

Go to www.un.org/ icty for more about the International Criminal Tribunal for the former Yugoslavia (ICTY).

Claims that Osama Bin laden (1957–), the Saudi leader of the Islamic terrorist group Al Qaeda, ran terrorist training camps in Bosnia are disputed. Reports that he was given a Bosnian passport in 1993 in return for helping Muslims in the Bosnian Civil War have yet to be confirmed.

See www.un. org/icty/glance/ index.htm for up-to-date information about those people in the custody of the ICTY. How successful have its proceedings been?

Give the ICC a chance

[I]t is far too early to assume [the International Criminal Court] will become the virulently anti-American institution that administration officials fear. The best way for the U.S. to guard against this is to reserve self-fulfilling judgment and work with the court to supply advice on personnel and procedures. What one can say with certainty is that genocide, crimes against humanity, and war crimes will abound in the next decade. And the ICC—because it is permanent and not ad hoc—can play an indispensable role punishing and incapacitating war criminals and thus deterring future atrocities—atrocities that typically come back to haunt the U.S.

NOT-SO-SUPREME COURT...
Gary Dempsey

NO

This article first appeared in the National Review Online, April 9, 2002. By April 11, 66 states had ratified the ICC treaty, and it came into force on July 1, 2002.

Fifty-six countries have ratified a treaty to create an international criminal court, or ICC, which could claim jurisdiction over American citizens whether the U.S. government ratifies the treaty or not. Only four more countries need adopt the treaty before the ICC becomes a reality. The sixtieth ratification is expected later this week.

A clash with Europe

[George W. Bush's] administration opposes the creation of the ICC for a variety of sound reasons. But virtually every European leader backs the treaty, and the European press is howling that Washington's opposition is merely another example of American "unilateralism." According to diplomatic sources, Britain's foreign minister has even warned Secretary of State Colin Powell that the United States "does not want to be in a head-on clash with Europe" over the issue.

In truth, the transatlantic row over the ICC reveals far more about Europe's confusion than about America's motives.

"Unilateralism" means acting without the agreement of others. Do you think it can ever be justified in foreign policy?

A rejection of supranationalism

For starters, the "unilateralism" slur arises from Europe's failure to distinguish between multilateral treaties and supranational treaties: Multilateral treaties rest on cooperation between independent nation-states pursuing overlapping interests. Supranational treaties seek to subordinate sovereign nation states to new forms of international authority. The ICC falls in the latter category, and thus rejecting it is not really an example of "unilateralism" but a rejection of supranationalism.

European proponents of the ICC will scoff that the court is not meant to subordinate national courts and point to the treaty's preamble, which states that the court "is intended to be complementary to national criminal justice systems in cases where such trial procedures may not be available or may be ineffective." Trouble is, it's the ICC that ultimately gets to decide what constitutes an "effective" trial and has the last word on whether one must be made "available" in a given circumstance. The ICC, in other words, will have de facto supreme judicial oversight. So even when the court remains silent, it's making the final judgment.

See Topic 4 Should human rights come before national sovereignty? Do you agree with the author's view that rejection of the ICC by the United States is not a case of unilateralism?

The Latin phrase "de facto" means "from the fact." It is used here to mean "in reality" or "in practice."

Suspected Al Qaeda and Taliban prisoners arrive at "Camp X-Ray," the prison at Guantánamo Bay naval base in Cuba, January 2002. U.S. treatment of such prisoners has provoked much criticism. See Topic 13 Does the United States have a good human rights record?

Go to Volume 7,
The Constitution
for discussion of 16
topical issues.

To "extradite"
means to hand over
an alleged criminal
to a country that
has jurisdiction to
try his or her case.

American defendants brought before the ICC, moreover, will not be accorded the rights guaranteed to them by the U.S. Constitution—the right to a trial by jury, the right to confront witnesses against them, the right to compel witness in their favor, and the right against double jeopardy [being tried twice for the same offense].

The court's European proponents argue that this is not a problem because the United States already extradites American citizens to foreign countries where they are not guaranteed constitutional protections. But that misses the point: The U.S. government is not a party to the conduct and maintenance of foreign courts. If it ratifies the ICC treaty, however, the U.S. government would be a party to the conduct, maintenance, and indeed creation of a court that can try American citizens, which means their rights must be guaranteed or the court is unconstitutional.

Open-ended amendment

The court's European cheerleaders counter that the constitutional question is unimportant because the ICC will be limited to only the most heinous crimes—war crimes, crimes against humanity, and genocide—so it's unlikely that even the most anti-American prosecutor will be in a position to haul Americans before the court. But to say "it will never happen" is a statement of faith, not law, especially because the ICC treaty covers such vague offenses as causing "serious injury to mental health" and committing "outrages upon personal dignity."

But the greater concern is that the court will expand its jurisdictional purview through an open-ended amendment process. Other crimes that have already been suggested for the court include environmental crimes, cyber-crimes and drug trafficking. But the most likely first addition to the court's jurisdiction will be the crime of "aggression," which is already included in the treaty's text but is awaiting a formal definition. According to proposed wording, "aggression" could include such things as the "bombardment by the armed forces of a state against the territory of another state" and "the blockade of the ports or coasts of a state by the armed forces of another state." Including those actions under the rubric of "aggression" would sharply reduce the military options available to U.S. policymakers by outlawing preemptive strikes and the kind of naval blockade President John F. Kennedy employed during the Cuban Missile Crisis. In an age when international terrorists are bent on acquiring weapons of mass destruction and targeting … [U.S.] civilians,

In October 1962 the
U.S. government
found out that the
Soviet Union had
installed nuclear
missiles on the
island of Cuba.
President John F.
Kennedy imposed a
naval blockade
on the island
and demanded
the removal of
the missiles. A
standoff between
the superpowers
followed, during
which many feared
a nuclear war, but
on October 28 the
Soviets backed down.

ruling out preemptive strikes and blockades is suicidal. And ratifying the ICC treaty won't change the outcome much. The United States would have exactly as much say in the amendment process as other ratifying countries like San Marino and the Pacific atoll of Nauru.

Why does the author cite these countries? Go to www.cia.gov/cia/ publications/ factbook/index.html for some facts about them.

Legal perversities

What's more, the ICC treaty contains worrisome legal perversities. For example, a state that ratifies the treaty today can exempt itself from the jurisdiction of the court for seven years, but a country that doesn't ratify the treaty, for whatever reason, could have its citizens subjected to the court's jurisdiction as soon as it is created.

In practical terms that means that signatory countries like Iran and Syria, which have been implicated in the use of torture and sponsoring terrorism against civilians, could have a free pass for the next seven years, but the United States, which is unlikely to ratify the treaty for constitutional and security reasons, could have its armed forces subjected to the ICC's scrutiny immediately. That is hardly an idle concern given that the United States is currently involved in hostilities overseas and has lately been the subject of near-hysterical European criticism over the detention of al Qaeda and Taliban fighters in Guantanamo Bay, Cuba.

In October 2001 the United States and its allies had launched an attack on Afghanistan. Its fundamentalist Islamic Taliban regime had been sheltering the Islamic terrorist group Al Qaeda— suspected of the September 11, 2001, attacks on the United States. The Taliban soon fell from power, but U.S. forces remained through 2002, imprisoning Al Qaeda suspects at Guantánamo Bay, a U.S. naval base in Cuba. Go to www. globalissues.net/ article/294 for an example of the criticism that has been provoked.

The United States is vulnerable to the ICC

Finally, consider this: The United States currently maintains more than 200,000 soldiers and sailors outside its borders and has base rights in more than 40 countries. Because of that global presence the United States will automatically face far more exposure to the ICC's second-guessing than Europeans, who no one seriously expects to do any real fighting anytime soon. For that reason alone, European complaining should be ignored and the ICC treaty should be vigorously opposed.

Why might the author say that no one expects the Europeans to do any "real fighting"?

211

Summary

There is considerable debate about whether or not the United States should recognize the jurisdiction of the International Criminal Court (ICC).

In the first article, from the *Wall Street Journal*, Samantha Power argues that the ICC is not only good for human rights but good for the United States. She dismisses as scare-mongering the idea that members of the U.S. armed forces require ICC immunity to protect them from anti-American judges. Drawing on recent history to support her case, she claims that U.S. interests would be well served by the ICC. She points out that the lack of a recognized international court of law in which to try the Iraqi leader Saddam Hussein for his crimes against humanity has not helped the United States. In Bosnia she claims that a permanent court would be more effective than the special tribunal that was created in response to war crimes committed there.

In the second article, first published in the *National Review Online*, Gary Dempsey supports George W. Bush's rejection of the ICC. He argues that the court would undermine U.S. sovereignty and infringe the constitutional rights of U.S. citizens. He also predicts that it would gradually expand its jurisdiction and probably conflict with U.S. security requirements. He fears that the crime of "aggression," for example, might be defined by the ICC in such a way as to outlaw U.S. military action in cases where it was in fact justified.

FURTHER INFORMATION:

Books:

Bass, Gary Jonathan, *Stay the Hand of Vengeance: The Politics of War Crimes Tribunals*. Princeton, NJ: Princeton University Press, 2000.

Kaysen, Carl, Sarah Sewall, and Michael P. Scharf (eds.), *The United States and the International Criminal Court*. Lanham, MD: Rowman & Littlefield, 2000.

Schabas, William A., *An Introduction to the International Criminal Court*. Cambridge: Cambridge University Press, 2001.

Useful websites:

www.amacad.org/projects/iccarticle.htm
"The United States and the International Criminal Court: The Choices Ahead," Carl Kaysen and Sarah Sewall.
www.cato.org/pubs/pas/pa-311.html
"Reasonable Doubt: The Case against the Proposed International Criminal Court," Gary T. Dempsey.
www.facts.com/icof/warintro.htm
Facts On File News Service site. This section is about the history of War Crimes Tribunals.

www.heritage.org/Research/InternationalOrganizations/BG1249.cfm
"The International Criminal Court vs. the American People," Lee A. Casey and David B. Rivkin Jr.
www.hrw.org/campaigns/icc/index.htm
Human Rights Watch site. Section on the ICC.
www.un.org/law/icc
United Nations Rome Statute of the ICC site.
www.un.org/icty
International Criminal Tribunal for the Former Yugoslavia site, including information on the Milosevic trial.

The following debates in the Pro/Con series may also be of interest:

In this volume:
 Topic 4 Should human rights come before national sovereignty?

SHOULD THE UNITED STATES RECOGNIZE THE JURISDICTION OF THE INTERNATIONAL CRIMINAL COURT?

YES: It is a unilateralist gesture that shows that the United States believes it does not need to answer to anyone

YES: The court will be used by people with grievances against the United States to indict Americans on spurious charges

HUMAN RIGHTS
Does U.S. rejection of the the ICC mean a rejection of human rights?

ABUSE
Could governments use the ICC for their own political ends?

NO: The United States believes that in the event of its own citizens being accused of committing war crimes, they should be tried domestically

NO: The ICC is an international court with international jurisdiction, and it is open to public scrutiny. Abuse of it by individual governments is very difficult.

SHOULD THE UNITED STATES RECOGNIZE THE JURISDICTION OF THE ICC?

KEY POINTS

YES: It is important for the United States to be able to act in the interests of both its citizens and the international community, and the ICC may prevent both those things

YES: After September 11, 2001, everyone should understand why the United States is so concerned with national sovereignty and anything that might undermine it

NATIONAL SOVEREIGNTY
Should U.S. interests come before the jurisdiction of the ICC?

NO: Even democracies have been known to commit crimes, and they must be accountable to an appropriate international body, such as the ICC

NO: The U.S. role in law enforcement would have more credibility if the United States accepted ICC jurisdiction

GLOSSARY

Amnesty International (AI) an international group that campaigns for basic human rights, such as freedom of conscience and expression, for all individuals.

arranged marriage a marriage in which the parents or immediate family select marital partners for their children or relatives. The arrangement is usually motivated by economic gain, religious motives, or social status, rather than love.

Bill of Rights a bill ratified in 1791 that contains the first 10 amendments to the U.S. Constitution. The amendments protect certain rights, such as freedom of speech, assembly, and religion.

citizenship the relationship between an individual, or citizen, and a state or nation. Citizens have certain rights and duties.

civil rights rights guaranteed to people by certain laws, such as the right to vote and the right to equality. *See also* Bill of Rights.

Convention on the Rights of the Child (CRC) a treaty adopted by the United Nations (UN) in 1989. The CRC affirms the right of all children to life, survival, personal development, and freedom of expression.

discrimination the act of treating others unfairly on the basis of their race, color, gender, sexuality, nationality, religion, education, or economic status.

ethnic cleansing action to remove or extinguish members of a certain minority ethnic group from a country or region, as seen in former Yugoslavia and Rwanda in the late 20th century. *See also* genocide.

female genital mutilation (FGM) procedures involving the partial or total removal of external female genitalia, performed for cultural, religious, and medical reasons.

fetal rights the idea that a fetus has the right to a safe and healthy environment and to be born.

freedom of speech the right to freedom of expression of one's views and opinions, and freedom of the press, as protected by the First Amendment.

gender inequality the condition of people being discriminated against economically, politically, socially, and culturally on the basis of their gender.

Geneva Convention Relating to the Status of Refugees adopted by the UN in 1951, the first formal international code to protect the rights of refugees.

genocide action intended to destroy or kill an entire national or ethnic group.

human rights the rights people have as human beings, irrespective of citizenship, nationality, race, ethnicity, language, sex, sexuality, or ability. Human rights become enforceable when they are codified as conventions, covenants, or treaties, or as they become recognized as customary international law. *See also* natural rights.

human trafficking the recruitment, transportation, harboring, or receipt of people by the threat or use of force or other forms of coercion, abduction, fraud, or deception.

inalienable refers to the rights that belong to everyone that cannot be taken away.

indigenous people original inhabitants of a particular region or country, usually new members of minority groups such as Native Americans, Maoris, or Australian Aboriginal people.

inequality disparity in distribution of a specific resource or item, such as income, education, employment, or health care.

International Bill of Rights the combination of three documents: the Universal Declaration of Human Rights (UDHR), the International Covenant on Civil and Political Rights (ICCPR), and the International Covenant on Economic, Social, and Cultural Rights (ICESCR).

International Criminal Court (ICC) an independent permanent court with jurisdiction over persons committing the most serious crimes of concern to the international community. Established in 1998, the ICC was adopted by 120 world states; 21 abstained and 7 voted against it, including Iraq and the United States.

minority rights the rights of ethnic, religious, and linguistic minorities and indigenous peoples to be treated equal to majority groups.

natural rights a political philosophy in the 17th and 18th centuries which held that people were entitled to certain "natural" rights as human beings, regardless of their nationality or status.

noncooperation a philosophy of nonviolent resistance to oppression developed by the Indian leader Mahatma Gandhi and later taken up by the black civil rights leader Dr. Martin Luther King, Jr. *See also* satyagraha.

national sovereignty the freedom of a country to conduct its internal affairs without external interference.

nongovernmental organizations (NGOs) public-service organizations formed by people independent of government, such as the Red Cross and Amnesty International.

Nuremberg Trials the first international war-crimes trials, which took place during 1945 and 1946 in Nuremberg, Germany. An International Military Tribunal (IMT) was set up by Britain, the United States, France, and the Soviet Union at the end of World War II. Prosecutors indicted 22 Nazi German officials for war crimes. The trials ended with 11 of the accused being sentenced to death, three acquitted, and the rest receiving prison terms.

political asylum the right of an individual who has been forced to flee his or her country to receive sanctuary, or "asylum," in a foreign state.

prisoner of conscience a term coined in 1961 by Peter Benenson, the founder of Amnesty International. It refers to those people who are imprisoned for their beliefs, politics, race, or national origin.

racism a belief that some races are inherently superior to others, which often gives rise to discrimination against or harassment of certain races.

refugee a person living outside of his or her country of nationality who is unable or unwilling to return because he or she fears persecution on the basis of their race, religion, nationality, or political opinion.

satyagraha a policy of nonviolent resistance developed in South Africa by Mahatma Gandhi as a peaceful, nonretaliatory method to redress injustice.

stateless people people without nationality or rights of citizenship in any country. Many are refugees who flee their country of nationality because of persecution.

suicide bomber a person who detonates a bomb to kill others regardless of the fact that the explosion will kill them. Suicide bombing became a favored tactic of terrorist groups in the 1990s.

sanctions economic embargoes or boycotts taken against nations as a penalty for disapproved conduct.

Taliban an Islamic fundamentalist political and religious group that emerged in Afghanistan in the mid-1990s following the withdrawal of occupying Soviet troops.

terrorism the unlawful use or threat of violence by a person or organized group against people or property with the intention of intimidating or coercing societies or governments, often for ideological or political reasons.

Universal Declaration of Human Rights (UDHR) UN declaration in 1948 establishing human rights standards. Although intended to be nonbinding, its provisions are now regarded as customary international law.

USA PATRIOT Act (2001) an act introduced after the September 11 terrorist attacks which allowed for tribunals to try noncitizens charged with terrorist offenses.

Acknowledgments

Topic 1 Do Human Rights Exist?

Yes: From "Human Rights and Universal Responsibility" speech given at the Non-Governmental Organizations United Nations World Conference on Human Rights, June 15, 1993, Vienna, Austria by His Holiness the XIV Dalai Lama of Tibet. Used by permission of www.tibet.com operated by the Office of Tibet, London, representing His Holiness the Dalai Lama and the Tibetan government in exile.

No: From "The Tyranny of Human Rights" by Kirsten Sellars, *The Spectator*, August 28, 1999. Copyright © 1999 by *The Spectator* and Kirsten Sellars. Used by permission.

Topic 2 Can Human Rights Be Applied Universally?

Yes: From "Are Human Rights Universal?" by Shashi Tharoor in *World Policy Journal*, Vol. XVI, No. 4, Winter 1999/2000. Copyright © 2000 by World Policy Journal (www.worldpolicy.org/journal/tharoor.html). Used by permission.

No: From "Human Rights in Islamic Perspectives" by Abdul Aziz Said in *Human Rights: Cultural and Ideological Perspectives*, edited by Adamantia Pollis and Peter Schwab. Copyright © 1979 by Praeger Publishers. Used by permission of Greenwood Publishing Group Inc., Westport, CT.

Topic 3 Are the Rights of the Individual More Important than Group Rights?

Yes: From "Liberalism and Human Rights: A Necessary Connection" by Rhoda E. Howard and Jack Donnelly, originally published in *The American Political Science Review*, Vol. 80, No. 3 (Sept. 1986) under the title "Human Dignity, Human Rights, and Political Regimes." Copyright © 1986. Used by permission of Cambridge University Press.

No: From "Minority Rights: The Failure of International Law to Protect the Roma" by Mary Ellen Tsekos, *Human Rights Brief*, Vol. 9, Issue 3, Spring 2002. Copyright © 2002 by Mary Ellen Tsekos. Used by permission.

Topic 4 Should Human Rights Come before National Sovereignty?

Yes: From "Sovereignty, Human Rights and Legitimacy in the Post-Cold War World" by Michael Joseph Smith. Copyright © by Michael Joseph Smith. Used by permission.

No: "Hands Off Domestic Politics, Say Asian Nations" by Thalif Deen, Interpress Third World News, September 27, 1999. Copyright © 1999 by Interpress Third World News Agency. Used by permission.

Topic 5 Has the Universal Declaration of Human Rights Achieved Anything Significant?

Yes: "The Universal Declaration of Human Rights: A Guarantee of Universal Good" by Asma Jahangir, Index No. ACT 30/023/1997. Copyright © 1997 by Amnesty International Publications, 1 Easton Street, London WC1X 0DW (www.amnesty.org). Used by permission.

No: From "50 Years of the Universal Declaration of Human Rights and 50 Years of Human Rights Abuses" by Amnesty International, Index No. POL 10/041/1998. Copyright © 1998 by Amnesty International Publications, 1 Easton Street, London WC1X 0DW (www.amnesty.org). Used by permission.

Topic 6 Do Threats to National Security Ever Justify Restrictions on Human Rights?

Yes: "Is There a Torturous Road to Justice?" by Alan M. Dershowitz, *Los Angeles Times*, November 8, 2001. Copyright © 2001 by Professor Alan M. Dershowitz. Used by permission.

No: From "Item 4: Report of the United Nations High Commissioner for Human Rights and Follow-up to the World Conference on Human Rights," Introductory Statement by Mary Robinson at the 58th Session of the Commission on Human Rights, March 20, 2002 (www.ohchr.org). Used by permission.

Topic 7 Do Stateless People Have Rights?

Yes: "All Refugees and Migrants Have Rights" by Human Rights Watch, International Catholic Migration Committee, and the World Council of Churches (With Other NGOs). Background Paper on the Refugee and Migration Interface presented to the UNHCR Global Consultations on International Protection, Geneva, June 2001. Used by permission.

No: From "Sadiq's Story" by Maggie O'Kane. *The Guardian*, Special Report, Refugees, May 21, 2002. Copyright © 2002 by Alan Howarth. Used by permission.

Topic 8 Is Violence Acceptable as a Means to Attain Human Rights?

Yes: From "Martyrdom (Istish-had)—The Only Option to Achieve Freedom" by Firoz Osman (www.mediareviewnet.com/martyrdom.htm). Used by permission.

No: "Nonviolent Resistance" by Dr. Martin Luther King, Jr. Copyright © 1960 by Dr. Martin Luther King, Jr., copyright renewed Coretta Scott King. Reprinted by arrangement with the Estate of Martin Luther King Jr., c/o Writers House as agent for the proprietor New York, NY.

Topic 9 Are Human Rights Women's Rights?

Yes: From "Women's Human Rights: An Introduction" by Charlotte Bunch and Samantha Frost (www.cwgl.rutgers.edu/whr.html). Originally published in the *International Encyclopedia of Women: Global Women's Issues and Knowledge*, edited by Cheris Kramarae and Dale Spender, Routledge, 2000. Copyright © 2000 by Routledge. Used by permission.

No: "Are Women Human?" by Catharine MacKinnon (www.nostatusquo.com/ACLU/mackinnon/mackin1.html). Used by permission of the ACLU.

Topic 10 Are Arranged Marriages an Abuse of Human Rights?

Yes: "Love, Honour and Obey?" by Jennie Christian, *The Alternative*, February 1997 (www.pastornet.net.au/alt/feb97/arranged.html).

No: From "Arranged Marriages: A True Family Affair" by Leena Kamat, *Campus and Culture*, Vol. 94, Issue 38, November 18, 2000. Used by permission.

Topic 11 Do Fetuses Have Rights?

Yes: "Unborn Victims Act Exposes a Lie" by Don Feder, townhall.com, May 4, 2001. Copyright © 2001 by Don Feder and Creators Syndicate Inc. Used by permission.

No: From "What's Wrong with Fetal Rights" by the American Civil Liberties Union, July 31, 1996. Used by permission.

Topic 12 Is the UN an Effective Advocate for Children's Rights?

Yes: From "Children's Rights" by the United Nations. United Nations Background Note. Used by permission.

No: "Bush to UN—U.S. Is Pro-Family: A Report from the Front" the National Center for Home Education, *Issue Analysis*, March 2001. Copyright © 2003 by Home School Legal Defense Association. Used by permission.

Topic 13 Does the United States Have a Good Human Rights Record?

Yes: From "The Role of Human Rights in Foreign Policy" by Lorne W. Craner. Remarks to the Heritage Foundation, Washington D.C., October 31, 2001. Courtesy of U.S. Department of State.

No: From "United States of America: Human Rights vs. Public Relations" by Amnesty International, Index No. AMR 51/140/2002. Copyright © 2002 by Amnesty International Publications, 1 Easton Street, London WC1X 0DW (www.amnesty.org). Used by permission.

Topic 14 Is the Government Doing Enough to Protect the Rights of Indigenous Peoples?

Yes: From "The Right to Freedom" by Tara M. Sweeney, Arctic National Wildlife Refuge. Address before the International Brotherhood of Teamsters Conference on Human Rights (www.anwr.org/features/tara_Sweeney.htm). Used by permission.

No: "No Caribou for Oil: An Arctic Tribe Struggles for Survival" by Nadine Pedersen, August 2001 (www.alternatives.ca). Used by permission.

Topic 15 Should the United States Have Relations with Countries that Abuse Human Rights?

Yes: From "Defending Liberty in a Global Economy" by Richard B. Cheney, Collateral Damage Conference, Cato Institute, June 23, 1998. Used by permission.

No: From "Strategies for Transnational Civil Society: Business: Target or Partner in Promoting Positive Economic Political Change" by Jennifer Davis, (www.africaaction.org/docs98/nig9803.htm). Used by permission.

Topic 16 Should the United States Recognize the Jurisdiction of the International Criminal Court?

Yes: "The ICC Can Serve the U.S." by Samantha Power. Reprinted by permission from *The Wall Street Journal*, July 10, 2002. Copyright © 2002 by Dow Jones & Company, Inc. All rights reserved.

No: "Not-So-Supreme Court: The Problem of an International Criminal Court" by Gary Dempsey, National Review Online, April 9, 2002. Copyright © 2002 by National Review Online, www.nationalreview.com. Used by permission.

The Brown Reference Group plc has made every effort to contact and acknowledge the creators and copyright holders of all extracts reproduced in this volume. We apologize for any omissions. Any person who wishes to be credited in further volumes should contact The Brown Reference Group plc in writing: The Brown Reference Group plc, 8 Chapel Place, Rivington Street, London EC2A 3DQ, U.K.

Picture credits

Cover: Corbis: Randy Faris; **Corbis:** Adrian Arbib, 121, Bettmann, 86/87, Bob Krist, 135; **Corbis Saba:** Najlah Feanny, 143; **Corbis Sygma:** Jacques Langevin, 185; **Franklin D Roosevelt Presidential Library:** 6/7, 65; **Rex Features:** James Fraser, 91, Profile Press, 55, Sipa, 104, 126/127, 209; **Richard Jenkins:** 46/47; **The Kobal Collection:** 77; **Topham Picturepoint:** Richard Lord, 160

SET INDEX